Ancient Greece
Documentary Perspectives
Second Edition

Translated and Edited by

Stylianos V. Spyridakis
University of California, Davis

Bradley P. Nystrom
California State University, Sacramento

KENDALL/HUNT PUBLISHING COMPANY
4050 Westmark Drive   Dubuque, Iowa 52002

Copyright © 1985, 1997 by Kendall/Hunt Publishing Company

Library of Congress Catalog Card Number: 97-68465

ISBN 0-7872-3924-0

Printed in the United States of America

10   9   8   7   6   5   4   3

Contents

II Philosophy 97

III Religion 155

Preface

We are pleased to offer this second edition of *Ancient Greece: Documentary Perspectives*, which first appeared in 1985. Our purpose now, as then, is to make available to students of ancient Greece a balanced collection of texts representing all aspects of Greek civilization from the Classical Age through the Roman era. Thus, this volume contains chapters on politics and society, philosophy, religion, the military, the role of women in Greek life, drama, poetry, and science. Many of the selections are standard fare in anthologies such as this one; Thucydides' account of Pericles' funeral oration, for example, and Demosthenes' *Third Philippic*. Others, such as funerary inscriptions and poems from the *Greek Anthology*, are less commonly found but offer unique and important insights into the ideals, attitudes and daily lives of the Greeks. In addition to a reworking of much of the material that appeared in the first edition, we have added new selections from Hesiod, Lysias and Xenophon. Our purpose throughout has been to make available highly readable translations of important texts that will illuminate the history and culture of ancient Greece.

S.V.S.
B.P.N.

Politics and Society

Portrait of the Tyrant: Aristotle, *Politics*, 1313a.34–1313b.29.

In his *Politics* Aristotle analyzed the constitutions of the Greek *poleis* with the same analytical intensity he brought to his study of botany and zoology. Thus, the *Politics* includes his review of theories concerning the ideal state, descriptions of actual states which he believed approached the ideal, his theories of citizenship and constitutions, descriptions of actual constitutions, the causes of revolution and constitutional change and related topics. In the following selection the philosopher describes the means by which tyrants may keep their rule secure.

There are two very different ways of preserving tyrannies. One is the traditional method which is still employed by most tyrants. Periander of Corinth is said to have been its originator, though many of its features may be derived from the Persian system of government. This method includes some of the measures for the preservation of tyranny (insofar as this is possible) which we have already mentioned; namely, the tyrant must cut the proud down to size and destroy men of spirit. But it also includes other measures. One is the prohibition of common meals, clubs, education and other activities of a similar nature; that is, he must guard against anything that might inspire courage and confidence among the people. A second measure is the prohibition of cultural assemblies and public discussions; in other words, the tyrant must take advantage of every opportunity to prevent citizens from getting to know each other (for mutual acquaintance breeds mutual confidence). Thirdly, the tyrant must require every resident in the city to be constantly in public and to linger at his palace gates. In this way he will not only always know what they are doing, but by keeping them perpetually under his control he will teach them humility. This strategy for fostering tyranny may be applied in other ways, some of them common among the Persians and other barbarians. A fourth measure available to the tyrant is to acquire information about everything that each of his subjects says and does. To do so he will have to employ spies like the female "tale-tellers" at Syracuse and the "eavesdroppers" Hiero sent to resorts and public meetings (for people aren't likely to speak freely if they fear informers; and, if they do, they aren't as likely to go undetected). Yet another measure is to encourage quarrels among the people, pitting friend against friend, the common people against the nobles and one group of wealthy citizens against another. Finally, the tyrant must reduce his subjects to poverty and keep them busy struggling to make a living, for then they will have no time to conspire against him. One example of this tactic is the building of the pyramids in Egypt. Others include the lavish gifts the Cypselid family made to temples, the building of the temple of Zeus by the Pisistratids and the additions of Polycrates to the monuments at Samos. All of these had the same effect: they kept the people occupied and they kept them poor. This is also true of the levying of taxes. A good example is Syracuse where, in the days of the tyrant Dionysius, people were forced to contribute every bit of their property to the state within a period of just five years. The tyrant must also be a warmonger, for war will keep his subjects occupied and always in need of a leader. Finally, while kings can look to their friends for support, it is typical of the tyrant to mistrust his friends in the extreme because he knows that while all people want to depose him, his friends, above all others, have the power to do so.

Poetry and Politics: Theognis of Megara, *Elegies*, 39–68.

Between the seventh and fifth centuries B.C. the aristocrats who had dominated politics and society in the Greek *poleis* lost their grip. This trend often involved the rise of tyrants, men who claimed to be champions of the lower classes and took power with their support. The bitter response of the displaced aristocrats is nowhere better illustrated than in the poems of Theognis of Megara, a sixth-century aristocrat who lost his property and was forced into exile when a tyrant seized power in his city. His words are addressed to his friend, Cyrnus.

Our city is pregnant, Cyrnus, and I fear that
she will bear a man who will smash our wicked pride;
for though her citizens still have sense, their
leaders are turning, falling into great evil.
Good men never yet destroyed a city, Cyrnus,
but when the wicked in their pride corrupt
the common folk and condemn the just
in order to seize their wealth and power,
then, Cyrnus, you can be sure that the city
will not have peace much longer.
When wicked men take pleasure in private gains
that bring with them public ills,
then factions and violence follow, and tyrants—
God save us from them all!
Cyrnus, our city still stands, but her people have changed.
In former times there was a breed who knew neither
laws nor manners, but wore goatskins for clothing
and grazed like deer outside the city walls.
But now, Cyrnus, these same men are nobles,
and the nobles of old are scum.
Who can bear to see such things?
These new men don't know the difference
between right and wrong;
they smile while they cheat each other!
Don't give your heart to them, Cyrnus,
no matter how much profit there may be in it.
Appear to be a friend to all, but

when it comes to serious business you had
better keep your distance; for they have
miserable little hearts, and like men
no longer sure of life they love
only mischief, tricks and deceit.

The Fundamentals of Democracy:
Aristotle, *Politics*, 1317b.18–1318a.10.

Aristotle's evaluation of various political institutions in the *Politics*, a work based on a lifetime of research and reflection, is of great significance to students of history and political theory. The philosopher began with an examination of the elementary forms of society and then, on the basis of his extensive knowledge of the existing constitutions of his time, proceeded to consider the best form of government. He concluded that all forms of government can be legitimate when the rulers, whether they are one, few or many, serve the interests of the people rather than their own. He noted, however, that all forms of government degenerate and become dangerous and destructive. Aristotle's discussion of the nature of true democracy, given here, reveals his deep understanding of politics and the nature of power, and no one has improved on his observation that the essence of democracy is to "rule and be ruled."

On the basis of these principles and in view of the nature of power we may now proceed to examine the characteristics of democracy: that rulers should be chosen *by* all citizens and *from* the whole body of citizens; that all citizens should rule each citizen and that each citizen, in his turn, should rule all; that offices should be filled by lot, either all of them or at least those which require no practical experience or technical knowledge; that the possession of property should not be a qualification for holding public office or, if such a qualification must exist, that it should be minimal; that, with the exception of military offices, no one should serve in the same office twice or, at any rate, only on rare occasions and in just a few offices; that the tenure of all offices, or as many as possible, should be short; that those who sit on the jury-courts should be chosen from the whole body of citizens and should pronounce judgments on all matters, or at least on most, and always on the greatest and most important, such as audits of government accounts, questions of constitutionality and issues involving private contracts; that the Assembly should be sovereign in all matters or, at least, in the most important, and that, on the other hand, no official should be sovereign in any but the most unimportant matters.

In states where there are not adequate means for paying all citizens to attend the Assembly the Council is the most democratic of offices. But where there *are* adequate means the Council is deprived of its powers, for the people, if they are paid, want to handle all matters themselves, as I have noted previously. This system of payment is itself a characteristic of democracy and should extend to every office—to everyone who attends the Assembly, sits on the jury-courts or serves as a magistrate. If this is not possible payment should be made to the magistrates and members of the jury-courts, Council and ordinary assemblies or, at the very least, to those officials whose duties require them to take their meals together. Again, while oligarchy is defined by noble birth, wealth and education, democracy is characterized by their opposites: low birth, poverty and plain tastes. Another feature of democracy is that it does away with all offices held for life (or, in cases where a life-term office does exist because of some ancient custom, a democracy appoints to it men chosen by lot rather than by election).

These, then, are the characteristics of democracies in general. But if we look at that form of democracy and sort of population which are generally considered to be the most *purely* democratic we find there that conception of justice according to which all people must count equally. Equality here does not mean that the poor should rule instead of the rich or that they alone should hold power, but that all people should share power equally, each group in proportion to its number. In this manner democrats believe that they will secure equality and freedom in government.

Solon's Abolition of Debts: Aristotle, *Constitution of Athens, 12.4.*

Solon's place in Athenian history is unique. He was the great lawgiver who laid the foundations of Athenian democracy with his wise legislation and prudent policies. Solon may well have been the first poet of Athens, but his work has survived only in fragments. The two hundred and fifty verses of his poetry which have come down to us are an important historical source which reveals his unique personality and the true nature of his reforms. His cancellation of debts and mortgages, which freed the land of Attica and put an end to serfdom, was an act that Solon proudly recounted in his poetry. In the well-known poem given here he justly claimed that by abolishing debts he became the savior of Athens.

And as for me,
did I ever abandon the goals
for which I brought the people together
before they had been accomplished?
My best witness before the tribunal of time
may be the revered mother of the Olympians—
Black Earth, from whom I removed
the many boundary stones of bondage
which pierced her everywhere:
She who was once a slave is now free!
I restored many of her citizens to Athens—
this country founded by the gods—
citizens who had been sold into slavery, justly or unjustly,
and others who had been driven into exile by poverty,
men who no longer spoke the Attic tongue
after many years of wandering.
And those who had been reduced to shameful servitude
here at home, who trembled before their masters,
these, too, I set free.
By my authority I accomplished these things,
blending force and justice harmoniously,
fulfilling all my promises.
The laws I wrote brought even-handed justice
to all men, whether good or evil.
Had a foolish and greedy man held my power
he could not have restrained the people,

and if I had favored one party over another
the city would have mourned the loss of many lives.
And so I defended myself on every side,
turning about like a wolf beset by hounds.

The Democratic Reforms of Cleisthenes:
Aristotle, *Constitution of Athens*, 20–22.3.

Politics was one of Aristotle's great passions but, unlike his teacher Plato, the philosopher based his political views on a detailed study of all the known constitutions of his day. In the Hellenistic Age there existed one hundred and fifty-eight separate treatises attributed to him or his close associates that dealt with the constitutions of various ancient states. All of them have been lost except the major part of his *Constitution of Athens*, which was preserved in an Egyptian papyrus discovered in 1891. The first part of this work consists of an historical discussion of the evolution of the Athenian constitution beginning with Solon. The second gives us a reliable account of the workings of the Athenian democratic system in Aristotle's time. The *Constitution of Athens* is a basic source for the study of the emergence of the first democracy in Athens, as the following account of the reforms of Cleisthenes clearly illustrates.

After the tyranny had been overthrown Isagoras, the son of Tisander, who was a friend of the tyrants, and Cleisthenes, who belonged to the family of the Alcmaeonids, faced each other in the political arena. When Cleisthenes lost support in the political associations he cultivated the support of the people by promising to give them power in the state. Isagoras, realizing that he would now lose his political influence, invited Cleomenes, who had been associated with him by the bonds of hospitality, to return to Athens and convinced him to "wipe out the curse," for the Alcmaeonids were thought to be among those who were under a curse. After this Cleisthenes fled secretly and Cleomenes arrived with a small force that expelled from the city seven hundred Athenian families. He then attempted to dissolve the Council and install Isagoras, with three hundred of his friends, as ruler of the city. But when the Council resisted and the people gathered in order to protest, the supporters of Cleomenes and Isagoras fled to the Acropolis where the Athenians besieged them for two days. On the third day they allowed Cleomenes and his followers to leave under a truce and recalled Cleisthenes and the other exiles. When political power was thus returned to the people Cleisthenes became their leader and protector. For the Alcmaeonids had been the clan most responsible for the expulsion of the tyrants, since they had almost incessantly opposed their schemes. Even before the Alcmaeonids, however, Cedon had attacked the tyrants, and for this he was praised in a drinking song:

Pour wine for Cedon, servant, and don't forget him,
if it is proper to drink to the good and the brave.

It was for these reasons that the people had placed their trust in Cleisthenes. As the leader of the people, then, four years after the dissolution of the tyranny, in the archonship of Isagoras, he first divided the entire population into ten tribes instead of the four which had previously existed, with the intention of mixing them up so that more Athenians would participate in public affairs. This gave rise to the proverbial saying, "don't investigate the tribes," which was addressed to those who wanted to inquire into family backgrounds. He then instituted the Council of Five Hundred in place of the old Council of Four Hundred, choosing fifty men from each tribe, whereas before one hundred men were chosen [from each of the four old Ionian tribes]. He did not place them into twelve tribes because he did not want to divide them according to the preexisting *trittyes*. For the four tribes had been made up of twelve *trittyes*, and this division could not have produced a completely new mixture of the population. He also divided the entire country into thirty parts made up of demes, ten from the areas of the city, ten from the regions of the shore and ten from the interior districts. He named these parts *trittyes* and allotted three of them to each tribe, so that each tribe would include one portion from each of the three main regions of the country. He also made fellow-demesmen all those who resided in each of the demes so that they would not, by calling each other by their father's names, discover who were the new citizens; instead, they would now address each other by the name of the deme to which they belonged. That is why the Athenians refer to each other by the names of their demes. Likewise, he established demarchs who functioned in the same way as the former *naucraroi*; in fact, the demes took the place of the naucraries. He named some of the demes after their locations, and others after their founders; for not all of them were situated in the localities for which they were named. He allowed, however, everyone to maintain ties with his family, brotherhood, and the sacred religious rites in accordance with the ancestral practice. He established ten *archegetae* as eponymous heroes of the tribes, these being selected by the Pythia from a group of one hundred who had been previously chosen.

After these reforms had been enacted the government became much more democratic than the government of Solon; for it happened that the laws of Solon were not enforced under the tyranny and were eventually lost, and that Cleisthenes passed new laws in order to win the support of the people; among these was the law regarding ostracism. Five years after these reforms, when Hermocreon was archon, they first introduced the oath which the members of the Council of Five Hundred still take today. In those days they elected the generals by tribes, one from each tribe, but the Polemarch was the commander-in-chief of the entire army.

11

Pericles' Funeral Oration: Thucydides, *History of the Peloponnesian War*, II.35–46.

In 430 B.C., at the end of the first year of the Peloponnesian War, the city of Athens honored its dead in a state funeral. Three days before the funeral the bones of the fallen were laid out so that friends and relatives could bring them offerings. Then, on the day of the ceremony itself, the remains were placed in ten chests of cypress (one for each of the Cleisthenic tribes) and conveyed in procession to the public sepulcher located outside the city wall. In addition to the ten litters which bore the chests, an eleventh, empty, was included in honor of those soldiers whose bodies had not been recovered. According to the customary order of the state funeral for those who had fallen in battle, when the dead had been interred a eulogy was to be given by a man chosen for his wisdom and prestige. On this occasion it was Pericles who spoke.

His speech is among the most famous in history. After noting that the actions of such brave men could never be honored adequately by words, Pericles went on to describe the greatness of the city for which they had died. Government by rule of the majority, political and legal equality of citizens, tolerance, respect for the law, openness to foreigners and the recognition of individual excellence—these and other qualities, he said, made Athens a model state unrivaled by any other Greek city.

The original text of Pericles' oration was not preserved. We have instead the version of the historian Thucydides, who almost certainly attended the funeral. He included Pericles' speech as he remembered it in his great history of the conflict which resulted in the defeat of Athens.

"Most of those who have spoken from this place have praised him who added this speech to our funeral rite, for they thought it good that a speech be made at the burial of those who have died in wars. I have been of the opinion that it is enough for men who have demonstrated bravery in action to be honored with action, and publicly, as they are in this funeral which you see has been prepared by the state, for then the honor of many men would not be endangered by one who, depending on whether he is a good or bad speaker, may or may not be believed. It is a difficult thing for a speaker to strike a proper balance in his words when it is hard to establish what the popular opinion is concerning the truth. For the well-informed listener who holds the dead in high regard will most likely think that the speaker's words do not meet with his expectations or his knowledge of the matter, and yet he who does not know the facts may (due to jealousy) think that the speaker is exaggerating if he hears something attributed to the dead which he himself is not capable of doing. This is because praises spoken of others are tolerable only so long as each listener thinks himself capable of doing the things about which he has heard; but when a eulogy goes beyond this the audience becomes jealous and disbelieving. Still, our ancestors approved this custom, and so I must obey the law and try my best to satisfy somehow the desires and beliefs of each of you.

I will begin by speaking of our ancestors, for at a time like this it is right and fitting that we should honor their memory. They dwelled in this land from time immemorial, and by their bravery they bequeathed it to us as a free land through generation after generation. They deserve our praise, and our fathers are even more worthy of it; for in addition to their own inheritance they gave us a great empire which they did not acquire without great effort. Our generation has enlarged that empire and has enabled her to be self-reliant in all respects, both in war and in peace. I will not speak of the wars through which the various territories of our empire were won or of the zeal with which our fathers defended themselves against their enemies, both Greeks and barbarians, for you know the story and it would take a long time to tell it. However, before I go on to eulogize the dead I will point out the means by which we have arrived at our present situation and what kind of constitution and way of life led us to greatness. I don't think that this would be inappropriate, and, in fact, every one of the citizens and foreigners here will benefit by listening carefully to what I am about to say.

Ours is a constitution which has no rival; it is a paradigm, not a copy. Our government is called a democracy because it exists for the sake of the majority and not for the few. The law guarantees that all citizens are equal with respect to their private interests, and yet claims of individual excellence are also recognized, so that when a citizen distinguishes himself in some way he is chosen for public office because of his merit, and not on the basis of his social status. Poverty is no obstacle to a man of humble origin if he can somehow benefit the city. We are free men, and we manage our public affairs as such. We are not suspicious of each other as we go about our daily business. We are not angry with our neighbor for doing what pleases him, nor do we give him looks of annoyance which, though harmless, are still irritating. While we are relaxed in private society, we are most careful not to transgress the law. We respect those who hold public office and the laws, and especially those which have been promulgated for the benefit of the injured and the unwritten laws which everyone agrees it is shameful to violate.

Moreover, more than any other city we make available to the human spirit various forms of relief from toil. We hold athletic contests and sacrifices throughout the year, our homes are nicely furnished, and the enjoyment we find daily in these things drives away sadness. Because our city is great all sorts of products from all over the world are brought to us, and so we enjoy the good things of other lands just as we do those of our own country.

In addition, we handle our military affairs in a manner which differs from that of our enemies with respect to the following. Ours is a city open to all people. We never resort to the expulsion of foreigners or keep anyone from learning or seeing anything which might help our enemies if not kept secret. For we place our trust primarily in courageous action, not in secret plans and deceptions. As far as education is concerned, our enemies seek to make themselves brave by vigorous training begun in early youth; but, even though our lifestyle is an easygoing one, we are just as prepared as they are to meet dangers. This is proved by the fact that the Lacedaemonians do not invade our territory by themselves, but bring all their allies with them. We, on the other hand, attack a neighbor's country without help, and we usually prevail without much difficulty even though we are fighting on foreign soil and against men who are defending their homes. They have not yet experienced the fullness of our strength because we must give our attention to the navy and, at the same time, send out our own citizens on land expeditions. And yet, if they attack some small part of our army and win, they boast that they have routed us all; but when they are defeated they say that it was our entire army that worsted them. Indeed, we are better off because we have chosen to meet danger in a relaxed fashion and without severe training, and with a bravery which is inspired by our way of life and not by laws; for we are not distressed beforehand at the prospect of pain, and yet when the time comes we prove that we are just as courageous as those who are always undergoing strenuous training.

But this is not the only reason why our city is worthy of admiration. For we love beauty without exaggerating its value, and we love knowledge without becoming soft and effeminate. We use wealth to accomplish our purposes, not as something to boast about; and while there is no shame in admitting one's poverty, we believe it is shameful for a man not to try to avoid it. We participate both in household and municipal affairs, and though we pursue various forms of business we are not ignorant of politics. We Athenians are the only ones who regard a man who takes no interest in public affairs not as apathetic, but as completely useless; and all of us have the right to criticize actions taken by the city although not everyone actually participates in the formulation of policy. We believe that action is not hindered by debate but by the lack of that instruction which is gained through discussion prior to taking whatever action is necessary. What makes us different from others is this: we boldly execute our plans after giving them careful consideration, but other men are brave in their ignorance and yet cowardly upon reflection. Indeed, the men who ought to be considered the bravest of all are those who most clearly understand the difference between pain and pleasure but do not turn away from danger because of this. And we differ from most men, too, in our goodwill; for we make friends not by receiving favors, but by doing them. The man who does a favor is a better friend because he causes the recipient to remember his indebtedness by his continued kindness; but the debtor is less concerned, for he knows that what he gives in return is not a favor, but the repayment of another's kindness. We are the only ones who help others, not because we coldly calculate that it will conduce to our advantage, but because we believe in freedom.

In short, I maintain that our city is the school of Greece, and that each citizen seems to me to be capable of coping with the widest range of circumstances with the greatest grace and versatility. This is not just an idle boast in a speech, but a truth borne out by actions and demonstrated by the power which the city has acquired because of our way of life. For among all the cities of the present time Athens is the only one which surpasses her reputation in times of crisis. She is the only city whose enemies feel no disgrace when they march against her and are defeated by men such as hers. No subject of ours has reason to complain of being ruled by unworthy masters. We need no one to testify to this, for there are great signs of our power which will make our city the wonder of this and all future ages. We need no Homer or any other poet whose words will be pleasing for a while, though truth will ultimately shatter their fanciful imaginings. Our daring spirit has forced every land and sea to open to us, and everywhere we have established everlasting memorials to our noble accomplishments. This, then, is the city for which the men whom we honor here nobly fought and died, for they did not want to lose her; and it is only natural that we who remain, every one of us, should be ready to give our all for such a city.

Indeed, this is why I have spoken at such length about the city, to make clear to you that what we are striving for is something greater than that which is sought by men who do not enjoy similar advantages, and at the same time to justify my eulogy of these men by pointing to the concrete proofs of what they have done. In praising the city I have already praised them, for the virtues of these men and men like them have adorned Athens. There are not many Greeks who are their equals, men of whom it can be said that their actions measure up to their reputations. And it seems to me that a death like theirs, whether it is only the first sign or a final proof, demonstrates the true worth of a man. Even in the case of men of dubious character it is right that their valor in defending the land of our fathers should be set above everything else; for the good cancels the bad, and their public service more than makes up for whatever damage they may have done in their private lives. Not one of these men lost his nerve because of a desire to enjoy a soft life. Not one of them shrank from danger, hoping, as poor men do, to escape from poverty to wealth. No, they thought that taking vengeance on their enemies was more desirable and that there was no nobler cause for which they could risk their lives. And so they decided to get revenge before allowing themselves to enjoy any other thing. They consigned to hope the uncertainty of ultimate success; but when they saw the task immediately before them they decided that it would be best to rely on themselves alone. And in doing so they thought it better to fight and suffer than to save their lives by giving in. They fled only from dishonor, for on the field of battle they stood their ground until, in a moment ordained by chance, a moment not of fear but of the highest glory, they died.

Yes, these men conducted themselves in a manner worthy of our city. As for those of us who remain, we must pray for our safety, and yet we must resolve to fight just as boldly as they did. Don't judge the advantage of such an attitude merely on the basis of what is said about it. (Indeed, anyone could speak to you at length about the good reasons that exist for defending ourselves against the enemy, but why discuss what is already obvious to you?) Rather, it would be better for you to contemplate day by day the greatness of our city until you come to love her; and when her magnificence becomes apparent to you, remember that it was gained by brave men who knew their duty and feared disgracing themselves in battle, men who, even if they failed in some undertaking, still did not withhold their valor from the city, but offered their very selves to her as the greatest contribution they could make. By giving their lives for the common good they have earned undying praise and the most honorable of all sepulchers; not the one in which they lie, but that in which their glory survives, to be remembered on every appropriate occasion in word and deed. For every land is a tomb for famous men. They are commemorated not only by inscribed stone monuments in their own country, but their memory lives on even in foreign lands—not in inscribed words, but in the minds of men. Let them be an example to you; realize that happiness is freedom, and that freedom comes from courage; and do not be overly concerned about the dangers of war. What kind of man has the best reason for generously and willingly giving up his life? It is not the man who has fared badly and has no hope that his life will improve, but rather the one who runs the risk of a change for the worse in his life and who would have to endure great changes if he were to fail in battle. Indeed, for a man with spirit it is worse to be oppressed like a weakling than it is to die without pain when filled with strength and the aspirations of the state.

That is why I do not now mourn with the bereaved parents who stand here. I will comfort them instead. They know that they have lived in a time of many changes and that those who are fortunate are those whose lot it has been to gain the most honor, whether an honorable death, like the death of their sons, or an honorable grief, like their grief, and in whose lives there have been equal measures of happiness and hardship. I know that it is hard not to long for those of whom you will often be reminded by the good fortune of others—the same good fortune which you once enjoyed. One does not grieve for the good things he has never known, but for those to which he had grown accustomed before they were taken away. But you must take heart. Some of you are still young enough to hope to have other children. Your new sons will help you to forget those who are no longer alive, and the city will gain in two ways: she will not be left without men and she will be more secure. For a man's voice in the political life of the city cannot have the same influence and value as that of other citizens unless he, like them, has sons to risk for the sake of the city. As for those of you who are too old to have children, remember that you have been happy for a long while, and let the glory of your dead sons make the short time left to you easier to bear. For the love of honor is the only thing which does not grow old; and when men grow old it is not money that brings contentment (as some say), but honor.

For those of you who are the sons and brothers of the dead, I can see that the struggle to live up to the standard they have set will be difficult. For even if your virtue were to surpass theirs you would not be considered their equals, but slightly inferior to them. Men bear ill will toward their rivals while they live, but when a rival is no longer in the way he is honored with undisputed goodwill. And, if I may say something about woman's virtues to those of you who will now be living as widows, I will make my point in one brief exhortation: for you, great glory consists in displaying no weaknesses other than those which are natural in women, and in being talked about among men as little as possible, whether they speak well or ill of you.

I have fulfilled my obligation by saying what is appropriate, and this is in accordance with our custom. As far as actions are concerned, the dead have already been honored in the performance of these funeral rites, and their children will be cared for at public expense until they are grown up. This is the prize which Athens bestows on these men and their survivors in recognition of what they have endured. For where the reward for virtue is greatest, there men give the best they have to offer for the benefit of the state. And now, when you have finished the mourning which is due to the dead, return to your homes."

An Athenian Statesman and Politician— Aristides the Just: Plutarch, *Aristides,* 7–8.

Aristides was one of the leading figures of Athens in the fifth century B.C. A distinguished soldier and politician, he saw action at Marathon and Salamis and commanded the Athenian forces at Plataea. He worked with Themistocles after the Persian Wars to rebuild the walls of Athens and is best known for his role in assigning just and equitable quotas for the contributions which the allies were to make to the Delian League. Aristides became the prototype of the upright politician even in his own lifetime, when the epithet "the Just" was attached to his name. The following excerpt from Plutarch recalls his ostracism in 483–482 B.C. and reveals that even his reputation for moral integrity did not endear him to all citizens of Athens.

It happened that Aristides was at first loved because of his surname [the Just], but afterwards he was envied, especially when Themistocles spread the word to the masses that Aristides had destroyed the courts by personally judging and pronouncing verdicts on all matters and that he had quietly set himself up as a monarch without a bodyguard. In addition, the people, now elated by their victory and demonstrating the greatest of pretensions, must have disliked all those individuals whose reputation raised them above the masses. So they gathered together in the city from all parts of the country and ostracized Aristides, disguising under the name of "fear of tyranny" their envy of his reputation. For ostracism was not a punishment for wickedness, but was deceptively said to be merely the humbling of a man and the suppression of his self-importance and excessive power; it was, in fact, a humane way of providing relief for feelings of envy which made it possible for people to express their ill will, not by inflicting irreparable injury, but by imposing ten years of banishment. When, however, they began to employ it against ignoble and knavish individuals they had to abandon the practice, and thus it was that Hyperbolus was the last man to be banished. It is said that Hyperbolus was ostracized for the following reason: Alcibiades and Nicias, the two most powerful men in the city, were political opponents. As the people were about to proceed with ostracism and it became obvious that one or the other would be the victim, they got together and, uniting their factions, schemed to banish Hyperbolus. The people, however, were offended by this tactic, thinking that ostracism had now become the object of derision and had been foully abused, and so they abandoned and abolished it. In short, ostracism was performed as follows: Each citizen, taking an *ostrakon* [a potsherd], wrote on it the name of the person he wanted banished and brought it to a certain location in the agora that was fenced with a circle of wooden rails. The archons counted all the sherds collected, for if their number was less than six thousand the ostracism was not valid. Then, placing every name separately, they declared banished the one whose name was written most often, but gave him the right to enjoy the income from his estates. Once, as they were writing on the *ostraka*, it is said that an illiterate and very boorish fellow gave his to Aristides, whom he had mistaken for a common citizen, and begged him to write "Aristides" on it. He was surprised and asked him if Aristides had ever done him anything harmful. "Nothing at all," he replied. "I don't even know the man, but hearing everyone call him 'Just' bothers me." When he heard this Aristides gave the man no answer but wrote his name on the sherd and gave it back to him, and as he left the city he raised his hands to heaven and made a prayer which, it seems, was the opposite of that of Achilles, that the Athenians might never find themselves in a position that would constrain them to remember Aristides!

A Critique of Athenian Democracy:
The "Old Oligarch," *The Constitution of the Athenians.*

This is one of the most important, and most puzzling, of all the political texts which have come down to us from ancient Greece—important, because it gives us a description of the highly praised Athenian system by one who knew it well and disapproved, and puzzling, because we know so little about its author and the circumstances which led to its composition. Modern scholarship has rejected the traditional view that this treatise was written by Xenophon, maintaining that he could hardly have been responsible for a work of such poor literary quality. It has been attributed instead to an anonymous figure of the late fifth century B.C. known only as the Old Oligarch. It is not certain even that this individual was an Athenian, for while he occasionally numbers himself among the Athenians by using the first person plural, he usually distances himself from them by employing the third person.

The designation of the author as an oligarch is quite appropriate, for he is strongly opposed to the rule of the many while favoring that of the few—oligarchy. For him, as for many among the privileged minority who resented the encroachment of democracy on their traditional rights and prerogatives, "the few" are also "the best," men who are in every way superior to those who constitute "the rabble." He acknowledges (though not without a hint of sarcasm) the ability of the Athenian democrats to preserve their system, but believes that democracy can never rise to the level of oligarchy because of the inferior moral character of "the many."

I

With regard to the constitution of the Athenians, I cannot praise them for having chosen this kind of government, for in choosing it they have given the advantage to the rabble at the expense of those who are upright and deserving. This is why I do not commend them. But, given the fact that they have made their choice, I want to demonstrate that they safeguard the constitution well and effectively manage the other matters in which the rest of the Greeks think they do wrong.

The first thing I have to say is this: it seems right that the rabble, the poor, and the common people should have more influence than the highborn and the rich, for they are the ones who sail the ships that give strength to the city. Helmsmen, boatswains, commanders of fifty, lookout men, shipwrights— these are the men who give far more strength to the city than do the *hoplites*, the highborn and the good. This being the case, it seems just that everyone participates in holding office, either by being chosen by lot or by election, and that any citizen who wishes to do so is allowed to speak.

But then there are offices which ensure the safety of the whole community when they are well executed, but endanger it when they are not. The people do not wish to serve in these, nor do they think it is good for the generals or the leaders of the cavalry to be chosen by lot. For the people understand that it is not to their advantage to hold these offices and that they should be reserved for those who are best qualified; but they do seek to serve in paid positions which will profit their households.

Some people are amazed that in everything they give the greater share to the lowly, the poor, and the common people, rather than to men of distinction, but it is apparent that by doing so they preserve the democracy. For if the poor, the common, and the insignificant are prospering and increasing in number the democracy grows stronger; but if the rich and the highborn prosper the common people are only building up the strength of their opponents.

In every land the aristocracy is opposed to democracy, for among the aristocrats there is the least licentiousness and injustice, and moral perfection is held to be the highest good; but among the common people there is much ignorance, disorder, and wickedness. For it is poverty which leads them into shameful acts, and the same is true of lack of education and the ignorance which results from insufficient money.

Thus, it might be said that not everyone should share equally in the right to speak [*i.e.*, in the Assembly] or to serve on the *Boule* [*i.e.*, the Council of Five Hundred], but only the most clever and best of men. But in this matter, too, they have chosen to do the best thing in allowing the rabble to speak. For if only the aristocrats spoke and served on the *Boule* it would be of benefit to the members of their own class, but not to the common people; but now, when anyone who wants to may stand up and speak, no matter how miserable a man he may be, he will strive to gain what is good for him and others like him.

Someone might ask, "How can such a person understand what is good for him or for the people?" Well, the people recognize that this man's ignorance and vulgarity, because they are combined with his goodwill, are of greater benefit to them than the virtue and wisdom of the distinguished man, for these are combined with malice.

Of course, a city with such social organization will never be the best, but this is the most effective way to preserve the democracy. For the common people do not want a city with good laws in which they are subject to others, but to be free and to rule, and so they are not much concerned about bad laws. That which *you* think is not a good constitution is the very thing which strengthens the common people and makes them free.

But if you seek a good constitution, you will first see to it that the most capable men establish the laws; after this the good men will chastise the bad ones, and the good men will be the ones who consult together on the affairs of state and refuse permission to crazy men to serve on the *Boule* or to speak in the Assembly. Moreover, as a result of these good measures the common people would quickly sink into bondage.

The slaves and metics [*i.e.*, resident aliens] in Athens have the greatest license, for it is not lawful to beat a slave there, nor will a slave step aside to make way for you in the street. Now I will tell you the reason for this local custom: if it were permissible for the free man to beat the slave, or the metic or the freedman, he would often assault an Athenian citizen, mistakenly supposing him to be a slave; for the common people there are clothed no better than the slaves and metics, nor are they better in appearance.

One may be surprised by this, that they allow the slaves there to live in comfort, some of them even in outright luxury, but in this, too, they seem to be acting purposefully. For wherever there is a naval power it is necessary for the slaves to work for pay, so that we may take the wages they receive for their labor and set them free. In a place where slaves are rich it is no longer of any advantage to my slave to be afraid of you; but in Sparta my slave *does* fear you. If your slave were afraid of me he would very likely pay his own money to avoid exposing himself to danger.

This is why we have given slaves the right to speak out against free men, and also the metics against citizens, for the city needs metics for the sake of the many trades in which they engage and that of the fleet. Thus, it is most likely because of this that we have given the right of free speech to metics.

The common people have ruined the profession of gymnastics and the study of music, thinking that these serve no good purpose, and because they know that they are incapable of practicing them. But with regard to the *choregoi,* the *gymnasiarchs* and the *trierarchs*, they know that rich men will be choregoi, and so the people will have choruses, and that since the gymnasiarchs and trierarchs are also rich men, these offices will also be provided for them. The common people think that they deserve to receive money for singing, running, dancing, and sailing the ships, in order that they might profit while the rich become poorer. And in the courts they are not as concerned with justice as with what will work to their advantage.

As for the allies, it seems that they [*i.e.*, the Athenians] sail out to their cities making false accusations and despising the aristocrats, for they recognize that a ruler is hated by those whom he rules, and that if the rich and powerful hold sway in the cities the empire of the Athenian people would last only a short time. This is why they dishonor the aristocrats, rob them of their fortunes, drive them out of the cities, and kill them; and all the while they exalt the vulgar people. However, the Athenian aristocrats protect their counterparts in the allied cities, for they know that it is always in their interests to protect the best men there.

Someone might say that the strength of the Athenians is increased if the allies are able to pay taxes. But the people think it is better still if each Athenian possesses a share of the wealth of the allies, and that the latter should have just enough to live on and be so busy with their work that they are unable to plot a rebellion.

It would seem that the people of Athens are making a mistake by forcing their allies to sail to Athens for the settlement of lawsuits. And yet this policy has certain advantages for the Athenians. First, throughout the year they receive the fees which must be deposited by the opposing parties prior to the adjudication of a lawsuit. Second, they can sit at home and manage the affairs of the allied cities without having to sail out in their ships, and in their courts they can protect the common people and destroy those who oppose them. If each of the allies handled its own lawsuits at home, their discontent with the Athenians would prompt them to ruin the people in their own cities who were friends of the common people of Athens.

In addition, the people of Athens benefit in the following ways from having the legal conflicts of the allies settled in Athens. First, there is the one percent tax levied by the city on all ships which sail to the Piraeus. Second, people who let rooms do better, and so do those who hire out carriages and slaves. And then there are the heralds, who also profit because the allies come and stay among us.

In addition to the above, if the allies were not required to go to Athens to settle their lawsuits they would only respect those Athenians who actually sail to their cities; namely the generals, trierarchs and ambassadors; but, as things stand now, every one of the allies must grovel before the Athenians, knowing well that when he arrives in Athens justice will be rendered by the common people and no one else, for this is the law in Athens. And he will have to enter the court as a supplicant with outstretched hand. In this way the allies have more and more been made the slaves of the people of Athens.

Moreover, because of their overseas possessions and the government positions which they hold outside their own borders, both they and those who travel with them learn to handle an oar without giving it a second thought; for when a man sails it is frequently necessary for him to take an oar and row, both him and his slave, and to learn nautical terminology. And they become good helmsmen through experience with ships and through study. Some receive their training by piloting ordinary ships, others in cargo ships, and from these they move on to the triremes of the navy. The majority of them are ready and able to sail as soon as they board the ships, for they have practiced for this all their lives.

II

The army, which even in Athens itself is thought to be inferior, is organized with this in mind: they see themselves as weaker and fewer in number than their enemies, but they are a stronger land power than any of the allies who pay them tribute, and they consider the army to be sufficiently powerful so long as they are stronger than the allies.

Chance has ordained the following circumstance for them: the subjects of a land power can unite their small cities and fight, but island-dwellers who are the subjects of a sea power cannot unite their city-states because they are separated by the sea, and because those who rule them also rule the sea. Even if the islanders were able to join together secretly on one island they would perish for lack of food.

Of the mainland cities which are governed by the Athenians, the larger ones are ruled by fear and the smaller ones entirely by their need; for there is no city which is not dependent upon importing and exporting. But a city will not be able to engage in these at all unless it obeys those who rule the sea.

Further, it is also possible for the rulers of the sea to do what land powers sometimes do, namely to destroy the land of a stronger opponent. For it is possible to sail to a place where there is no enemy or only a few enemies, and, if these attack, to go back on board the ship and sail away. By doing this they have an easier time of it than do those who come to the rescue by land.

Moreover, it is possible for the rulers of the sea to sail as far away from their own land as they wish, but land powers cannot go on a march of many days from their own country; for marches are slow, and an army on foot cannot carry enough food to last for a long time. Also, one who advances on foot must either go through friendly territory or win its passage by fighting, but he who sails can go ashore where he is stronger, and where he is not he can choose not to go ashore and sail past that land until he arrives at either a friendly region or one where his strength is superior.

Further, even the strongest of the land powers endure with difficulty the crop diseases which are sent by Zeus, but the sea powers bear them easily. For not every land is stricken by disease at the same time, so that the rulers of the sea may get what they need from the area which is flourishing.

If mention may be made of unimportant things, then, in the first place, through their rule of the sea and their contact with other lands the Athenians have discovered new ways of enjoying themselves; for whatever delights are to be found in Sicily or Italy or Cyprus or Egypt or Lydia or Pontus or the Peloponnesus or anywhere else, all of these are brought together in one place through the rule of the sea.

And then, because they have occasion to hear every language, the Athenians have chosen for themselves a word here and a word there; and while the other Greeks make use of their own dialects, ways of life, and forms of dress, the Athenians blend everything together, both barbarian and Greek.

The people know that the poor cannot afford to procure and enjoy sacrifices, religious services, feasts and temples, and to live in a great and beautiful city, and yet they have found a way to make these things possible. Thus, they sacrifice many victims at public expense, and it is the people who divide the sacrificial offerings and feast on them.

24

Some of the rich people have their own gymnasia and bathing places and dressing rooms, but the people have built for themselves many schools for wrestling and exercise, dressing rooms and public baths, and the masses derive greater enjoyment from these than do the privileged few and the prosperous.

The Athenians are the only ones among the Greeks and the barbarians who are able to take possession of the wealth which derives from the sea trade. For if a certain city is rich in timber for ship-building, where will it sell this product if it does not have permission from the rulers of the sea? And what if a city is rich in iron or copper or flax, where will it find a market for these if it is not obedient to the rulers of the sea? Yet these are the same cities from which I get the materials to build my ships: timber from one, iron from another, and copper, flax and beeswax from still others.

In addition to this, they will not allow any of our commercial rivals to ship cargo to any other city, or these will be denied use of the sea altogether. Thus, although I myself do not labor to produce anything from the earth, I still get all of these goods because of the sea, and yet no other city possesses any two of them. Flax and timber are not found in the same place, for where there is an abundance of flax the countryside is flat and treeless; nor are copper and iron to be found near the same city, or any two or three commodities, but one in one city and one in another.

Further, add to this the fact that every mainland territory has a protruding cape near to it, or an island nearby, or a strait of some kind; this makes it possible for the rulers of the sea to rush forward from that place and harass the mainland-dwellers.

But they have one weakness. If the Athenians held power over the sea as island-dwellers they could injure others, if they wanted, without suffering themselves. As long as they ruled the sea their own land would not be destroyed, nor would they expect enemies to come upon them. But as things stand now the farmers and the rich people of Athens seek to accommodate the enemies, while the common people, who know quite well that the enemies will neither set fire to anything that is theirs nor destroy it, live without fear of them and without fawning on them.

Moreover, if they were island-dwellers another reason for fear would be eliminated, for then the city could never be betrayed by a few malcontents, nor could the city gates be opened to allow enemies to burst in. How could this happen to island-dwellers? Nor could there be a rebellion against the people if they were islanders; for if there were a rebellion now it would be undertaken in the hope that the enemy would come by land to help out. But if they lived on an island they could rest assured that this did not constitute a danger to them.

But then, since from the beginning it has not been their good fortune to live on an island, they do as follows: they keep their property on the islands, relying on their control of the sea; and they are even willing to turn a blind eye to the devastation of the soil of Attica, for they know that if they were soft-hearted concerning it they would lose things of greater value.

Further, cities ruled by oligarchs must stand by the alliances and oaths they make, for if they do not live up to their agreements, or if you are wronged by one of them, the names of the few men who made the agreement will be a matter of public knowledge. But when the people as a whole make an agreement it is possible for the blame to be placed on the individual who made the proposal or the one who put it to a vote, and everyone else can deny personal responsibility by saying "I was not present" or "I was not pleased" by what was agreed on in a well-attended meeting of the popular assembly. And if some measure passed by the assembly does not suit them, the people concoct ten thousand excuses for not carrying out what they do not wish to do. And if something bad results from that which the people have decreed they accuse a few persons of working against it and corrupting it, but if the result is some good thing they take the credit for themselves.

The Athenians do not permit the people to be ridiculed in a comedy or to be defamed lest they hear bad things said about themselves, but in private they encourage anyone who wishes to do so, for they know well that the person ridiculed would not normally be a man of the common people or the masses but a rich or well-born or influential person. Of course, there are a few poor men and democrats who have been satirized in comedies, but this would never have happened if they had not been overly meddlesome in public affairs or sought to gain in some way at the expense of the people. This is why they do not become upset if such people are ridiculed in a comedy.

I am of the opinion that the common people in Athens know who the honest citizens are and who are the villainous ones. And yet, even though they know this they love those persons who are useful and profitable to them, and if these men happen to be wicked then they hate honest men even more. For the common people do not think that the virtue of honest people produces any good effect for them, but works to their disadvantage. On the other hand, there are some who truly belong to the people who are not democratic by nature.

Personally, I forgive the common people of Athens for their democracy, for everyone ought to be pardoned for looking out for his own interests. But anyone who is not one of the people and yet prefers to live in a democratic city rather than one ruled by an oligarchy is a person prepared to commit an injustice, for he knows that it is easier to commit a crime and escape notice in a democratic city than in an oligarchy.

III

I do not approve of the type of constitution which the Athenians have, but since they have decided to live in a democracy, I think they are doing a good job of preserving their government by means of the things which I have already mentioned.

But I have seen some people raise a complaint against the Athenians, that sometimes it is impossible for a man to bring a matter before the *Boule* or the Assembly even if he waits for a year.

This happens in Athens because the number of cases is so large that they are unable to deal with all of them and be done with them.

Indeed, how could they be capable of handling all these cases, when they have such a great amount of business to attend to? First, they must celebrate more festivals than any other Greek city (and during these it is difficult to execute public business); and then they have to settle both private and public lawsuits and perform audits, more than all the rest of mankind combined could take care of; next, the *Boule* must frequently debate about the war, public finance, laws which have been proposed, matters which are always turning up concerning the city and the allies, and it must collect tribute and manage the shipyards and sanctuaries. Is it any wonder, then, that with such a huge amount of business to be done it is impossible for them to serve everybody?

But there are some who say: "If someone goes to the *Boule* or the Assembly with money they will listen to him." I am prepared to concede that in Athens much can be accomplished with money, and that still more would be accomplished if more people offered money. But I know, too, that the city is unable to take care of all those who come asking, regardless of the amount of gold and silver they offer.

But there are also legal matters to be settled, such as if someone who is commissioned by the state to repair a ship doesn't do his work, or if somebody builds something on public property. Further, they have to settle the claims of the *choregoi* at the Dionysia, the Thargelia, the Panathenaea, the Promethia, and the Hephaestia, and this must be done every year. Four hundred *trierarchs* must be appointed each year, and any of these who so desire may have their legal cases decided every year; moreover, government officials are to be examined and resulting lawsuits settled, orphans must be considered, and prison guards must be appointed.

These are things which they must do every year; but occasionally they must also pass judgment when soldiers shun their military duty, or if certain other crimes should be committed unexpectedly, or if people commit some unusually outrageous offense or an act of irreverence against the gods. I am omitting a great many things, but the most important ones have been mentioned except for the assignments of quotas for tribute, and these usually take place every five years.

Now then, isn't it clear that all of these matters should be adjudged? Someone might say that there are some which need not be settled right away. But if, on the other hand, it is agreed that all cases must be dealt with, then this must be done within a year; and yet, even as things are now, when they are sitting in judgment all year long, it is impossible to control crime because of the sheer number of people.

Still, someone might say that, while judgment must take place, a smaller number of people should do the judging. But if the number of courts is not decreased the number of persons serving on each court will necessarily be smaller, so that it would be easier to influence a small number of jurors and bribe them to judge much less fairly.

In addition, it should be kept in mind that the Athenians must hold festivals during which it is impossible for the courts to function. They do hold twice as many festivals as the other cities, but I am comparing Athens to the city which has the fewest.

In view of all these things, I would say that it is not possible to direct the affairs of Athens in any way other than that in which they are handled now, except that minor changes could be made here and there. But it is not possible to make big changes without somehow weakening the democracy.

Many ways can be found in which to improve the constitution but, assuming that the democracy will continue to exist, it is not easy to find a way to improve the functioning of the government unless, as I have just said, small changes are made in areas of minor significance.

In my opinion the Athenians have erred in taking the side of the lower classes in cities where there are rebellions. But they do this intentionally. For if they took the side of the better people they would be supporting those who do not share their opinions. For there is no city in which the aristocracy takes kindly to the common people, but in every city it is the worst kind of people which wishes them well; for like is kindly disposed towards like. This is why the Athenians take the part of those who are of their own ilk.

On those occasions when they have attempted to support the aristocrats things have not worked out to their advantage: in Boeotia it did not take long for the common people to be reduced to servility; when they favored the aristocrats of Miletus these soon forsook them and slaughtered the common people; and when they supported the Lacedaemonians against the Messenians the Lacedaemonians lost no time in defeating the Messenians and then attacking the Athenians.

Someone might assume that no one in Athens was ever unfairly stripped of his citizenship. But I claim that there are persons who have been wrongfully deprived of their rights, although these are very few.

But it would take more than just a few to make an attack on the democracy in Athens, and these few would not come from among those who lost their rights for a legitimate reason, but from those who are angry because they were unjustly deprived of their citizenship. And how can anyone believe that the majority of those who are disenfranchised in Athens have been unjustly victimized, when the people themselves are in control of the government? Men are expelled from Athens for ruling unjustly or for not speaking or acting justly. In view of this, it should not be expected that those who have been deprived of citizenship constitute any danger to the city.

The Mixed Constitution: Aristotle, *Politics*, 1265b, 33–42.

Ancient political theorists, including Aristotle, admired Sparta for its "mixed" constitution which combined characteristics of the three basic forms of government—monarchy, oligarchy and democracy—in a harmonious blend that served satisfactorily all elements of Spartan society. Aristotle's views on Sparta are also expressed in other passages of his *Politics*.

Some people claim that the best polity is a mixture of the three basic forms, and as a consequence they praise the Spartan constitution because it is a combination of oligarchy, monarchy and democracy. They call the king the monarchic element, the *Gerousia* the oligarchic element and say that the *Ephors* represent the democratic element, since they are selected from among the people. Others, however, declare the Ephorate to be a characteristic of tyranny and see democracy expressed in the common meals and the other habits of daily life.

The Spartan Constitution and Society:
Xenophon, *Constitution of the Lacedaemonians*.

This laudatory account of Spartan society and its institutions appears to have been widely read in antiquity, though for many years its authorship was in doubt. Today, most scholars attribute it to Xenophon, an Athenian historian whose admiration of Sparta and its constitution is well-known. For Xenophon, the greatness of the Spartan system should be credited to the ingenious Lycurgus, whom the Spartans themselves regarded as their city's great lawgiver and founder of its *eunomia* ("good order"). Xenophon's account is cursory and of uneven quality, but its idealization of Sparta has influenced historical perceptions of this remarkable state and society for centuries.

I

Having realized that Sparta has clearly become one of the most powerful and renowned states in Greece, despite the fact that it is one of the least populous, I began to wonder how this success had been achieved. However, after reflecting on the nature of Spartan institutions my wondering ceased, for I understood that the achievement of the Spartans is the result of their obedience to the laws given to them by Lycurgus. I have the greatest admiration and respect for this wisest of men who made his city extremely successful not by imitating others, but by following a course contrary to that pursued by most of the other Greeks.

Let us begin with the most important issues, such as the procreation of children. In other states prospective young mothers are allowed to eat only simple foods and are given as few luxuries as possible. They are never given unmixed wine; rather, it is always diluted with water. It is also the practice of the other Greeks to require girls to be sedentary, so that they spend their time sitting still and working wool in the same way that craftsmen do. But how can girls brought up in this sedentary fashion give birth to strong and healthy children?

In contrast, Lycurgus was of the opinion that slave women are capable of producing enough clothing to meet society's needs and that the primary duty of a free woman is to produce children. Thus, he made it an absolute requirement for girls to engage in the same physical exercises as boys. Moreover, he required women to compete against each other in athletic

30

contests of speed and strength in the same way as men, for he was convinced that children issuing from the union of two strong bodies are sturdier than other children.

Lycurgus also chose a different approach in another matter. Noting that in other states men had unlimited access to sexual relations with their wives in the early days of marriage, he maintained that it was disgraceful for a man to be seen entering or leaving his wife's room. He reasoned that a couple's desire to enjoy one another would never be satiated if they were limited to having sex only under difficult circumstances and that the children born of such unions would be stronger than if their parents had exhausted their vigor by easy access. In order to further ensure the birth of fine children, Lycurgus no longer permitted men to marry when they pleased but only when they had reached their physical peak. And when it came to his attention that older men married to young wives tended to be very jealous and watchful over them, he took corrective action by requiring an elderly husband to introduce his wife to some young man whose physical and personality traits he admired so that he might be the father of her children. If a man was unwilling to marry but still wanted children, Lycurgus made it lawful for him to father children by a well-bred woman with children of her own, provided that her husband gave his consent. Lycurgus gave his personal approval to many of these relationships. They appealed to women since they offered them the opportunity to have two households, and Spartan men approved of them because they allowed them to provide "brothers" for their sons who would enhance their power and influence without having claims on their property.

These are the unique practices established by Lycurgus concerning the procreation of children. Their effectiveness in endowing Sparta with men of superior size and strength can be seen by anyone who wishes to investigate Spartan society.

II

Having given an account of Lycurgus' views on procreation, I would like to proceed to a thorough discussion of education in Sparta and how it is different from education elsewhere. Now, in other parts of Greece parents who claim to give their sons the best possible education place them, as soon as they are able to understand what is said to them, in the care of servants who act as their tutors. After this they send them to schools where they are taught reading, writing, music and the art of wrestling. They also soften their children's feet by requiring them to wear shoes and make their bodies delicate with changes of clothing. Further, they allow their children to eat as much as their stomachs can hold. Lycurgus, however, instead of assigning to each boy a slave who would be his tutor, required that a man known as the *paidonomos*, who belonged to the select group of Spartans eligible for appointment to the higher state offices, should be responsible for the boys. Lycurgus gave this official the right to assemble them and to discipline them if they did not behave properly while under his supervision. He also assigned to him a squad of young men armed with whips to punish those who misbehaved. As a result of measures such as these, there is a high degree of respect and obedience in Spartan society. Rather than following the practice of allowing the feet of boys to grow soft in shoes, Lycurgus instructed them to strengthen their feet by not wearing shoes at all. He was convinced that this practice would allow children to walk uphill without much difficulty and to walk downhill more safely. He also believed that a boy used to going barefoot would jump, leap and run farther and faster than one who wore shoes. In order to avoid making Spartan children delicate by the wearing of clothes, he required them to wear a single garment for the entire year; in this way he believed they would be better prepared to endure both cold and hot weather. As for their diet, Lycurgus instructed the *Eiren* in charge to serve for the common meal only as much food as was necessary so that the children would not become sluggish by overeating and in order that they might learn what it is like not to have enough food. He believed that boys raised according to these practices would be better able to work hard without food, if they were required to do so, and to make their rations last longer if so ordered. Thanks to this regimen, they would be perfectly able to cope with a plain diet, adapt to whatever food was available to them, and enjoy better health. Lycurgus also thought that a plain diet would encourage children to grow taller, while a rich one would only fill them out.

It should be noted that, while Lycurgus made it difficult for boys to get what they needed, he permitted them to engage in limited stealing in order to avoid excessive hunger and the suffering it causes. He did not introduce this practice of encouraging them to procure food through theft and cunning because he was unable to provide for their needs. This should be obvious to everyone. Clearly, those who steal must stay alert at night while practicing deception and lying in wait during the day. They must also have associates to assist them. It appears, then, that by having boys practice these things Lycurgus hoped to make them more capable of satisfying their need for food and thereby make them better soldiers as well.

But the question arises: If he viewed theft as a good thing, why did he punish with so many lashes a boy who was caught stealing? The answer is that in this, as in all other forms of training, those who do not perform satisfactorily are punished. The Spartans, then, chastise those boys who are caught stealing because they are not stealing well. And yet, while Lycurgus made it an honorable thing to steal as many cheeses as possible from the altar of Artemis Orthia during her festival, he also ordered others to whip the thieves. In this case his message was that a few moments of pain would be rewarded by the lasting prestige enjoyed by those who were flogged. This practice shows that in matters requiring quick action the sluggard gains little but suffers much.

In order to ensure that boys would not be left unattended even in the absence of their appointed supervisor, Lycurgus authorized any Spartan citizen who happened to be present to order them to do whatever he deemed appropriate and to punish them for any violation of his instructions. In giving citizens this authority, he strengthened the boys' sense of respect. In fact, it is well-known that in Sparta both boys and men have the greatest respect for those placed in charge of them. Also, wanting to be certain that boys would not be left unsupervised even when there was no adult present, Lycurgus appointed the smartest of the *Eirens* as commander of a squadron so that it would not be left without someone in charge.

At this point I think that I should say a word or two about the love of men for boys, since this practice is a part of the education of the latter. The attitude of the Greeks generally is well illustrated by the example of Boeotia, where a man and a boy form a bond of love together, and that of Elis, where beautiful boys are won by gifts and favors. On the other hand, there are places in Greece where would-be lovers are strictly forbidden from talking to boys.

Lycurgus' position on this matter was entirely different. If a man of good character innocently sought to befriend and keep the company of a boy whose personality he admired, Lycurgus approved of the bond and considered it the finest form of mentoring. However, if a man lusted after the boy's body he was absolutely opposed to this attraction, for he considered it disgraceful. In fact, he determined that in Sparta men who loved boys should not molest them, just as parents do not molest their children or brothers their sisters. I am not surprised that many people do not believe this, since in many parts of Greece there are no laws against indulging one's lust for boys.

I have now discussed the educational system of Sparta and other cities. It is up to anyone who wishes to do so to further investigate these matters in order to determine whether the Spartan approach or that of the other Greeks produces the most disciplined, respectful and self-controlled men.

III

While other Greeks remove their sons from school once they have grown to become youths, leaving them unsupervised and free to do as they please, Lycurgus opposed this practice. Realizing that at this stage of their lives young men become selfish and cocky, qualities that produce urgent desires for the fulfillment of physical desires, Lycurgus gave them much work to do in order to keep them occupied as much as possible. Moreover, by prescribing that youths who avoided this work would be ineligible for any of society's honors in the future, he not only made this a matter of public concern but a family concern as well, since the families of youths did not want the behavior of their sons to ruin their reputations in the Spartan community.

Furthermore, in order to instill in youths a sense of modesty, Lycurgus legislated that they should keep both hands in their cloaks even in the streets, walk in silence, and fix their eyes on the ground before them rather than allow their gaze to wonder in one direction or another. Thus, Spartan males are stronger than females even in the matter of self-control. Indeed, you would sooner expect to hear a cry from a stone statue or catch the eye of a bronze one than hear a peep or catch a look from a Spartan youth, who seems more bashful than a virgin girl. In fact, when youths attend the public mess the elders expect to hear nothing from them other than replies to the questions they ask. Clearly, Lycurgus gave much attention to the education of the Spartan youths.

It must be noted, however, that he paid much more attention to the young adults in Sparta, for he was convinced that they would be of the greatest benefit to the state if they were endowed with the right character. On the basis of his observation that competitive people produce the most noteworthy choruses and stage the most spectacular athletic contests, he concluded that if young men could be persuaded to compete in the pursuit of excellence they would achieve the highest degree of manly perfection.

I will now explain the means by which he put this principle into practice. The Ephors select three of the very best of the young men as *hippagretai*— that is, as leaders of an elite unit of soldiers known as the Three Hundred. Each of the three in turn selects one hundred others and clearly explains why they were chosen and the others rejected. This practice creates tension between those who are chosen and those who are not, the result being that each group is always looking for any conduct on the part of the other that may be in violation of the accepted code of honor. This sort of competition is the one most favored by the gods and most useful to the community. It clearly delineates the sort of conduct expected of a brave man and pits the two groups against each other as each strives to excel and prove itself superior to the other. And yet, when some external force threatens the city the two groups are able to join forces and fight as a single unit to defend it. Since their rivalry can bring the two groups to blows whenever they meet, both must keep themselves physically strong. And it is interesting to note that when they are fighting any passerby has the right to call for an end to the conflict and that those who ignore his command are brought by the chief trainer before the Ephors, who impose a stiff penalty on them. The principle conveyed by this punishment is that anger should never be placed above a citizen's respect for the law of the land.

IV

Concerning the Spartans who have progressed beyond the earliest stage of adulthood and constitute the group from which the highest state officials are actually selected, the training they receive also differs from that of other Greeks. The latter require mature adults to continue their service in the army but excuse them from any obligation to remain physically fit. Lycurgus, on the other hand, made hunting the most noble activity for men in this age group and excused only those whose public duties made it impossible for them to participate. Such discipline enabled mature men to endure the rigors of a military campaign just as well as younger men.

V

This completes my account of the training which Lycurgus imposed on each age-group in Sparta. I will now turn to the way of life he prescribed for Spartans generally.

Now, when Lycurgus took charge of Spartan affairs his people, like the rest of the Greeks, lived in separate households, a lifestyle which he believed was the cause of much bad behavior among them. In order to cut down on disregard of orders, he established public messes and fixed the food ration in such a way that the people would have neither too much nor too little to eat. However, extra food would be supplied on occasion by hunting expeditions, and rich men would donate bread made of wheat, so that there was some variety in their diet. As a result, there is never a shortage of food on the table, although there is never an excess of it either. As for wine, Lycurgus did not permit the excessive drinking which causes both physical and mental harm but allowed a man to drink whenever he felt thirsty, for he believed that this was the healthiest and most enjoyable way to drink wine. Clearly, the institution of the public messes made it unlikely that anyone would destroy himself or his family by gluttony or excessive drinking.

In the rest of the Greek world, men tend to congregate with others of the same age; as a result, the level of respect shown among them is generally low. At Sparta, however, Lycurgus brought together men of different ages in the belief that the younger ones would benefit greatly from the experience of their elders. In fact, it was customary for discussion in the public messes to focus on noble deeds performed by Spartan citizens, and so few opportunities were offered there for the display of rowdy and drunken behavior or for offensive words and actions. Another benefit of the custom of eating outside the home is that the Spartans must walk home afterwards (since they are not allowed to remain in the dining area) and must take care not to trip and fall under the influence of wine while they are on their way; for Spartan men of military age are not permitted to carry lighted torches, and so they must also do in the dark what they do by daylight.

Lycurgus also noted that the same rations improve the complexion, physique and strength of those who work hard while causing lazy people to look ugly, bloated and weak. He did not ignore this fact but, being aware that people who are glad and eager to work possess reasonably attractive physiques, he instructed the senior man in each gymnasium to make certain that each man's physical training was suited to his diet. In my opinion, this was the correct action on the part of the legislator, for it would be hard to find men anywhere in the world who are healthier or more physically fit than the Spartans, for through exercise they strengthen equally their legs, arms and necks.

VI

Lycurgus' opinions also differed from prevailing views in the following ways. While in other city-states each man is the master of his own children, slaves and property, Lycurgus made each Spartan man the master of other people's children just as much as his own, for he wished to create a society in which citizens might benefit each other without doing any harm. Clearly, when a man knows that fathers are to conduct themselves in this fashion he is bound to give orders to the children under his control in the same manner in which he would have others instruct his own children. If a boy should reveal to his father that he was beaten by another man, it is disgraceful for the father not to give him another beating. This illustrates how much they trust one another not to give improper orders to their children.

Lycurgus also went so far as the authorize citizens to use the domestic servants of their fellow citizens if they needed them, and he ordered that hunting dogs should be shared among them, so that when those who have no dogs ask to borrow them the owner gladly consents if he is not using them himself. The same applies to horses, so that a man who falls ill or needs to transport something or must go someplace quickly may use a horse, if he should see one, and then promptly bring it back to its owner.

Another Spartan practice which has no parallel elsewhere in Greece was also instituted by Lycurgus. This relates to hunters who find themselves in need of food because they have been delayed out in the country without provisions. Lycurgus ordered that hunters who had brought a supply of food should leave part of it behind in the country, so that those who were in need could break the seals, eat what they needed, and leave the rest sealed up again for needy hunters in the future. This practice of sharing allows even the poorest of citizens to benefit from the resources of the land whenever they are in need.

VII

The following practices devised by Lycurgus also differ from those of the other Greek city-states, where every citizen earns as much money as he can, whether by farming, owning ships, trading or craftsmanship. In Sparta, Lycurgus forbade all free citizens to engage in the pursuit of material wealth and required that their only concern should be those matters which ensure the freedom of their city. Indeed, it is hard to see why anyone in Sparta would be concerned with the acquisition of wealth, when Lycurgus prescribed a

36

uniform lifestyle for all citizens by requiring that provisions should be contributed equally among them, thus eliminating people's selfish passion for money. Beyond this, there is no point in earning money even for the sake of purchasing clothing, since in Sparta it is not fine clothes but a powerful physical presence that gives men a look of distinction. It is even pointless to earn money so that one might spend it on the other members of the mess, for Lycurgus made the contribution of physical labor for the sake of one's companions more important than monetary assistance. Thus, he showed them that a contribution of physical labor comes from the heart, whereas the contribution of money is simply a function of being wealthy.

Lycurgus prevented the acquisition of wealth by illegal means in the following manner. To begin, he introduced a system of coinage that made it impossible to conceal even the minuscule amount of ten minas from a master or servant, for it would take a wagon to transport it and much space inside in which to store it. In addition, the authorities make searches for gold and silver, and when they make a discovery they subject those found in possession of them to fines. Since the trouble that comes from making money outweighs the pleasures it affords, what is the point of pursuing wealth?

VIII

It is generally known, of course, that the strictest obedience to laws and authority is practiced at Sparta. Yet, it is my view that Lycurgus made no attempt whatsoever to institute such discipline until he had acquired the consent of the most important people in the state. This personal observation is based on the fact that in other states people of power and influence do not want even to appear as though they fear the authorities, for they consider obedience to be demeaning to free citizens. In Sparta, however, the most prominent citizens are especially submissive to and respectful of the city's magistrates. As a matter of fact, they are proud of their humility and their custom of responding to the summons of their leaders at a run rather than by simply walking to them. They do this because they believe that their example in showing complete obedience will be followed by the rest of the people, and this has been shown to be true. Moreover, it is likely that the most prominent Spartans also contributed to the establishment of the office of the Ephors, since they recognized the fact that obedience benefits the state as greatly as it benefits an army or household. They thought that the more powerful the office, the more it would be able to coerce the people into obedience. As a consequence, the Ephors are authorized to impose fines on any person they choose, to exact payment on the spot, to dismiss officials, and even to put them into prison and on trial for their lives. Armed with such tremendous power, the Ephors do not always allow officials to perform their duties as they see fit for an entire year, which is the standard practice in other states. Instead, acting like tyrants or referees in athletic games, they punish on the spot those whose behavior they consider improper.

Lycurgus may be credited with introducing many other admirable means of making the citizens willingly obedient to the laws of the city. In my opinion, though, the most admirable was that he enacted his legislation only after he had visited Delphi, along with the most influential Spartan citizens, in order to ask the god [i.e., Pythian Apollo] whether it would be beneficial for the Spartans to adopt the laws he had drawn up. It was only after the god had responded affirmatively that he issued them, along with the decree that to disobey the laws ordained by Pythian Apollo would be considered not only unlawful but impious as well.

IX

We admire Lycurgus for other contributions as well. He was the man who made the Spartans think that an honorable death was preferable to a life of infamy. And yet, as anyone interested in this matter will discover upon further investigation, war casualties among the Spartans are lower than among those who prefer to retreat from danger. In fact, it should be noted that survival in war is more closely related to courage than to cowardice, since to be courageous is really easier and more pleasant than being cowardly, and since courage brings greater resources and strength. And it is obvious that the close companion of courage is glory, so that everyone wants to be associated with brave men.

But we should not neglect the means by which Lycurgus promoted this Spartan attitude. To begin with, he rewarded brave men with prosperity, while adversity was the fate of cowards. In other cities, when someone acts in a cowardly manner he earns the name of coward, but the coward may still go out in public, sit down with other men, and exercise in the gymnasia along with the citizens who are brave. In Sparta, however, everyone is ashamed to associate with a coward, to sit with him in his mess, or to have him as a wrestling partner in the gymnasia. The coward is usually left out when sides are chosen for ball games and assigned to the worst places in the public dances. Moreover, he is required to give way when he meets someone in the streets and to give up his seat even to younger men. He is also obligated to support at home the young women of his family and to explain to them why no one wants to marry them. He must not only get along without a wife in his home, but must also pay a penalty for being unmarried. The coward is forbidden to walk around town with a cheerful face and must avoid imitating people of good character and reputation, for a violation of this rule would lead to his being beaten by reputable citizens as punishment. When I consider all the forms of disgrace imposed on cowards there, I am not at all surprised that in Sparta death is preferable to a life of dishonor and infamy.

X

Another of Lycurgus' laws is, in my opinion, an important means of encouraging men to cultivate excellence throughout their lives. By requiring that election to the Gerousia should occur at an advanced age, Lycurgus ensured that the Spartans would continue to care about their morals even in later life. Another thing for which we must admire him is the protective attitude he displayed towards older men of virtue by making the Elders the supreme judges in capital cases, thus making old age more respectable than the age at which a man is at the peak of his physical strength. It is certainly reasonable to assume that of all human competitions this should elicit the greatest rivalry, for although athletic contests are admittedly honorable, they are merely physical in nature, while the competition for election to the Gerousia tests the noble qualities of the human spirit. As the spirit, then, is superior to the body, it follows that contests of the spirit elicit fiercer competition than those which merely test the powers of the body.

Another of Lycurgus' measures which is undeniably worthy of admiration is the following. He saw clearly that in those places where the attainment of virtue is left to those who desire it, the small number of such people is insufficient to glorify their country. Thus, he made it compulsory for all Spartans to cultivate all virtues as a duty to the state. Since individuals who develop excellence are clearly better than those who do not, it is obvious that Sparta, which alone among the city-states has mandated the cultivation of high morality as a public duty among its citizens, is superior to all other cities in this respect. And I should also mention another admirable measure of Lycurgus, that while other cities punish individuals for injuring one another, he imposed even more severe penalties on those who openly neglected to be as good as they were capable of being. In his view, men who enslave others or commit crimes of fraud or theft wrong only their particular victims, but those who display unmanly cowardice betray and victimize the entire community. Therefore, in my view it is quite proper that the heaviest penalties were imposed by Lycurgus on such people.

Lycurgus also made the exercise of all the high qualities of citizenship a duty for all citizens. Thus, an equal share in the state was given to all loyal citizens regardless of their physical or financial status. But he made it absolutely clear that those who shirked their duty and made no effort to obey the state's laws would forfeit their right to be considered among the Equals [the name by which full citizens of Sparta called themselves].

These Spartan laws are certainly very old, for according to tradition Lycurgus was a contemporary of the Heraclids, and yet even today other peoples find them to be very relevant. Indeed, it is a paradox that despite the universal praise they have received as a code of behavior, not a single city wants to imitate or adopt them.

XI

These, then, are the advantages that the Spartans have over others in times of both peace and war. Those who are interested in learning how Lycurgus organized their military campaigns so that they were superior to all others should read the following passages.

First, the Ephors announce to the members of the cavalry and the heavily armed infantry which age-groups will be asked to serve. After this the craftsmen are notified as well. As a result, while on campaign the Spartans are equipped with all the provisions that are useful in civil life in peacetime. Orders are issued for all the required equipment to be supplied to the army, some to be carried in wagons and some by pack animals; as a result, a missing item is not likely to go undetected. Concerning their battle gear, Lycurgus directed that each soldier should be given a red cloak and a bronze shield. This was done because he believed that the red cloak is much different from female dress and very warlike in appearance, while the bronze shield could be easily polished and is very slow to tarnish. Moreover, he allowed soldiers who had reached adulthood to wear their hair long, for he believed that long hair gave them a taller, nobler, and more awe-inspiring appearance.

The men thus supplied and equipped were then divided into six *moras* of cavalry and heavily armed infantry. Each *mora* of infantry is led by a *polemarch*, four *lochagoi*, eight *pentecosters*, and sixteen *enomotarchs*. When the order of assembly is given, the *enomotiae*, which are subdivisions of the *moras*, are arrayed either in single file, three abreast, or even six abreast.

The prevalent view that the entire battle formation of the Spartans is extremely complicated is very far from the truth. In fact, in the Spartan battle formation the officers stand in the front line and all of the soldiers, regardless of rank, work together in performing their assigned duties. Anyone who can tell men apart would have no difficulty in understanding the Spartan formation, for some have been assigned to lead while others are obliged to follow their orders. Deployment commands are shouted out by the *enomotarch*, who acts as a herald, and the phalanxes of the heavy infantry respond by thinning out or becoming thicker. There is nothing about these maneuvers that is difficult to understand. What is difficult to grasp, unless one has been raised under the laws of Lycurgus, is the Spartans' ability to continue to fight effectively after the line has been thrown into confusion.

It should also be noted that the Spartans manage to smoothly execute maneuvers that military instructors consider very difficult. For example, whenever they march in column formation one unit naturally marches behind another. Now, if an enemy phalanx suddenly appears in front of the marching Spartan column, each *enomotarch* is given the command to form a front to the left; thus, the first unit halts, the one behind it lines up to the left of it, and so forth down the entire length of the column until a center-phalanx is formed. In case the enemy appears in the rear while they are in this formation, each line counter-marches itself with the result that soldiers of superior ability always face the enemy. Although under these circumstances the commander finds himself on the left of the formation, instead of in his normal position on the right, there are times when they see this as an advantage rather than a disadvantage; for if the enemy makes an attempt to outflank them his encircling movement takes place on their protected left side, where the soldiers are protected by their shields, rather than on their exposed right side, where they hold their weapons in their right hands. However, in those instances where it is advantageous for some reason for the commander to hold the right wing, they proceed to form the unit in file and then reverse the phalanx formation so that the commanding officer finds himself on the right side and the rear of the column is on his left. In cases where an enemy appears to the right of a marching Spartan column, all they must do is simply position each unit like a trireme [a warship with three banks of oars] with its prow facing the enemy. With this movement, the unit in the rear finds itself once again positioned on the right. This does not mean that they allow the enemy to approach on the left side; instead, they push it back or turn the units to face the enemy so that the rear unit finds itself once again on the left.

XII

I would now like to discuss Lycurgus' views regarding the way in which a camp should be laid out. Since it is clear that the angles of a square cannot be defended, he formed his camps in the shape of a circle unless there was a protective hill, wall or river in the rear. During the day he posted sentries by the weapons. These soldiers faced the camp, for their responsibility was to guard against their fellow soldiers rather than the enemy. The cavalry kept watch on the enemy from positions where approaching enemy soldiers could be spotted a great distance away. During the night hours, Lycurgus placed Sciritae [hardy soldiers from Sciritis, a hill region of Laconia] to guard the perimeter of the camp. In our own time they are assisted by foreign mercenaries, if they are available. It is clear that the Spartan practice of always walking about with a spear in hand has the same purpose as that of forbidding the slaves from coming near the weapons. Nor should we be surprised that even when they leave their posts to perform some necessary function, the Spartans do not distance themselves too much from their fellow soldiers or their weapons, so that they do not cause each other distress. All of these customs are aimed at providing security in the camp. In addition, the Spartans move their camps frequently in order to cause difficulties for their enemies and to assist their friends.

Spartan soldiers are also required by law to continue their gymnastic training while campaigning; this enhances the pride they take in themselves and makes them appear superior to other men. But they are not allowed to walk or run beyond the area assigned to their unit, so that no soldier ventures far from his weapons. When the exercises are concluded, the senior *polemarch* issues the order through a herald for the soldiers to sit down and have breakfast, and at the same time relieves the scouts and conducts a kind of inspection. After this there is a period of relaxation and leisure until the evening exercises commence. When these have been completed, a herald gives the order for the preparation of the main meal, following which the soldiers sing hymns to the gods who have responded with good omens to their sacrifices. After this they go to sleep with their arms close by.

The length of my discussion should not come as a surprise to anyone, since it is easy to see that when it comes to military matters the Spartans have overlooked nothing that requires attention.

XIII

I will now proceed to describe the power and prestige that Lycurgus gave to the king when he was on a campaign. During such times the king and his attendants are maintained by the state. In fact, the *polemarchs* mess with him; this allows them to be with him at all times and provides them with the opportunity to confer with him whenever this becomes necessary. Three of the Equals are also assigned to be members of the king's mess. They serve the king's staff so that no mundane distractions or concerns will interfere with their conduct of the war.

But now I will go back to the beginning of the campaign and describe how the king sets out with his army. The first thing he does, while still at home, is to sacrifice to Zeus the Leader and to the other relevant gods. If the omens are favorable, the fire-bearer takes the fire from the sacrificial altar and brings it to the frontier. Here the king again offers sacrifices to Zeus as well as to Athena. It is only after he receives favorable responses from both of these divinities that he crosses the country's borders. The fire from these sacrifices is then carried ahead and is never extinguished. They also carry along with them animals for future sacrifices. The king begins these rituals before daybreak in the hope that he will be the first to win the favor of the god. The sacrificial ritual is attended by officers of all ranks, *polemarchs*, *lochagoi*, *pentecosters*, commanders of mercenary units, supervisors of the supply trains and even commanders of contingents of allies who wish to participate. Two Ephors are also present. Although they do not interfere in the proceedings in any way unless called upon by the king, they carefully observe everyone involved and make certain that all behave in a correct manner. When the sacrifices have been concluded, the king calls a general assembly and issues the orders for the day. Anyone who has witnessed these proceedings would come to the conclusion that in military matters all other peoples are mere amateurs, while the Spartans alone are the real masters of the art of war.

When the enemy is not in sight the king personally leads the army. No one goes before him except the Sciritae and the cavalry on reconnaissance. When they think that a battle is imminent, however, the king takes command of the first *mora* and leads right until this unit is placed between two *moras* and two *polemarchs*. Then the eldest member of the king's entourage leads the troops which are to be positioned behind the king's unit. These troops are made up of all the Equals who mess with the king: seers, doctors, pipers, the supervisors of the supply train, and any volunteers who happen to be present. Thus, nothing essential for the conduct of the war is lacking since everything has been thoughtfully considered in advance.

Other wonderful and, in my opinion, useful arrangements affecting actual military combat were made by Lycurgus. When the enemy is close enough to see what happens in the Spartan camp a she-goat is sacrificed, and the law dictates that all pipers present are to play and every Spartan is to wear a garland. Also, an order is given to polish their weapons. The young soldiers are required to go into battle with their hair well-groomed and to present a joyful and noble appearance. In addition, they shout positive, encouraging words to the *enomotarchs* because each one singly, as he stands outside his unit, cannot be heard over the entire line of soldiers. The responsibility for seeing that this is done properly is assigned to the *polemarch.*

The king is also responsible for finding the right location in which to pitch camp when the time comes to do so. It is also his duty to send embassies to both friends and enemies. All relevant business, in fact, is conducted by approaching the king first. In cases concerning judicial matters the king refers the person seeking advice to the *Hellanodicai*, those who approach him about money matters are sent to the treasurers, and in cases dealing with the spoils of war the inquirer is directed to the sellers of booty. As a result of these practices, the only concerns of the king while he is on a campaign are his duties as priest in his dealings with the gods and as general in his dealings with men.

XIV

I would also like to discuss the relationship between the kings and the state that was worked out by Lycurgus. This is necessary because Spartan kingship is a unique institution in that it retains its original form, whereas other forms of government have been modified and even now are subject to evolution and alteration.

Lyrcurgus ordained that, because of his divine ancestry, the king should perform all sacrifices offered on behalf of the city and that he should lead the army in all campaigns ordered by the state. He also ordered that certain parts of the sacrificed animals should be granted to the king and gave him enough land in the communities of the *perioeci* to ensure that his basic needs were satisfied but not so much as to give him excessive wealth. In addition, in order to ensure that the kings did not eat at home, Lycurgus required them to take their food at a specific state mess where they were honored with double portions at meals. This was not done so that they would have twice as much to eat as others, but so that they might have something to offer as a mark of royal respect to anyone they chose. In addition, Lycurgus allowed the king to choose two of his companions at mess, who are called *Pythii*. He also allowed each king to take a piglet from the litter of every sow so that he would always have sacrificial victims when he wished to consult the gods.

A pool located near the king's residence supplies him with an abundance of water, which is a great convenience, as those who do not have it can attest. All rise from their seats when the king appears, with the exception of the Ephors sitting in their official chairs. A monthly exchange of oaths is also required, the Ephors swearing on behalf of the city and the king for himself. The king swears to rule according to the laws of the state, while the Ephors pledge to leave the king undisturbed as long as he abides by his oath. These are the rights granted to a king during his lifetime, prerogatives which are barely above those of private citizens. This is so because Lycurgus had not intended that the kings should assume the attitude of tyrants or that the citizens of Sparta should be envious of their power. As for posthumous royal honors, Lycurgus' intention was that the Spartan kings would be honored not as mere humans, but as heroes.

XV

If someone were to ask whether I believe that the laws of Lycurgus are still applied today in an unchanged form, I would not be able to say, by Zeus, that they are. I know that in earlier years the Spartans chose to live modestly at home instead of allowing themselves to be corrupted by flattery while serving as the *harmosts* [military governors] of foreign cities. I know, too, that in the past they feared being found in possession of gold, while today some of them are even proud of having acquired it. In the past, foreigners were expelled from Sparta and the Spartans themselves were forbidden to live abroad so that citizens would not be influenced by the permissive habits of foreigners. In our day, however, those who are recognized as leading citizens have demonstrated that their ambition is to serve abroad as *harmosts* all their lives. In former times such people would have done their best to ensure that they were worthy of their prominent positions, but today their primary concern is to exercise their authority rather than proving that they are worthy of their power. The Greeks in past years would come to Sparta to request that the Spartans provide them with leadership against those who did them harm. Today, however, they call upon each other to help prevent the further expansion of Spartan rule. It is no wonder that this attitude toward them exists now, for it is clear that they obey neither the divine will nor the laws of Lycurgus.

Defects of the Spartan Constitution:
Polybius, *History*, 6.48.2–50.

Polybius, a second century B.C. Greek historian from Megalopolis in Arcadia and author of an ecumenical and pragmatic *History*, is considered to be one of the giants of ancient historiography. He is famous for his interest in constitutional history and his studies of the constitutions of Sparta, Carthage and Rome are justly viewed as masterpieces. Unlike other Greek thinkers, however, he considered the Roman, rather than the Spartan, as the ideal "mixed" constitution. His judicious analysis of the strengths and weaknesses of the Spartan constitution in the following passages from his work are indicative of his unique appreciation of the true potential, as well as the limits, of the Spartan form of government.

It seems to me that in matters concerning the maintenance of harmony among the citizens, the security of the land of Laconia and the preservation of Spartan freedom, Lycurgus' legislation and foresight were so great that one may consider them to be divine rather than human in origin. The even distribution of land and the simplicity of their common meals were intended to make the citizens temperate in their private lives and to eliminate civil disorder, while training in the toleration of pain and suffering were meant to produce men who are strong and brave. Evil will not grow in the individual or in the city in which these qualities of temperance and strength are found, nor will those who possess them be easily subdued by their neighbors. Thus, by drafting such a constitution Lycurgus brought complete security to the entire region of Laconia and bequeathed to the Spartans a long and lasting freedom.

However, with regard to matters concerning the occupation of the territory of their neighbors, the establishment of Spartan hegemony in Greece and the exercise of foreign policy in general, it seems to me that Lycurgus made no provision whatsoever, either in the constitution itself or in any other legislation. He neglected to introduce to the citizens some necessity or principle by which, just as he had made the Spartans simple and self-sufficient in their private lives, he might likewise have made the general ethos of the whole state one of self-sufficiency and temperance. As it turned out, however, he made the Spartans the least ambitious and most sensible of peoples as far as their laws and private lives are concerned, but left them the most ambitious, emulous and greedy of the Greeks in matters of foreign policy. For who does not know that the Spartans were among the first Greeks to covet the land of their neighbors, making war on the Messenians out of

45

greed and with the intention of reducing them to slavery? And what historian does not tell how, for the sake of contentiousness, they bound themselves by an oath never to abandon the siege before taking Messene by storm? Isn't it common knowledge that their ambition to dominate the Greeks led them to obey the orders of the same people they had conquered in war? For they defeated the Persians when the latter marched against Greece, fighting to the end for the freedom of the Greeks, but when the enemy turned back they betrayed the Greek cities [of Ionia] and delivered them to Persia by the Peace of Antalcidas in order to get money with which to establish their supremacy over the Greeks. It was then that a serious shortcoming in their constitution became obvious. As long as the Spartans were content to rule over their immediate neighbors, or even the rest of the Peloponnesians, the resources of Laconia met all their needs. They lacked nothing and, whether they traveled by land or by sea, they were always close to home. But when they began to undertake naval expeditions and to engage their land forces outside of the Peloponnese it became clear that their customs of using iron currency and bartering their crops for whatever they needed, both established by the laws of Lycurgus, were no longer useful; for these new enterprises demanded a universal currency and supplies drawn from foreign lands. Thus, they were forced to knock as beggars at the gates of the Persians, to impose taxes on the islanders and to exact money from all the Greeks, for they realized that under the laws of Lycurgus they would never achieve hegemony or any kind of prominence in Greece.

The Oligarchic Constitution of Crete:
Aristotle, *Politics,* 1271b.10–1271b.23.

It is generally recognized that Aristotle's examination of ancient constitutions in the *Politics* presents us with authoritative historical evidence and demonstrates his profound regard for institutional essentials. It is not surprising, therefore, that he grasped the fundamental unity of the Cretan system, which transcended the fragmented political state of the island and its division into several independent city states. Thus, Aristotle's model of the Cretan constitution reflects the oligarchic institutions of the aristocratic societies of ancient Crete. It should be noted that the abundant epigraphic records from the Hellenistic Age lend credence, for the most part, to his historical analysis and philosophical reflections on Cretan society and institutions. The tenacity of the Cretan laws, whose antiquity Aristotle traces to King Minos, not only excited the admiration of great thinkers such as Plato, but defied the changes brought about by the intervention of foreign powers in Hellenistic Crete. In fact, the conservatism of the islanders explains their stubborn resistance to Roman expansionism and the conquest of the Cretan city-states nearly a century after the fall of Corinth and the loss of Greek independence on the mainland.

The Cretan constitution is similar to the Spartan; not inferior in a few respects, but in general less polished. It is said, and it is probably true, that the Laconian constitution was, for the most part, modeled after the Cretan, for in ancient times most institutions were less elaborate than their modern counterparts. They say that when Lycurgus gave up the guardianship of King Charillus and went abroad he spent most of his time in Crete because of the ties of kinship which existed between Crete and Sparta. For the Lyctians were Spartan colonists who adopted the laws they found in existence among the native inhabitants when they came to establish their colony. Even now the *perioeci* use them in the same form in which they had been promulgated by Minos. It seems that the island has been intended by nature to rule over Greece, and that it is well-situated. It lies right across the sea around which nearly all of the Greeks dwell and is located a short distance from both the Peloponnese on one side and from the region of Asia about Triopium and Rhodes on the other. Because of this Minos became the ruler of the seas, conquering some of the islands and colonizing others until, in the end, he attacked Sicily and lost his life there near Camicus.

These are some of the similarities between the Cretan and Laconian institutions. The *helots* cultivate the land for the Spartans and the *perioeci* do the same for the Cretans, and both peoples have common meals which the Spartans originally called by their Cretan name, *andreia*, and not *phiditia*. It is clear, then, that this institution derives from Crete. This is also true of their constitution. For the Spartan *ephors* have the same powers held in Crete by the magistrates called *kosmoi*, with the difference that the number of *ephors* is five, while the board of *kosmoi* consists of ten members. The Spartan elders correspond to the elders of Crete, who are called by the Cretans their Council. Kingship also existed in Crete in early times, though the Cretans abolished it and leadership in war is now exercised by the *kosmoi*. Everyone is allowed to participate in the assembly, but it has no powers except the ratification of the decisions of the elders and the *kosmoi*. The common meals are better managed among the Cretans than among the Spartans. At Sparta everyone contributes a stipulated per capita amount, and failure to contribute results in the loss of citizenship, as has been previously explained; in Crete, however, there is more communal sharing. Out of all the produce from the public lands and the revenues from state-owned cattle and the tribute paid by the *perioeci* a portion is reserved for the gods and for public services in general, and another portion is set aside for the communal meals so that all people, men, women and children, are maintained by the state. The lawgiver has also given much thought to finding ways of encouraging moderation in eating as a useful practice, and of controlling the growth of the population by separating men from women and by sanctioning the companionship of men with other men; whether this practice is good or bad will be considered at a later time. It is obvious, then, that the communal meals in Crete are better managed than those in Sparta, although the *kosmoi* as an institution are even worse than the *ephors*. For what is wrong with the *ephors* is wrong with the *kosmoi* as well, since both are indiscriminately chosen; in Crete, however, they do not enjoy the compensating political advantages which the *ephors* have in Sparta. There, because the *ephors* are chosen from the entire citizen body, the people want the constitution to be preserved since they themselves share in the highest office. In Crete, however, the *kosmoi* are not selected from the whole people, but from certain clans, and the *elders* are chosen from the ranks of those who have served as *kosmoi*. With regard to them we may repeat the same objections that have been already made about the Spartan *elders*, namely that the lack of accountability for their acts and the life tenure of their office are greater privileges than they deserve, and that it is dangerous for them to rule according to their own judgment rather than by the law. The fact that the people who do not hold the office remain quiet is no proof of the goodness of this practice. Neither is there any profit to be gained from service in this magistracy, as is the case with the *ephors*, for the *kosmoi*, who are confined on an island, are far removed from the temptation of foreign corruption.

The means they employ to cure the ills of this magistracy are absurd, being unconstitutional and arbitrary. For quite frequently the *kosmoi* are driven out of office either by some of their own colleagues or by the conspiracies of private citizens. However, it is also possible for them to resign before the expiration of their term of office; but all of these matters can be best regulated by the rule of law rather than by the will of individuals, for the latter is an unsafe practice. Worst of all, however, is the condition of not having *kosmoi* at all, which the powerful often bring about as a means of avoiding justice. It is very clear, then, that although their government has some characteristics of a constitutional state, it is in reality a closed oligarchy [*dynasteia*]. The powerful are accustomed to forming bands composed of their friends and the people and stirring up quarrels and fights with each other, thus causing a state of anarchy. How does this differ from the temporary cessation of government and the dissolution of the political community? A city in this condition would be in greater danger from those who are willing and able to attack it. But, as I have already remarked, they are saved by their geographical situation: remoteness has kept foreigners away as effectively as the expulsion of strangers in Sparta. This is why the Cretan *perioeci* remain quiet, whereas the Spartan *helots* often rise in revolt. The Cretans have no foreign dominions, either, though recently a foreign war reached the island and revealed the weaknesses of their institutions. But enough has been said about the Cretan government.

The Delian League and Athenian Power:
Thucydides, *History of the Peloponnesian War*, I.95–99.

In his *History of the Peloponnesian War* Thucydides describes the rise of Athens in the years following the Persian Wars. His account begins with the fall of Pausanias, son of the Spartan king Cleombrotus and nephew of Leonidas, who led the combined Greek forces in their victory over the Persians at Plataea in 479 B.C. but had been undone, after capturing Byzantium at the head of an allied Greek fleet a year later, by his arrogance and rumors of treason. Pausanias' fall left a power vacuum, and in the following excerpt Thucydides relates how the Athenians quickly took advantage of the opportunity to assume a leadership role in Greece. Of particular interest is his description of the origin of the Delian League in 478–77 B.C.

By that time Pausanias had already become domineering, thereby alienating the rest of the Greeks and in particular the Ionians and others who had been recently freed from the Persian king. They went to the Athenians and pleaded with them as kinsmen to be their leaders and to protect them against Pausanias if he tried to coerce them. The Athenians accepted their proposals and resolved both to put up with Pausanias' behavior no longer and to settle matters to their own advantage. Meanwhile, the Lacedaemonians called Pausanias back to Sparta in order to question him about rumors they had heard, for he had been accused of many crimes by Greeks who came to Sparta and had seemed more like a tyrant than a general in exercising his authority. His recall happened at the very time that their hatred for him led the allies, except for the Peloponnesians, to turn to the Athenians. When he arrived in Lacedaemon he was held responsible for his offenses against individuals, but he was acquitted on the principal charge, that he had been involved in treasonable negotiations with the Persians, even though his guilt had seemed obvious. He did not retain his command, however; the government gave it instead to Dorcis and a few others with a very small force. But the allies would not recognize these men as their leaders and so they returned home. After that the Lacedaemonians sent no more commanders, for they were afraid that these would be corrupted as Pausanias had been. They had also grown tired of fighting the Persians and so, believing that the Athenians were their friends, they acknowledged that they were competent to take command.

This, then, is how the Athenians became the leaders of the allies, who gave them the command voluntarily and because they despised Pausanias.

They determined which of the cities should contribute money and which should supply ships for the war against the barbarians, the avowed purpose of which was to compensate themselves and the allies for their losses by plundering the Persian King's country. And it was then that the Athenians created the office of Hellenic treasurers, who received the *phoros*, as the tribute was called. The first assessment was four hundred and sixty talents. The treasury was the island of Delos, where the allies held their councils in the temple.

Leaders of allies who, at least in the beginning, were autonomous and met in common councils, the Athenians in the interval between the Persian Wars and this war scored great military and administrative victories against the barbarians, their own allies when they rebelled, and against the Peloponnesians who sometimes became involved in those rebellions. I have gone out of my way to write about this interval because earlier writers have ignored it. They have focused either on Greek affairs prior to the Persian Wars or on the Persian Wars themselves. Hellanicus is the only one who has touched on this interval, but his account is brief and his chronology is inaccurate. My narrative of events during this interval will also serve to explain how the Athenian empire grew.

First, under the leadership of Cimon, son of Miltiades, the Athenians took by siege Persian-held Eion on the river Strymon, making slaves of its citizens. Then they enslaved the Dolopians who lived on Scyros and made that Aegean island their own colony. A war broke out between the Athenians and the Carystians in which the other Euboeans remained uninvolved, and after a while the parties settled on terms of surrender. The Athenians then waged war on the Naxians, who had revolted, and took them by siege. The Naxians were the first of the allies to be enslaved for violating the order established by Athens, enslavement being a practice which would later become common.

There were many factors which led to the rebellions of the allies, but the most important were their failure to pay the tribute or to supply ships and, in some cases, their refusal to perform their military service. For the Athenians were very severe in their exacting of the tribute and they offended by their coercive measures people who were neither accustomed to nor willing to put up with the hardships of forced service. And there were other ways in which the Athenians turned out to be less agreeable as rulers than they had been at first; they would no longer take part in joint campaigns unless they were in charge, and they found it easy to put down allies who rebelled. And yet it was the allies themselves who were really responsible for their fate, for most of them, because they disliked military service and did not want to be away from home, agreed to make their contributions in money rather than ships. Their contributions increased the size of the Athenian fleet, but they themelves were always untrained and unprepared when they rebelled.

The Melian Dialogue: Thucydides, *History of the Peloponnesian War*, 5.85–116.

In 416 B.C., in the midst of the Peloponnesian War, the Athenians sent an expeditionary force against the island of Melos. The Melians were colonists of the Spartans who, unlike most of the other islanders, were unwilling to submit to Athenian imperialism. At first they sought to remain neutral, but when the Athenians began ravaging their lands they resolved to fight for their freedom. However, before the outbreak of full-scale hostilities the Athenians sent envoys to negotiate with the Melians. When their efforts proved unsuccessful they besieged the city and, after breaking through its defenses, massacred its male population and sold the women and children into slavery. The following account of the dialogue between the Athenians and the Melian magistrates is from Thucydides, who almost certainly had no special knowledge of what was said in this secret meeting. Thus, his version of it no doubt reflects both his own view of what must have transpired there as well as his interpretation of Athenian imperialism and political relationships among the Greek states in general.

Athenians: "You are refusing us a public platform because you fear that the people, if they hear us speak persuasively and without interruption, might be swayed by us. We know that this is why you have brought us here to speak before only a select few. Well, suppose that you who sit here make yourselves safer still. Let us dispense with set speeches; instead, you may respond to every statement of ours which you find objectionable, criticizing it on the spot. Do you think that this is a good way to proceed?"

Melians: "It makes sense to exchange our explanations of our respective positions calmly and quietly, and so we do not object to that. But at this very moment you are engaged in acts of war against us, and these clearly belie your words. It seems to us that you are determined to decide this matter yourselves; if we prove that justice is on our side and refuse to surrender you will make war on us, and if you can prove that you are right you will enslave us."

Athenians: "If you are simply going to speak of your suspicions about the future, or if you have met with us for any purpose other than facing facts and saving your city from destruction, there is no point in our going on with this discussion. However, if this is not the case then let us proceed."

Melians: "It is only natural that people in our position should employ all sorts of arguments and consider different points of view. But you are right, we have met here to discuss the preservation of our city and so let us proceed in the manner you have suggested."

Athenians: "All right, then, we Athenians will not use fancy arguments to try to persuade you that we have a right to rule because we defeated the Persians or that we are attacking you now because you have harmed us in some way. You would never believe us. And we ask you not to try to convince us that you, although you are a colony of the Lacedaemonians, have never helped them in war or done us any harm. Each side should say what it really thinks and should hope only for what is reasonable, for we both know that in discussions like this one there can be no justice unless both sides have equal power and that, in the end, the strong will take what they can and the weak will give what they must."

Melians: "Well, then, since you want to talk about expediency rather than justice, in our opinion the expedient thing would be for you to respect a principle which works for the common good—namely, that every man who is in danger should be treated fairly and that every plea he makes in support of his cause ought to be taken seriously, even if it is not entirely convincing. You have as great a stake in this principle as we do since you, if you fall, will incur the most terrible vengeance and be made an example to the entire world."

Athenians: "We do not fear the fall of our empire, if such a thing is possible, because ruling states like Lacedaemon are not cruel to those they conquer. We are not as fearful of the Lacedaemonians as we are of our own subjects, who may one day rise up against us. But leave us to worry about that danger. What we want to do now is to show you that we have come here in the interests of our empire and that in what we are about to say we are seeking to save your city. We want to make you a part of our empire, but without trouble, since the survival of your city will be good for us as well as for you."

Melians: "It may be good for you to be our masters, but how can it be good for us to be your slaves?"

Athenians: "You, by giving in to us, will save yourselves from destruction; we, by not destroying you, will gain your city."

Melians: "But why must we be enemies? Would you consider us friends if we declared our neutrality?"

Athenians: "No, for friendship with you is more dangerous to us than your hostility. Our subjects would see the former as a sign of our weakness and the latter as proof of our power."

Melians: "But aren't your subjects able to distinguish between the free states in which you have no real interest and those which are your own colonies, some of which have revolted only to be subdued by you?"

Athenians: "They think that both can make good claims to being in the right, but they also believe that the free states remain free because we know their power and are afraid to attack them. Thus, by conquering you we will simultaneously increase the size of our empire and ensure its security. Besides, we are the masters of the sea and you are islanders, and insignificant islanders at that; thus, we must be especially careful to keep you from escaping us."

Melians: "But don't you see any advantage for yourselves in recognizing our neutrality? Once again, since you want to speak only of your own interests and not about justice, we must tell you what our interests are and hope to convince you that what is good for us is good for you as well. Won't you make enemies of the other states who are now neutral? When they see what you are doing to us won't they assume that you will one day turn against them too? And, if they do, won't you be strengthening the enemies you already have and forcing others to join them who would otherwise never dream of opposing you?"

Athenians: "We are not particularly concerned about the states on the mainland. They have their freedom, and so it will be a long time before they start taking defensive measures against us. We are much more fearful of islanders like you who still have their liberty and of subject peoples who are bitter because they have been forced into our empire. These are the ones who might recklessly throw themselves, and us, into some dangerous though foreseeable conflict."

Melians: "But surely, if you are willing to take great risks to preserve your empire and your subjects are ready to face dangers to escape it, then we who are still free would seem weak and cowardly if we were not ready to do and suffer anything rather than submit and become your slaves."

Athenians: "Not necessarily, if you think clearly about it. We are stronger than you are and so there would be no dishonor for you in submitting to us. The issue before you is not honor, but whether you will decide to save your city by not attempting to resist an irresistible force."

Melians: "But we know that in war fortune sometimes intervenes on the side with fewer men. If we yield to you now our hope is gone, but if we fight there is always the chance that we will succeed in defending ourselves."

Athenians: "Hope is a comfort in times of danger, and there is nothing wrong with hoping provided that one does not depend on hope alone; for then it may be harmful, but never ruinous. But when hope's 'go for broke' nature induces men to stake everything on her they don't see her for what she really is until

54

it is too late, in the moment of their destruction. It is only before that moment, when there is still time to take precautionary measures, that hope never fails them. You are weak, and a single turn of the scale might mean your destruction. So don't be deluded by hope. Don't make the mistake made by so many others who, though they could save themselves simply by doing what is sensible and practical when there are no longer good grounds for optimism, place their faith instead in smoke and mirrors, in prophecies and oracles and other intangibles which destroy men by encouraging them to be hopeful."

Melians: "We know very well how hard it would be to stand against your power, and against fortune too if she is against us. Still, we believe that the gods will be as kind to us as they are to you, for we are in the right and you, our enemies, are in the wrong. As for our weakness, we expect that our allies the Lacedaemonians will more than make up for it. They will help us because we are their kinsmen and for the sake of their honor. So you can see that our confidence is not so unfounded as you suppose."

Athenians: "We expect just as much from the gods as you do, for we are not striving for anything unusual, anything beyond what everyone agrees are the expectations of gods and men in human affairs. Our beliefs about the gods and our knowledge of men tell us that there is a law of nature according to which we seek to rule whatever we can. We did not create this law, nor are we the first to act upon it. We inherited it, and we will bequeath it to those who come after us. Moreover, the action we are taking against you is perfectly consistent with this law, and we know that you and all other peoples would do just what we are doing if you had our power. So much for the gods; we have no reason to fear their disfavor. Now, as for the Lacedaemonians—we admire you for your simple faith in them, but we do not envy you for your foolishness. The Lacedaemonians are, among themselves, a remarkably virtuous people. But their treatment of other peoples is another story, and a long one too. Let it suffice to say that of all the peoples we know the Lacedaemonians are the most notorious for believing that whatever they like is honorable and whatever advances their own interests is just. This attitude is absolutely inconsistent with your absurd belief that they will come and save you."

Melians: "But that is exactly why we *do* trust them to help us. They will look to their own interests, and so they will not betray us; for we Melians are their colonists, and they know that if they betray us they will lose the trust of their friends in Greece and thereby strengthen their enemies."

Athenians: "But don't you see that the self-interested seek safety, whereas doing what is just and honorable brings danger—something the Lacedaemonians prefer to avoid?"

Melians: "But we think that they would be willing to face dangers for our sake, and that they would even think the risk well worth taking since we are so close to their home in the Peloponnese and because we are their kinsmen and share their feelings."

Athenians: "But the good feeling of those who ask for help is not what induces a prospective ally to give it. What that ally wants is a clear superiority in real power over the enemy. Now, there is no people more intent on this than the Lacedaemonians. They have so little confidence in themselves that they won't even attack their own neighbors unless they have plenty of allies with them, and so it is not likely that they will come to your island when we are masters of the sea."

Melians: "But they might send their allies. The Cretan sea is large, and you would have more difficulty in intercepting enemy ships than they would have in slipping past you. And, if a rescue by sea should fail, they might invade Attica itself and even the lands of your allies who were left unharmed by Brasidas. Then you would have to fight close to home in order to save your own land and confederacy rather than for a country in which you have no legitimate interest."

Athenians: "It is possible that the Lacedaemonians may help you, for they have helped others. But you should remember that we Athenians have never withdrawn from a siege out of fear of others. And we are surprised that, though you have said your chief concern is the preservation of your city, not once during this long discussion have you said anything which would lead a reasonable man to believe that your salvation is likely. Your main points are all related to events you hope will take place in the future, and the power you do have cannot begin to compare with that which you see arrayed against you at this very moment. You really will be demonstrating a complete lack of common sense if, after we have left this meeting, you in your deliberations still do not come up with a strategy wiser than those you have already mentioned. Don't bring ruin on yourselves out of a false sense of honor, a thing which often destroys men when their pride is threatened by a dangerous situation. There have been many who, even though they were well aware of the likely consequences, nevertheless allowed themselves to be seduced by honor—a mere word, an idea! That it led them into irrevocable disaster was bad enough, but their disgrace and dishonor were made all the worse by the fact that they were brought about not by fortune, but by their own foolishness! You, if you are wise, will not make this mistake. You will see that there is nothing dishonorable in yielding to the greatest city in Greece when it invites you to join its empire on such reasonable terms, for we will allow you to keep your land and ask only that you pay us tribute. You will see that, given a choice between war and safety, there is no honor in obstinately insisting on war. Safety is achieved by standing up to one's equals, being deferential to superiors and treating one's inferiors with moderation. We will leave this meeting now. We ask that you consider this matter carefully, keeping in mind at every moment that your purpose is the survival of your country, the only one you have, and that its future hangs on the decision you are about to make."

The Athenians then left the meeting, and the Melians, after further discussion, determined to remain firm in their resolve to resist the enemy. They answered as follows: "Men of Athens, our position is unchanged. We will not surrender in one brief moment the freedom which our city has enjoyed for the seven hundred years since its foundation. We will put our trust in the good fortune which, by the grace of the gods, has kept us safe until now, in the Lacedaemonians, and in ourselves. Still, we are willing to be your friends and the enemies neither of you nor of the Lacedaemonians, and we ask you to make a treaty which is acceptable to both of us and then to leave our land."

This was the reply of the Melians, and the Athenians, as they departed, said: "Well, we must say, judging from your decision, that you are a people unique in your ability to see the future as more certain than the present and to regard uncertainties as certain just because you want them to be so. As you have entrusted your security mostly to the Lacedaemonians, fortune and hope, so shall these play the greatest part in your destruction."

The Athenian envoys returned to the army, and the Athenian generals, when they heard that the Melians would not surrender, began hostilities immediately. They built a wall around the entire city of Melos, dividing the work among the various contingents. Then they left some of their own troops and some of their allies to blockade the city by land and by sea and returned home with the bulk of their army. The force which stayed behind continued the siege.

At about the same time the Argives invaded Phliasia and lost eighty men when they were ambushed by the Phliasians and the exiles from Argos. It was then, too, that the Athenian force at Pylos plundered some Lacedaemonian lands. But the Lacedaemonians did not renounce the treaty; instead, they announced that if any of their people wanted to attack the Athenians they were free to do so. After this the Corinthians declared war on Athens for their own reasons, but the rest of the Peloponnesians remained at peace.

On one occasion the Melians made a night attack on the Athenians, capturing that part of the Athenian line which was opposite the agora, killing a few men and taking as much corn and other necessities as they could carry. They retreated and made no further move while the Athenians, for their part, took measures to tighten their hold on the city. And so the summer came to an end.

The Lacedaemonians had planned to attack Argos during the winter, but when the sacrifices they made at the Argive frontier turned out to be unfavorable they changed their minds. The Argives suspected that the planned invasion had been instigated by traitors within their own walls; some were arrested but others escaped.

At about this time the Melians again captured a part of the Athenian line, a section that was undermanned, and so the Athenians sent reinforcements under the command of Philocrates the son of Demeas and intensified their operations against the city. This led to treachery among the Melians themselves and, ultimately, to an unconditional surrender to the Athenians. The latter put to death all the men of military age and sold the women and children into slavery. They then took the land of Melos for themselves, sending five hundred of their own citizens as colonists.

The Thirty Tyrants: Xenophon, *Hellenica* II, 3.1–4.1.

After the defeat of Athens in the Peloponnesian War (404 B.C.), the victorious Spartans adopted the policy of supporting conservative Athenian oligarchs. Accordingly, the Spartan general Lysander allowed for the selection of thirty men who were to run the government and enact legislation they claimed would be more in line with the laws of Solon and Cleisthenes than the more radical democracy of the late fifth century. The Thirty were divided into two factions, the reactionaries led by Critias and the moderates by Theramenes. When the latter attempted to broaden the franchise beyond the three thousand citizens who were originally approved, Critias called for his condemnation and execution. The following excerpt from Xenophon's *Hellenica* describes these events which occurred even as Thrasybulus and other exiled democrats were organizing an opposition force that would topple the Thirty in 403 B.C.

The next year the Olympic games were held and Crocinas the Thessalian was the victor in the stadium. At that time Endius was ephor at Sparta and Pythodorus was archon at Athens. But since Pythodorus was chosen during the time of the oligarchy the Athenians did not name the year after him; they call it instead the "archonless year." This oligarchy came into being when the people voted to choose thirty men to form the ancient laws [*i.e.*, of Solon and Cleisthenes] into a new constitution on the basis of which the city would be governed. The men chosen were Polychares, Critias, Melobius, Hippolochus, Eucleides, Hieron, Mnesilochus, Chremon, Theramenes, Aresias, Diocles, Phaedrias, Chaereleos, Anaetius, Peison, Sophocles, Eratosthenes, Charicles, Onomacles, Theognis, Aeschines, Theogenes, Cleomedes, Erasistratus, Pheidon, Dracontides, Eumathes, Aritoteles, Hippomachus, and Mnesitheides. Once the Thirty had been chosen, Lysander sailed for Samos and Agis pulled his land force from Deceleia and sent the members of its various units home to their own cities. . . .

The Thirty had been chosen immediately after the long walls and the walls around Piraeus were destroyed. Although they were responsible for drafting laws for the city, these were never promulgated; instead, the Thirty created a council and appointed such officials as they thought necessary. Once this had been done their first action was to arrest those who were known to have made their living as informers under the democracy and to have brought grief to good and decent people. These people were put on trial for their lives. The council was glad to condemn them, and the rest of the citizens, seeing that they had nothing in common with them, seemed not at all unhappy with this judgment.

Once this had been done the Thirty considered how they might gain complete control of the city. As a first step, they dispatched Aeschines and Aristoteles to Lacedaemon with instructions to gain Lysander's support for the sending of a Lacedaemonian garrison to Athens, where it would remain until they could get rid of the "scoundrels," as they called them, and set up their government. The garrison would be maintained at their expense. Lysander agreed to their request and arranged for the soldiers to be sent under the command of Callibius, who would serve as governor.

Once they had their garrison, the Thirty flattered and fawned on Callibius at every opportunity in order to win his approval for their actions. Since he allowed them the use of soldiers to guard them wherever they went, they had the power to arrest whomever they wished—not just the so-called "scoundrels" and other small fry, but those they thought would be least likely to put up with being ignored by the government or, if they sought to topple it, could rally a large number of supporters.

In the early days Critias and Theramenes agreed on matters of policy and were on friendly terms. But as time passed Critias grew bloodthirsty and eager to get revenge on the democracy which had once banished him by putting to death those he associated with it. Theramenes resisted him, arguing that it made no sense to kill people who had never harmed the aristocrats just because they had been honored by the common people. "You and I, Critias," he would say, "have also said and done many things in order to make ourselves popular." But Critias, who at this point still considered Theramenes a friend, would reply that it was necessary for ambitious people to eliminate anyone who might get in their way. "You are a fool, Theramenes," he would say, "if you think that just because we are thirty rather than one each of us should not guard the government just as carefully as if he were ruling alone."

And so many people were put to death unjustly. But as their number grew, so did popular discontent. Finally, when the citizens began banding together and asking where the city was headed, Theramenes advised his colleagues that if they did not give enough citizens a share of power in the conduct of public affairs their regime would surely collapse. By this time Critias and the rest of the Thirty were alarmed by the possibility that the Athenians were about to throw their support to Theramenes, and so they invited three thousand of them to participate in the government. But Theramenes objected, saying that it was ridiculous for them in their effort to create a partnership with the very best citizens to limit themselves to three thousand, as if that were the precise number of good men in the state and that one could not find other good men outside the three thousand or some bad ones included among them. "Besides," he said, "we are being inconsistent, for we are trying to create a government which is based on force and yet weaker than the people we seek to govern." This was what Theramenes said. What the Thirty did was to hold a military review in which they disarmed the population. The Three

Thousand were assembled in the Agora, and the rest of the population, whose names were not included on this special list, were called together in various places in and around the city. The Thirty gave the order for all weapons to be piled, and then, when the men were off duty, they sent the Lacedaemonian soldiers and their sympathizers to seize the weapons of all but the Three Thousand and deposit them in the temple on the Acropolis.

The Thirty now believed that they were finally in a position to do exactly as they pleased. More citizens were put to death, some because the tyrants hated them and others because they desired their wealth. In order to pay for the garrison, it was decided that each of the Thirty would seize one of the foreigners living in the city, kill him and confiscate his property. When Theramenes was told he could seize anyone he pleased, he said, "I do not think it would be appropriate for people who represent themselves as the very best of citizens to surpass the informers in injustice. They allowed those from whom they took money to live. Will we kill innocent men in order to take their money? Wouldn't this make us worse than the informers?"

After this the rest of the Thirty began to plot against Theramenes, for they had come to regard him as an obstacle to their plans. They accused him of interfering with the government, each of them denouncing him in private conversations with members of the council. Then, after enlisting the help of some bold young men who agreed to attend a meeting of the council with daggers hidden under their arms, they called the council into session. As soon as Theramenes arrived, Critias stood and spoke as follows:

"If there is anyone here who thinks that too much blood has been shed, he ought to remember that bloodshed always accompanies a change of government. Furthermore, it is inevitable that we who are creating an oligarchy here in Athens should have many enemies, for this is by far the most populous of the Greek cities and the common people here have been accustomed to freedom for many years. To men like ourselves, and also to you, democracy is a detestable form of government, and so we aristocrats support the Lacedaemonians, who have saved us from it. But we know that the common people are of a different opinion, and that they will never give them their loyalty and friendship. This is why we are working with the Lacedaemonians to create an oligarchy. This is why we must make use of our power to eliminate anyone who stands in our way. And if one of our own number should resist us, he too must be punished. As it turns out, Theramenes is just such a man. He is bent on doing whatever is necessary to destroy both us and you. Is this a baseless accusation? Hardly. Consider the matter and you will realize that no one is more critical of the present state of affairs than Theramenes. No one opposes us more fiercely than he does when we seek to get rid of some troublemaker. Now, we would consider him an enemy, though not a scoundrel, even if this had been his attitude from the beginning. But this is not the case. It was Theramenes who took the lead in establishing friendly relations with the Lacedaemonians. He was the one who initiated the overthrow of the democracy and who called most loudly for the punishment of the first batch of prisoners brought before you for trial. But now that you and we are despised by the common people he has changed his tune. He no longer approves of our actions. Why? Because he wants to make sure that he will be able to save his own skin, and that we alone will be held responsible for what we have done if the political situation should suddenly change. He deserves to be punished, not only as an enemy of the state but as one who has betrayed both you and us. I might add that a traitor is far more dangerous than a common enemy. It is more difficult to defend oneself against a hidden danger than one that is out in the open. Moreover, traitors are especially hateful since, though men make peace with their enemies and may even become good friends with them, it is impossible ever to make peace with a man or trust him once he has been found guilty of treason. In order to demonstrate that Theramenes is a traitor by nature and that what he is up to now is nothing new, let me recall his past actions.

"In the beginning, although he was greatly esteemed by the democracy, he was just as eager as his father, Hagnon, to transform it into the oligarchy of the Four Hundred. Indeed, for a time he was the leader of that government. Later, when he sensed a growing opposition to that oligarchy, he made himself into the leader of the democrats in their assault on the oligarchs! This is how he earned the nickname 'Buskin,' for just as the buskin fits both feet, he faces both ways. Listen, Theramenes: a man who leads his friends into dangerous situations and then seeks to save himself at the first sign of trouble doesn't deserve to live. Rather, like a sailor on shipboard he ought to remain at his station until he comes into a fair wind. How in the world would sailors ever reach their destination if they turned their ship around and sailed in the opposite direction as soon as they encountered a contrary wind or tide? Any change in government brings death, Theramenes, but since you have been so quick to change sides you must share the responsibility for deaths on both sides: the slaughter of oligarchs by the common people and the killing of democrats by the aristocrats. Members of the council, remember that this is the same Theramenes who, though ordered by the generals to rescue the crews of ships disabled in the sea battle off Lesbos, not only failed to do so but put the blame for his failure on them. He sacrificed their lives in order to save his own!

"How can it be right to spare the life of a man who makes it clear that he is always looking out for himself and has no interest in honor or friendship? We know how quick he has been to turn on others; shouldn't we make sure that he doesn't turn on us? We must, and so we charge Theramenes with conspiracy and treason against us and you. The reasonableness of this is demonstrated by the following. Everyone knows that the constitution of the Lacedaemonians is the best of all constitutions. Can you imagine what would happen if one of their ephors were to criticize the government and stand in its way instead of going along with the majority? Wouldn't the other ephors— and, in fact, the whole state—consider him worthy of the most severe punishment? You, then, if you are wise, will spare yourselves rather than him.

If you allow him to live his example will inspire the courage of your enemies. Kill him, and you will destroy the hopes of all who oppose you, both inside and outside the city."

When Critias had finished speaking, Theramenes rose and said: "With your permission, gentlemen, I will begin by commenting on the last thing Critias said against me. He claims that by accusing the generals I brought about their deaths, but you know that my accusation was not the beginning of the matter. No, they accused *me* of failing to rescue the unfortunate men in the battle off Lesbos even though they had ordered me to do so. In defending myself, I pointed out that a violent storm had made it impossible for me to set sail, much less actually accomplish the rescue. It seemed to the city that my argument was a very reasonable one. The generals, on the other hand, condemned themselves by their own testimony, for although they maintained that it was possible to save the men they sailed away and left them to die. I am not surprised that Critias has misunderstood what happened, for it so happens that when these events were taking place he and Prometheus were establishing a democracy in Thessaly and arming the poor working people there against their masters. Heaven help us if any of the things he did there should happen here!

"And yet I must admit that I do agree with Critias on one point. Whoever seeks to remove you from power and strengthen those who are intriguing against you ought to suffer the very worst of punishments. But who is that man? This will become clear if you consider what Critias and I did in the past and what we are doing now. We were in agreement up to the time when you were formed into a council and officials were appointed and the most notorious of the informers were put on trial. But when the Thirty began to arrest good and decent people, I began to oppose them. From the moment Leon of Salamis was executed—a man who deserved his excellent reputation and who had never committed the slightest offense—I knew that others like him would have to fear the government, and that, being afraid of it, they would necessarily become its enemies. Similarly, when Niceratus, the son of Nicias, was arrested—a man who, like his father, had never made any attempt to make himself popular—I knew that men like him would begin to hate us. And when we put Antiphon to death—a man who contributed to the war effort by maintaining two fast-sailing triremes at his own expense—I knew that all true patriots would regard us with suspicion. I objected when the Thirty decreed that each of us should seize one of the foreigners living in the city, for it was obvious that the deaths of these men would turn the entire population of resident aliens against us. I also objected to the disarming of the people, for I thought it would be a mistake to thereby weaken the city. In fact, it seemed to me that the Lacedaemonians were of a similar opinion. Would they have stepped in to save us only to weaken us to the point where we would be of no use to them? If this had been their purpose they could easily have wiped us out simply by allowing the famine to continue a little while longer. I was not pleased by the hiring of the Lacedaemonian garrison, for it would have been very easy for us to make use of an equal number of our own citizens as we sought to establish ourselves as rulers of the city. Finally, when I saw that there was growing hostility to our regime and that many citizens were going into voluntary exile, I could not help but see the banishment of men like Thrasybulus, Anytus and Alcibiades as a mistake. I knew that such banishments would strengthen the opposition by giving it just what it needed: leaders for the common people and a mass of supporters for would-be leaders.

"I ask you, does the man who openly advises actions such as these deserve to be considered a benefactor or a traitor? Surely, Critias, the man who seeks to keep the state from making enemies and does what he can to assist it in making more friends cannot be accused of helping the enemy. Such a charge should be made against those who wrongfully strip others of their property and put to death people who are innocent of any crime. Men like these increase the number of our enemies and betray both their friends and themselves in order to satisfy their greed.

"If the logic of my argument is not clear, look at the matter this way. Do you suppose that Thrasybulus and Anytus and the other exiles would prefer to see us follow the path which I am advocating in words or that which my colleagues are taking in their deeds? I suppose that they must now be saying to themselves that the number of their allies here is growing by leaps and bounds. But if the best of our citizens supported us instead of opposing us, the exiles would be unable to find a welcome anywhere in the city.

"Now, concerning Critias' allegation that I am always changing sides, I would ask you to keep a few things in mind. First, it was the people, as everyone knows, who voted for the government of the Four Hundred. They did so because they had been told that the Lacedaemonians would trust any form of government more than a democracy. Later, when the Lacedaemonians continued their war against us and Aristoteles, Melanthius, Aristarchus and the other generals were clearly planning to build a fort on the peninsula commanding the Piraeus in order to admit the enemy and bring the city under the control of themselves and their associates, I saw what they were up to and foiled their plans. I ask you, is that being a traitor to one's friends? Second, Critias calls me 'Buskin' because, as he says, I try to fit in with both parties. But what about the man who pleases neither party? By the gods, what should we call him? I am talking about you, Critias! In the time of the democracy you were regarded as the most bitter despiser of the people, and under the aristocracy you have proved yourself the bitterest foe of the more respectable classes. But I, Critias, have always been the enemy of extremists, both those who think that a true democracy has not been created until slaves and poor people who would sell the city for a drachma have been given power and those who believe that the only good oligarchy is the one which subjects the entire city to the despotism of a very few. From the very beginning until today I have regarded the best government as that in which I might share power with those who can afford a horse and shield and are willing to put them into the service of the state. Critias, if you can mention a single occasion when I joined forces with despots or demagogues in order to deprive good and decent people of their property and citizenship, I urge you to speak up now. If it can be shown that I have committed such a crime, whether now or in the past, I admit that I deserve to die the very worst of deaths."

With these words Theramenes ended his speech, and the applause heard in the council showed that he had won them over. Realizing that the council would make the intolerable decision to allow Theramenes to go free if they were allowed to pass judgment on him, Critias quickly discussed the matter with the Thirty. He then ordered the young men with daggers to stand close to the bar separating the council from the onlookers, so that they were in plain sight of the council. After this he addressed the council once again with these words:

"Members of the council, I believe it is the duty of a good leader to step in and take action if he sees that his colleagues are being duped. This is what I will do now. Besides, the young men standing before you say that they will not allow us to acquit a man who is so obviously guilty of attacking the oligarchy. Now, the city's new laws forbid the execution of any of the Three Thousand without your approval, but the Thirty have the power of life and death over all those who do not appear on the list of their names. Therefore, I hereby remove Theramenes from the list, and I do so with the approval of the Thirty." Having said this, he added, "We now condemn Theramenes to death."

Hearing this, Theramenes leaped upon the altar of Hestia and shouted, "Members of the council, I ask you for nothing more than plain justice. Do not leave it to Critias to decide whether I or one of you shall be removed from the list. Such decisions should be made strictly in accordance with the law. By the gods, I know that this altar won't protect me, but I want everyone to see that the Thirty are impious toward the gods as well as unjust toward men. And I am amazed that you good and respectable men are doing nothing to protect yourselves, for you must know that your names are just as easily removed from the list as my own."

At that moment the herald of the Thirty shouted out, ordering the Eleven to seize Theramenes. An instant later they appeared along with their servants and led by Satyrus, the boldest and most shameless of them all. Addressing them, Critias exclaimed, "Theramenes has been condemned, and so we hand him over to you. Take him to the proper place and do what you must do."

Once Critias had said this, Satyrus and his servants took hold of Theramenes in order to drag him away from the altar. Theramenes, as was natural, called upon the gods and men to witness what was happening. But the council sat silently, for they could see that the men at the bar were of the same mind as Satyrus and that the space in front of the council building was filled with soldiers belonging to the garrison. They were aware, too, that many of these men were carrying concealed daggers. And so Theramenes was dragged through the Agora, all the while protesting loudly the wrongs that he was suffering. They say that when Satyrus told him to hold his tongue or he would regret it, he replied, "But won't I regret it if I keep silent?" And when he had drunk the hemlock he is said to have tossed out the last drops in the cup and, like a man playing *cottabos*, exclaimed, "Here's to my good friend Critias." I know that these sayings themselves have no particular merit, but they do point to what I consider an admirable trait in Theramenes, that even in the face of death he kept his composure and his playful spirit.

And so Theramenes died. As for the Thirty, believing that they could now play the tyrant without fear, they issued a proclamation forbidding all whose names were not on the list to set foot within the city. Those who sought safety in their country estates were evicted and their property confiscated for the enjoyment of the Thirty and their associates. Even those who fled to Piraeus were not safe; those who sought refuge there were driven away, so that Megara and Thebes were filled with refugees.

Justice in the Marketplace: Lysias, *Against the Grain Merchants*.

The Attic orator Lysias was well-known in antiquity. He appears in Plato's *Phaedrus*, was the subject of one of Plutarch's biographies, and wrote hundreds of published speeches, thirty-four of which are extant. His career coincided with the defeat of Athens in the Peloponnesian War (431–404 B.C.) and the political turbulence which followed. In these difficult times, Lysias spoke out on behalf of justice and democracy in both private and public cases. He delivered the speech which appears below *ca.* 386 B.C., when an irregular grain supply and the greed of the retail merchants threatened the security of the Athenians.

Members of the jury, many people have come to me expressing surprise that I have made an accusation against the grain merchants in the Boule. They say that, no matter how certain you may be of their guilt, you are likely to consider those who make speeches against them as slanderers [i.e., who bring charges against the unpopular grain-dealers in the hope of being bought off by them]. For this reason I would like to speak first about the reasons why I find it necessary to accuse them.

When the Committee presented this case in the Boule there was such anger against the grain merchants that some of the speakers called for them to be handed over without trial to the Eleven so that they might be put to death. I, however, thought it would be a terrible thing for the Boule to become involved in such a thing, and so I stood and said that it seemed to me that we should try the grain merchants in accordance with the law. My thinking was that if they had committed acts deserving of death you would be just as able as the Boule to render justice and that, if they were innocent, it would not be right for them to die without a trial. The Boule was persuaded by my remarks, but then attempts were made to discredit me by saying that my purpose in speaking had been to save the grain merchants. When the case came before the Boule for a preliminary hearing, I defended myself against my detractors in the following way: while everyone else remained silent, I stood and accused the merchants, making it clear to everyone that what I had said earlier was not in defense of these men but in support of the established laws. So, it was fear of these accusations that led me to begin this business. And now I think it would be disgraceful for me to abandon it before you have voted to judge them in whatever way you wish.

[Speaking to one of the grain merchants]

First of all, sir, please take the stand. Now, tell me, are you a resident alien?

Yes, I am.

Do you live here in order to obey the city's laws, or to do whatever you like?

To obey.

Shouldn't you expect to be put to death if you have committed a crime that carries the death penalty?

I should.

Then tell me, do you admit to buying up more than the fifty measures of grain allowed under the law?

Yes, but I bought it on the order of the archons.

Well then, members of the jury, if he can demonstrate that there is a law which requires the merchants to buy up grain on an order from the archons you must acquit him. If he cannot, then you must condemn him. For we have produced to you the law which forbids anyone in the city to buy up more than fifty measures of grain.

Gentlemen, my accusation should be sufficient to condemn this man, for he admits that he bought up the grain even though the law forbids him to do so, and you have sworn to judge him in accordance with the law. But in order for you to be persuaded that the grain merchants are lying about the archons we must say something more about the latter. Since the merchants pinned the blame on them, we called the archons before us and questioned them. Two of them claimed they had no knowledge of this matter. But Anytus said that during the previous winter, when the price of grain was high and the merchants were outbidding each other and fighting among themselves, he had urged them to end their rivalry so that, for the sake of their customers, they would be able to buy grain at the lowest possible price; for they were allowed to sell it for no more than an obol above the market rate. I am prepared to call Anytus himself to testify that he did not order the merchants to buy up grain to hold until the rate rose, but only advised them not to drive up the price by bidding against each other. Anytus made these statements during the term of the previous Boule, while these merchants appear to have bought up the grain during the term of this one.

So, now you have heard that the merchants did *not* buy up the grain on an order of the archons. In my opinion, even if they are telling the truth in saying that they did, they are not clearing themselves but only accusing the archons. For in the case of those laws which apply in this matter, surely there should be punishment both for those who break them and for those who order them to do so.

And so, members of the jury, I do not think the merchants will be able to argue that they were required to buy up the grain. I expect that they will instead repeat what they said earlier before the Boule, that it was out of kindness toward the city that they purchased it, so that they would be able to sell it to you at the most reasonable price possible. And I will give you a very powerful proof that they are lying. If they were in fact acting in your interests, they would have been seen selling it for the same price over the course of several days. As it turns out, they were selling the grain several times in the same day for the profit of one drachma, as if they were buying it a bushel at a time. You yourselves are witnesses to this. It seems strange to me that when these men are called upon to contribute to some special cause known to everyone they plead poverty and refuse, but when they commit illegal acts in secret they say they committed them out of kindness to you. But all of you know that they are the last people who ought to make such statements. Their aims are opposed to those of other men, for their profits rise when the price of grain is driven up by some report of bad news in the city. They are so happy to see disasters happen to you that they either manage to get word of them before anyone else or create rumors about the destruction of Athenian ships in the Black Sea, their seizure on the outward voyage by the Lacedaemonians, the blockade of commercial harbors, or the breaking of a truce that is about to occur. Their enmity is so great that they set their plots against you in motion just when you are being set upon by your enemies. For it is at the very moment when you are running low on grain that these men buy it all up and refuse to sell it. Once they do so we do not dare to dispute the price; we are happy to buy their grain at any price, no matter how high. And so there are times, even times of peace, when these men besiege the city.

The city has long known of the malice and deceit of the grain merchants. In the case of all other products you make the market clerks responsible for regulating trade, but in the case of grain alone you elect special market-controllers by lot. You have often imposed the death penalty on the controllers, who were citizens, for failing to put a stop to the schemes of these men. What penalty should you impose on the criminals themselves if you execute even those who cannot control them?

Keep in mind that it is impossible for you to vote for an acquittal, for if you ignore the accusation made against these men despite the fact that they have admitted to working against the importers it will appear that you are attacking the latter. If the accused were offering some other defense no one could criticize an acquittal, for it is up to you to decide which side's story is the most believable. But, under the circumstances, your decision to allow admitted lawbreakers to go free without punishment would be considered outrageous. Remember, members of the jury, that in the past there were many who responded to this charge by denying it and produced witnesses to support their testimony; yet you condemned them to death because you found the statements of their accusers more convincing. It would surely be astounding, then, if in passing judgment on persons who actually admit to the crime you appear to be less eager to punish them than those who denied their guilt. Furthermore, members of the jury, I imagine that it is obvious to all of you that cases such as this one are matters of the greatest concern to the people of this city. I expect that they will want to know your views in such cases, believing that if you sentence these men to death the behavior of others in their business will be more orderly and that, if you set them free without punishment, you will have given them permission to do as they please. Members of the jury, you must punish these men not only because of what has happened in the past, but to set an example for the future; yet even then the grain merchants will be barely tolerable. Bear in mind that many in their business have been put on trial for their lives; there is so much profit in what they do that they would rather risk death each day than give up making money illegally at your expense. You would not be justified in taking pity on them even if they were to beg and plead with you. In fact, you ought to pity the citizens who have been destroyed by their treachery and the importers against whom they have worked together. These victims will be gratified and made more zealous if you punish the accused. If you do not, how do you think they will feel when they learn you have acquitted the merchants who confessed to conspiring against the importers?

I see no reason to say anything more. When you hear cases against other criminals you must get your information from their accusers. But in this case all of you recognize the villainy of these men. If you convict them justice will be served and you will buy grain at a more reasonable price. If you do not the price will rise.

A Call to Arms: Demosthenes, *Third Philippic.*

Demosthenes (384–322 B.C.), perhaps the greatest orator in antiquity, was born in the deme of Paeania in Attica. His father, a manufacturer of swords and furniture, died when the boy was only seven, leaving him a not inconsiderable fortune of about fourteen talents. His guardians so mismanaged his inheritance that the young Demosthenes resolved to prosecute them himself. Thus it was that he began to study rhetoric under Isaeus, an authority on cases of inheritance, and undertook the prosecution of his former guardians when he was twenty. He won, recovered approximately ten percent of what he should have received, spent almost all of it in fitting out a trireme for the Athenian navy, and applied himself diligently to earning a living as a writer of speeches for litigants in Athenian courts. In time his hard work and talent made him one of the most famous and effective speakers in Athens.

Demosthenes' political career began in earnest in 351 when he delivered the first of a series of speeches against Philip II of Macedon known as *Philippics*. By this time Philip had forged the previously antagonistic Macedonian tribes into a unified nation animated by expansionist ambitions. Taking advantage of sharp divisions among the Greek states and employing innovative military tactics (such as the use of the phalanx, which he had learned while a hostage at Thebes), Philip used his national army and his political skill gradually to insinuate himself into a position of power over his southern neighbors. It was the inability of Athens and the other states to recognize the threat posed by Macedon that prompted Demosthenes to speak out. Accusing the Athenians of indolence and pointing to the growing power of Philip, he relentlessly urged that action be taken against Macedon.

The *Third Philippic*, which many regard as Demosthenes' greatest oration, appears below. It was given in 341, the immediate occasion of its delivery being an urgent request for supplies from the anti-Macedonian forces in the Chersonese.

Men of Athens, at almost every meeting of the Assembly speeches are made about the crimes which Philip has been perpetrating since the Peace was concluded, crimes committed not against you alone, but against the other cities as well. I know that all the speakers would say, though they may not *do* much, that the aim of both our words and deeds must be to put a stop to his insolence and to make him pay for it. However, I see that all our interests have deteriorated to the point where I fear a blasphemous statement may nevertheless be true: that even if all those who speak to you had wanted to propose measures designed to plunge our affairs into the worst possible condition, and if you had wanted to vote for such measures, I do not think that they could have been made worse than they already are. There may be many reasons for the decline of our interests to their present condition, and not just one or two, but if you look at the matter carefully you will discover that the blame lies primarily with those who seek to win your approval instead of giving you the best advice. Men of Athens, some of these men want only to maintain a system which gives them power and prestige, and so they have no real concern for the city's future. And there are others who, by falsely accusing and slandering those who are at work in public office, are keeping the city occupied with the punishment of its own citizens and thereby allowing Philip the freedom to say and do whatever he wants. Political practices like these are customary among you, but they are the cause of your present problems. So I think I have a right, men of Athens, to speak freely and tell you certain truths without your becoming angry with me for doing so. Look at it this way. In all other areas of public life you believe it is so necessary to extend freedom of speech to everyone in the city that even foreigners and slaves share in it. Many household servants can be seen in public saying whatever they wish with greater liberty than is enjoyed by citizens in some of the other cities, and yet you have completely eliminated this freedom in the area of political discussion. The result is that in the meetings of the Assembly you put on airs and listen only to what is flattering and pleasing, while circumstances and events are even now putting you in the greatest danger. I have nothing to say to you if you still have this attitude, but if you are willing to hear something useful, something other than flattery, I am ready to speak. Our position is weak in every way, and much has already been sacrificed, but it is still possible to set everything right if you will only resolve to do what must be done. Now, what I am about to say may seem paradoxical, but it is true. The worst feature of our past will be our greatest boon in the future. And what is this feature? It is that you do not do the things, both great and small, which are required of you, and this is why your affairs are in such a miserable state; for it is certain that if your condition remained the same even in spite of doing all that you should there would be no hope of improving it. But, as things stand now, it is your laziness and indifference that Philip has overcome; but he has not conquered your city. Nor have you been vanquished—you haven't made even the slightest effort. . . .

If it is possible for Athens to remain at peace, and if this decision is ours to make (and I will begin my argument with this), then I say we should make it; and if there is any man here who says that this can indeed be done, I ask him to write and propose a resolution, and not to trick us [by suggesting a measure which he is not willing to support actively]. But if there is another party with weapons in his hands and a powerful army at his command who proposes peace, though in name only, while all the while he commits acts of war, what choice do we have but to defend ourselves? If you wish to pretend, in the same way that he does, that peace exists, I will not argue with you. If anyone really believes that peace is a state of affairs in which Philip can take everything else and then march against us, then, in the first place, that man is out of his mind; and, secondly, this peace he speaks of is one which you observe towards Philip, though he does not honor it in his dealings with you. This is the favorable position which Philip is buying with all the money he is spending: he is at war with you, but you are not at war with him.

If we are waiting for him to admit that he is at war with us we are the most naive people of all. Indeed, if we are to judge by the way he has treated other cities, he wouldn't admit he is at war with us even if he were to invade Athens itself, and the Piraeus. . . .

Demosthenes goes on to describe Philip's treacheries and urge the Athenians to resist him lest they share the fate of other cities which he destroyed after having lulled them into a false sense of security.

Even though we Greeks see and hear all this we do not send ambassadors to each other. We don't even express our anger. We are in such a wretched state, and our cities are so deeply divided, that even today we are unable either to act in support of our interests or to do what duty requires. Not only are we unable to unite, we cannot even form an association for the purposes of mutual aid and friendship. Instead, we simply watch Philip's power grow greater, each of us determined to gain some advantage in the period during which another is being destroyed, or so it seems to me, neither caring nor acting for the salvation of the Greeks. None of you is ignorant of the fact that Philip is like the recurrence or the initial attack of a fever or some other illness in that he launches his attacks even against those who think they are out of his reach at the time. And you surely know this also, that the wrongs which the Greeks suffered at the hands of the Lacedaemonians or ourselves were at least inflicted upon them by true Greeks. One might suppose them to be like the acts of a legitimate son, born to great wealth, who does not manage his possessions in a good and proper way. For this he would deserve to be blamed and admonished, but at least no one could say that he was not related to those he harmed or that he was not the legal heir to the things he mismanaged. Yet if it had been a slave or an illegitimate pretender who spoiled and abused what was not his, why, Heracles! how much more terrible and senseless everyone would have declared such acts to be. But no one has anything bad to say about Philip and his present behavior, even though he is not Greek, or related to the Greeks, or even a barbarian from a country about which one can say anything good. No, he is a pernicious Macedonian from whose country it was previously not possible even to purchase a good slave.

And yet is there any limit to his insolence? Even the destruction of cities is not enough for him. Is he not holding the Pythian games, the contest in which all the Greeks participate, and sending his slaves to supervise them if he can't attend them himself? Does he not write to the Thessalians to tell them what kind of government they must have? Does he not send mercenaries to Porthmus to expel the democrats of Eretria, and to Oreus to establish the tyranny of Philistides? The Greeks see all these things happening and yet they put up with them. It seems to me that they observe him just as they would a hailstorm, each city hoping that the threat will not come its way, but none attempting to stop it. And it is not only Philip's wanton assaults on Greece as a whole that go unavenged, for no city resists even the crimes commited against itself. This is the extreme situation which presently exists. Has he not attacked Corinth's possessions, Ambracia and Leucas? Naupactus belongs to the Achaeans, but has he not vowed to hand it over to the Aetolians? Has he not stolen Echinus from the Thebans? And is he not marching against their Byzantine allies at this very moment? And what about our own possessions? To mention just one of them, does he not have control of Cardia, the greatest city in the Chersonese? These are the things we have suffered, and yet all of us hesitate and act like weaklings, watching our neighbors and distrusting one another rather than the man at whose hands we are all being victimized. Indeed, if he behaves this brutally towards all of us taken together, what do you think he will do when he has made himself the master of each of us separately?

Why have these things happened? It was not without reason or good cause that the Greeks of old were as ardent in their desire for freedom as the Greeks of today are for slavery. There was a certain something, men of Athens, something in the minds of many in those days which does not exist today—something which defeated the wealth of Persia, kept Greece free, and never yielded in battles at sea or on land. And it is the loss of this something which has led to universal destruction and reduced all our affairs to a shambles. What was it? It was that men who took bribes from those who sought to rule Greece or despoil her were despised by everyone; that to be found guilty of this crime was a most grievous thing; that the guilty man received the most severe punishment. The critical moment for taking action, with which Chance often arms the negligent against those who are on their guard, was not sold by orators and generals in those days. Nor did they put a price on harmony among peoples, or their distrust of tyrants and barbarians, or, in short, on anything of this sort. But now all these things have been sold as if they were items in the market, and in their place we have substituted their opposites which have ruined Greece and infected her with sickness. What are these? Envy of anyone who receives a bribe; laughter, if someone admits to having done so; hatred of anyone who objects to such criminal activity; and every other vice found in connection with bribery. We have numerous ships and men, an abundance of money and war matériel, and all the things by which the strength of cities is judged—and, together, we possess far more of these than the Greeks of days gone by. But these resources have been rendered completely useless, ineffectual and worthless by those who sell them for personal gain. . . .

Demosthenes goes on to illustrate the better attitude of the Athenians of former times by citing a record they had inscribed on a bronze pillar on the Acropolis. This concerned a certain Arthmius of Zelea who had conveyed gold to the Spartans from the Persians. Thinking this enough for him to be considered their enemy, and the enemy of their allies as well, the Athenians dealt with him as they would one of their fellow citizens: they declared him an outlaw.

Those who want to reassure the city offer a rather foolish argument. They say that Philip, after all, is not yet in the position of strength formerly held by the Lacedaemonians when they ruled over every sea and land and, having the king [of Persia] as their ally, could be withstood by no one; and yet our city resisted even them, and was not overcome. It might be said that great progress has been made since then in every field of human endeavor, and that today's world is a far cry from that of former times, but it is my belief that no field has seen more advances and improvements than the art of war. In the first place, I hear that in those days the Lacedaemonians and all our other enemies would spend the four or five months of summer invading our territory and destroying it with heavy infantry and citizen-soldiers, and would then return home again. The men of that time were so old-fashioned in the way they fought wars—or rather, they conducted themselves so admirably as citizens—that none of them ever bought any advantage in war. No, they waged war in a legal and open way. But I am sure you see that the majority of our losses now are the work of traitors, and that none are the result of conflicts between soldiers drawn up in the usual order of battle. And yet you are told that it is not because he leads a phalanx of heavy infantry that Philip marches wherever he pleases, but because he has created a force of light infantry, cavalry, archers, mercenaries, and similar troops. And when he uses this force to attack some city so plagued by internal strife and distrust that no one goes out to defend its territory, he simply moves his engines of war into position and lays siege to it. I need not mention the fact that Philip makes no distinction between summer and winter, and that there is no season which he sets aside for rest. All of you know this, and so you must give it due consideration and not allow the war to enter into Attica. Nor must you allow yourselves to be overthrown by using the simplistic tactics of the earlier war against the Lacedaemonians. Instead, you must guard your political affairs and military preparations as much as possible and make it your aim to prevent him from leaving his home base; and you must never engage him at close quarters in a fight to the finish. As far as war is concerned, men of Athens, we have many natural advantages, provided that we are willing to do what is necessary. One example is the nature of Philip's territory, much of which we can raid and pillage, but there are countless others. Nevertheless, his army is better trained than we are for a pitched battle.

It is crucial that you understand these things and that you resist him by military means—but this is not enough. You must also hate, in a calculated and deliberate way, those who speak to you on his behalf, keeping in mind that we will never be able to prevail against the enemies of our city until you have punished those who work as their representatives within the city itself. And this, by Zeus and all the other gods, you will be unable to do; for you have reached such a state of foolishness or derangement or—well, I don't know what to call it (for I am often seized by the fear that some inhuman power is driving our city's affairs to destruction)—that because you enjoy their abusive language or their ill will, or their wit, or whatever your reason may happen to be, you encourage men to speak out who are hired agents, some of whom would not even bother to deny it, and you laugh when they slander others. And yet, as bad as this may be, there is more. For you have given greater security in the pursuit of their political aims to these men than to those who speak in defense of your own interests. And yet, look at the disasters that are brought about by a willingness to listen to men such as these. I will cite some examples which are known to all of you.

At Olynthus there was one party which favored Philip and obeyed his every order and another which sought what was best for the city and to save its citizens from bondage. Which destroyed their country? Which betrayed the cavalry and thereby caused the destruction of Olynthus? Those who sided with Philip, men who, while the city still stood, so slandered and falsely accused the true patriots that the people of Olynthus were persuaded even to banish Apollonides.

Moreover, it was not only at Olynthus that this attitude produced every conceivable unfortunate result. When the people of Eretria had rid themselves of Plutarchus and his mercenaries and gained control of the city and of Porthmus, one faction desired to put their affairs in your hands while another wanted to entrust the city to Philip. Listening mostly, or rather only, to the latter, the strife-weary and hapless Eretrians were finally persuaded to banish the men who spoke out on their behalf. Philip, their "ally," sent Hipponicus with a thousand mercenaries, tore down the walls surrounding Porthmus and put three tyrants in power—Hipparchus, Automedon, and Cleitarchus. Since that time they have twice determined to free themselves, and on both occasions he has expelled them from their own country.

Is it really necessary to mention the majority of such cases? Perhaps it will be enough to recall how at Oreus Philip had as his agents Philistides, Menippus, Socrates, Thoas, and Agapaeus—men whom everyone knew to be his hirelings and who are now in control of the city—but Euphraeus, a man who once lived with us here in Athens, was championing the cause of freedom and striving to preserve freedom and save them from slavery. The tale of how this man was insulted and humiliated by the people of Oreus is a long one; but a year before the city was captured he realized what Philistides and his adherents were up to and publicly charged them with treason. A large group of men banded together and, with Philip financing and guiding them, put Euphraeus in prison for stirring up trouble in the city. When the democrats of Oreus saw this, instead of rushing to his aid and beating up the others, they were not angry with them at all but rejoiced and said that Euphraeus had got just what he deserved. After this Philip's men were able to do whatever they pleased, and so they conspired to seize the city and made ready to set their plan in motion; but anyone from among the common people who sensed what was happening maintained a terror-stricken silence, remembering what had happened to Euphraeus. Indeed, their condition was so miserable that, even though they were faced with this terrible threat, no one dared to speak until the plot was fully prepared and the enemy was marching against the walls. At that point some defended the city, while others favored surrender. After this shameful and dishonorable capture of the city the victors ruled as tyrants. As for those who had protected them before the city's fall, and who were prepared to do anything against Euphraeus, some were expelled from the city and others were killed. Euphraeus himself committed suicide, thereby establishing a testimony to the justice and purity of his opposition to Philip.

You are probably wondering why the people of Olynthus, Eretria and Oreus were more willing to listen to Philip's orators than to their own. The explanation also applies to you—that there are times when those who advocate what is best might want to please their audience, but cannot, for they must make the security of the city their primary concern; but their rivals, by the very act of saying what will please the public, are assisting Philip. One group urged that a war tax be levied, but the other said none was needed; the first group called upon the citizens to fight and to hold Philip in suspicion, but others counseled that peace be maintained—that is, until they were caught in his trap. Without mentioning each and every example, I believe that events transpired in the same way everywhere. Some spoke with the intention of gaining approval, others out of a desire to save their cities. In the end the majority of the people acceded to most of the demands of the former—not because it pleased them to do so, as had formerly been the case, or out of ignorance, but because they recognized that the absolute hopelessness of their situation had made submission inevitable. This, by Zeus and Apollo, is what I am afraid will happen to you when you take stock of your circumstances and realize that there is no way out. Men of Athens, may this never come to pass. For it would be better to die ten thousand of deaths than to do anything in compliance with Philip's wishes. A fine reward the people of Oreus received for putting themselves in the hands of Philip's friends, and for ignoring Euphraeus! A fine reward the people of Eretria have earned for expelling your ambassadors and submitting to Cleitarchus! They are slaves, whipped and slaughtered! What noble forbearance he displayed toward the Olynthians, who elected Lasthenes to lead their cavalry and sent Apollonides into exile! It is foolish and disgraceful to hope for such things, to be guided by bad counsel, to be unwilling to discharge your responsibilities, to listen to those who speak on behalf of your enemies, and to presume that you live in a city so great that nothing, however terrible, can overpower it. How shameful it would be to say, when it is too late, "What? who would have guessed that this would happen?" or "By Zeus, we should have done this, or ought not to have done that!" There are many things the Olynthians could tell you now which, if they could have foreseen them then, would have allowed them to escape destruction. Many things could be told by the people of Oreus, and of Phocis, and of every city which has been destroyed. But what use is a knowledge of such things to them now? It is while the ship (whether it is large or small) is safely under sail that the sailor and the helmsman and everyone else on board must take his turn in demonstrating genuine enthusiasm and making sure that it does not capsize, whether deliberately or by accident; for enthusiasm is worthless once the sea has overpowered it. This is how it is with us, men of Athens. As long as we are secure, as long as we have our great city, plentiful resources and the best of reputations, what should we do? Perhaps there is someone sitting here who has been waiting to ask just that question. Well, I will answer it, by Zeus, and will also move a resolution for which you may vote if you wish. First, we must see to our own defense by making preparations—I am talking about triremes, money, and soldiers. We must strive for freedom even if every other city yields and falls into slavery. Second, when we have finished all our preparations and our readiness for battle is evident to all, we must immediately rally the others and send ambassadors to inform them of our concern so that, if you succeed in persuading them, you will have companions who will share the dangers and the expense of war if the need arises; and, if you do not persuade them, you will at least be able to buy some time. For since the war is against a man and not against the strength of a league of cities, even procrastination has its value; valuable, too, were the diplomatic missions which you sent throughout the Peloponnese last year to decry Philip, when I and Polyeuctus, a fine man, and Hegesippus and the other envoys went from place to place and succeeded in stopping him, with the result that he neither marched against Ambracia nor launched a campaign against the Peloponnese. But I urge that we should not call upon the other cities for assistance unless we ourselves are willing to do what must be done; for it would be foolish to neglect our own interests while claiming that we are protecting those of others, or to disregard the present threat while frightening the other cities with talk about future dangers. This is not what I am suggesting. Rather, I am urging that we send money to the forces in the Chersonese and support them with whatever actions they deem necessary. And then, while we are making our own preparations, we must call together, assemble, instruct, and warn the rest of the Greeks. This is the course of action which a city with so great a reputation as yours should adopt. If you think that the Chalcidians or the Megarians will save Greece while you run away from your responsibilities you are mistaken. They will be content if they can save themselves. No, the salvation of Greece is your responsibility. It is an honor which your ancestors won and bequeathed to you in the face of many great dangers. But if each of you merely sits back, seeking to do only what he wants and looking to avoid doing anything on his own, then I fear for you: first, because you may not find anyone who *will* act; second, because all of the obligations we try to avoid may one day demand a response at the same time.

This is what I have to say, and this is the motion I make. I believe that even now, if you approve it, it is still not too late to restore our fortunes. If anyone has a better proposal, let him speak and give us his advice. I beseech all the gods that, whatever you decide, it may be for the best.

The Corinthian Congress—The End of Greek Independence: Diodorus, *Historical Library*, 16.89.

After the battle of Chaeronea in 338 B.C., when the combined forces of Athens and Thebes were demolished by Philip II and resistance against the Macedonian king collapsed, a congress of the new Hellenic League was called at Corinth, where Philip announced his plans to invade Persia. In essence, the Corinthian congress marked the end of an era, for the once independent Greek city-states were now brought under the sway of a single ruler.

At this time [337/6 B.C.] King Philip, proudly aware of the significance of his victory at Chaeronea and of the fact that he had astounded the most important of the Greek city-states, aspired to become the leader of all Greece. He circulated the word that he wanted to fight the Persians for the sake of the Greeks and to punish them for the violation of the temples, and so he won the goodwill of the Greeks. He treated everyone with kindness and consideration, both privately and in public, and declared to the city-states that he wanted to confer with them on matters of common interest. As a consequence, a general congress was held at Corinth where he spoke about the war against the Persians and, by raising great hopes, won over the delegates. After the Greeks had elected him general plenipotentiary of Greece, he began great preparations for his campaign against the Persians. Then, having decided on the number of soldiers which each city-state should contribute to the alliance, he returned to Macedonia.

Alexander and Oecumene: Plutarch, *On the Fortune of Alexander*, Discourse I, 5–8.

This short work *On the Fortune of Alexander* was written by Plutarch as an oration to be delivered in praise of the great conqueror, its main theme being that Alexander was the instrument of Fortune. Plutarch's objective in the excerpt given below is to show that Alexander was a great philosopher, even greater, perhaps, than Plato, Aristotle and Zeno. None of these had to contend with the difficulties faced by Alexander, yet their impact on history, he says, was far less than that of the man who subdued Asia; they sketched blueprints for ideal cities, but he built them; they wrote about how men ought to live, but he conquered the "barbarians," civilized them and taught them to be happy. Nor is any other conqueror his equal. Xerxes built a bridge over the Hellespont so that his horde could invade Greece, but Alexander joined Europe to Asia through marriages and the children resulting from them, so that the whole of the inhabited world (*oecumene*) would be united. Indeed, it seems that his commitment to the ideal of *oecumene* is what most impressed Plutarch about Alexander, and there are many today who believe that the Macedonian conqueror was the first to conceive of a united humanity.

First of all, consider, if you will, a paradox concerning the difference between the students of Alexander and those of Plato and Socrates. The two philosophers instructed men who had been blessed with natural gifts and who spoke the same language. Thus, if nothing else, they at least understood Greek. And yet Plato and Socrates did not persuade many of them to follow their teachings. Instead, their pupils—Critias, Alcibiades and Cleitophon—spat out their teachings like the bit of a bridle and turned away from the right path in life.

But if you look at the instruction given by Alexander you will see that he taught the Hyrcanians to marry and instructed the Arachosians in the art of agriculture. He persuaded the Sogdians to take care of their parents instead of killing them, and the Persians to honor their mothers rather than marry them. O wondrous philosophy! Through you the Indians came to revere the gods of the Greeks, and by your power the Scythians began to bury their dead, and no longer ate them. We marvel at the power of Carneades, who hellenized Cleitomachus, a Carthaginian formerly known as Hasdrubal. We stand in awe of Zeno, who convinced Diogenes the Babylonian to become a philosopher. But when Alexander civilized Asia her people began to read Homer, and the children of the Persians, Susianians and Gedrosians recited the tragedies of

Sophocles and Euripides. Socrates was convicted by the testimony of slanderers when he was brought to trial on the charge of introducing foreign deities in Athens, but through Alexander Bactria and the Caucasus learned to worship the gods of Greece. Plato wrote a book about the ideal constitution, but no one was persuaded to put its principles into practice because of their severity. Alexander, on the other hand, founded more than seventy cities among the barbarian tribes, sowed all Asia with Greek institutions, and thereby put an end to the savage and brutal way of life in that place. Only a few of us have read Plato's *Laws*, but countless thousands of men have obeyed, and continue to obey, the laws promulgated by Alexander. Those peoples who were subdued by him are more fortunate than those who escaped, for the conqueror caused the former to be happy, but the latter had no one to free them from a way of life that made them miserable. And so it is quite appropriate to cite here a saying of Themistocles, who received great gifts from King Artaxerxes of Persia when he was in exile in that land. These gifts included three cities from which he received tribute, one of them supplying him with wheat, another with wine, and yet another with meat. When he had taken possession of these cities Themistocles said, "My children, if we had not already been undone this would be our undoing." This statement might be applied more justly to the peoples conquered by Alexander, for they would never have been civilized if he had not subdued them. Egypt would not have Alexandria; Mesopotamia would be without Seleucia; Sogdiana would not have Prophthasia; India would not have its Bucephalia; and the Caucasus would be without that Greek city [*i.e.*, Alexandria in the Caucasus] which lies close by. It was by living as citizens of these cities that the wildness of the conquered peoples was extinguished, and the inferior qualities in each of them were improved through familiarity with better ways of life. Indeed, since philosophers pride themselves most on their ability to refine the harsh and boorish aspects of human nature, Alexander, who has manifestly reformed the bestial natures of countless nations, may quite reasonably be considered a great philosopher.

Zeno, the philosopher who founded the Stoic sect, wrote the popularly acclaimed *Republic*, a work whose substance is expressed by this one point: we should not live in such a way that we are divided by cities and towns and their different conceptions of justice, but should think of all humankind as constituting a single people and a single polity and sharing a common life and society, just as a flock of sheep graze together in a common pasture. When Zeno wrote this it was as though he was committing to writing an image from a dream, an image of a state built on good laws and philosophy. And yet it was not Zeno, but Alexander, who transformed the written word into a reality. Alexander did not take the advice of Aristotle, who urged him to be a leader to the Greeks and a master to the barbarians, to care for the former as friends and relatives while treating the latter as if they were only animals or plants. If he had followed this advice his leadership would have been undermined by many wars, banishments and rebellions. But Alexander believed that he had been sent by the gods to bring the whole world together as its governor and arbiter, and whenever a people was not convinced by reason to join with the others he subdued them by the power of his weapons, thereby uniting all peoples from all places. And then, as if blending them together in a cup of friendship, he mixed together their lives, customs, marriages and ways of life. He decreed that every man should regard the whole of the inhabited world as his native country, consider his camp as a fortress guaranteeing his safety, think of all good men as members of his family, and regard only the evil as foreigners. He desired that no one should identify another as Greek or barbarian on the basis of such insignificant criteria as his cloak, shield, sword and garment, but that a man should be considered a Greek if he is virtuous and a barbarian if he shows himself to be wicked. And it was his wish, too, that customs, foods, marriages and ways of life should be the same everywhere, mixed together by the mingling of blood and children. When Demaratus the Corinthian (one of Philip's good friends) saw Alexander in Susa he was overjoyed and said that the Greeks who had died before then had been robbed of a great delight, for they had not seen Alexander sitting on the throne of Darius. But, by the gods, I do not envy those who beheld this sight. It was, after all, only something brought about by Fortune, a thing common to all kings. No, I think I would rather have been present at that beautiful and sacred wedding when a hundred Persian brides and a hundred Macedonian and Greek bridegrooms stood within a single golden tent and at a common hearth and table. Alexander himself, crowned with a wreath of flowers, began the chanting of the wedding hymn, and it was as if he was singing a song of friendship between the two greatest and most powerful nations in the world. He was the bridegroom of one bride, but for all the others he assumed the roles of escort, father and marriage-arranger as he united them with their grooms in wedlock. Had I been there to behold this sight I would have been overcome with happiness and shouted, "O barbaric and foolish Xerxes, who worked so hard and so senselessly to bridge the Hellespont! Wise kings do not join Asia to Europe with boards or planks, nor with ties which are inanimate and without feelings; no, nations are joined together by the bonds of love sanctioned by law, wise marriages, and sharing in the begetting of children."

With this in mind Alexander gave much thought to styles of dress and preferred Persian clothing to Median, since the Persian was plain and simple. Indeed, he had no use for the strange and ostentatious styles of the foreigners such as the headdress, the flowing robe and trousers. Thus, according to the account of Eratosthenes, he wore a combination of Persian and Macedonian fashions. Of course, since he was a philosopher he was not much concerned with what he wore; but, as the leader and philanthropic king of many conquered peoples, he sought to cultivate their goodwill by showing his respect for their various forms of dress so that they would remain firm in their love for the Macedonians as rulers instead of hating them as enemies. This attitude set him in direct opposition to the stupid and vain men who admire tunics of solid color and turn their noses up at those with purple borders, or perhaps scorn the former while approving of the latter. Men such as these are like foolish children who cling tenaciously to whatever kind of clothing the custom of their country, like a child's nurse, has dressed them in. Now, when men go off to hunt wild beasts they dress themselves in deerskins, and when they want to snare birds they wear chitons covered with feathers; similarly, they make sure that bulls do not see them when they are dressed in red, or elephants when their clothes are white, for these animals are provoked to anger when they see these colors. How, then, can we criticize a great king who takes advantage of this same principle when he attempts to civilize stubborn and warlike peoples and succeeds in calming and controlling them simply by wearing clothes which they know and like, taming them by living as they do? Shouldn't we be impressed by the wisdom of a man who, by making a minor change in the way he dressed, made himself the leader of all Asia, a man who triumphed over the bodies of the foreigners by force of arms but won their hearts with his clothes? How strange it is that men are in awe of Socrates' disciple Aristippus because he managed to project an aura of elegance whether he wore a worn out cloak or a Milesian robe, and yet blame Alexander for respecting the dress of conquered peoples along with that of his native land while he was building a great empire. He did not trample on Asia like a robber or ransack and pillage it as if the land had been given to him as booty and loot by an unexpected stroke of luck. This was how Hannibal behaved when he invaded Italy, and the Treres when they despoiled Ionia, and the Scythians when they fell upon Media. But Alexander's wish was to unite all the earth under one law of reason and a single government, and to make all human beings members of one nation. Indeed, he directed his every action toward this goal.

If the god who sent the soul of Alexander down into the world had not called it back so quickly all men would now be governed by one law and would look to a single form of justice as if to a light shining on them all. But this was not to be, and so a part of the earth remains without sun—that part which never saw Alexander.

A Hellenistic Federal Experiment–The Achaean League: Polybius, *History*, 2.37.7–38.9.

The ancient Achaean cities had experimented with the principles of federalism since early times. However, the Achaean League of the Hellenistic Age, founded in 280 B.C. by the union of four cities, eventually encompassed most of the Peloponnese by the incorporation of Dorians and Arcadians who enjoyed equal rights with the original Achaean members of the federation. The historian Polybius, an Arcadian from Megalopolis who had served as General of the League, naturally knew intimately its organization and functions and understood clearly the reasons for its success in the world of the perpetually antagonistic and mutually jealous city-states of Greece. The League was dissolved by Rome in 146 B.C. after the Achaean War, and its dissolution marks the end of Greek independence in antiquity.

But concerning the nation of the Achaeans and the Macedonian royal house, it will be fitting to look back briefly to earlier years since in our time the latter has suffered total extinction while the Achaeans, as I explained previously, have experienced a remarkable growth in power and political unity. For though in the past many people tried to unify the Peloponnesians for their common good but failed because each city was concerned with the preservation of its own power rather than the freedom of the entire region, in our days this policy has made so much progress and has been implemented so fully that not only have the Peloponnesians formed a community of allies and friends, but they have also adopted identical laws, weights, measures and currency. In addition, all states have the same magistrates, senate and judges, and the entire region of Peloponnesus would be but one single city if it were not for the fact that its people are not enclosed within the same city-walls; all other things, both general and those that concern each individual city, are nearly identical.

It may be worthwhile to learn how and in what manner the name of Achaeans came to be applied to all Peloponnesians, for the people who originally bore it as their ancestral name were by no means superior to others in the size of their territories, the number of their cities, their wealth or the valor of their men. The nations of the Arcadians and the Laconians are by far superior to them with respect to population and the extent of their territories, and neither of them could ever be induced to concede to any other Greek people the first place in fighting ability. How, then, and for what reasons have these two nations and the rest of the Peloponnesians consented to adopt both the political institutions and the name of the Achaeans? Obviously, to attribute this to chance would be improper, for that is no explanation. Rather, we should seek a cause; without a cause nothing ever happens, whether probable or unexpected. In my opinion, the cause in this case may be this: no political system can be found anywhere in the world which favors more the principles of equality, freedom of speech and true democracy than that of the Achaeans. Because of this, many of the Peloponnesians freely chose to adopt it, many others were brought to it by persuasion and argument, and some who had originally been coerced to accept it gradually acquiesced to their place in the alliance. Since no special privileges were reserved for the original members and all newcomers were given equal rights, the aims of the league were attained by the use of the two most powerful of co-workers, equality and love of humanity. This, then, is the source and cause of the Peloponnesian unity and prosperity.

Music as a Civilizing Force—The Case of the Arcadians: Polybius, *History*, 4.20.4–21.

A land of small cities and villages in the center of the Peloponnese, mountainous Arcadia with its harsh climate and few resources was proverbial for its pastoral and idyllic way of life. In antiquity Arcadia was known chiefly for its brave soldiers who often served with distinction as mercenaries in foreign service, but it also gave birth to Polybius, the famous historian who commented on the beneficial effects of music in tempering the rustic character of his Arcadian compatriots.

The cultivation of music, and I mean genuine music, bestows positive benefits on all peoples, but to the Arcadians it is an absolute necessity. Thus, we must disagree with Ephorus who, in the preface to his *History*, advances a theory quite unworthy of him, namely that music was introduced to humanity for the purpose of deception and delusion. The ancient Cretans and Lacedaemonians did not act thoughtlessly when they substituted in war the flute and its rhythmic movements for the trumpet, nor were the early Arcadians acting haphazardly in allowing music to permeate their public life to the point that not only children but young men up to the age of thirty were required to practice it, although in other respects they were extremely austere in their habits. It is common knowledge that only among the Arcadians are the children trained from infancy to sing the hymns and paeans by which the local heroes and gods are honored and that, afterwards, they learn the odes of Philoxenus and Timotheus, which they perform each year with great distinction in the theater to the accompaniment of the Dionysiac orchestras, the children competing in the juvenile and the young adults in the so-called men's contests. Likewise, throughout their lives they entertain themselves at social functions, not by hiring professional musicians, but by performing themselves, calling on each other to sing in turn. And while they do not consider it a disgrace to confess their ignorance of some other subjects, they cannot possibly deny a competence in singing because they are all required to learn it; neither can they excuse themselves if they have admitted it, for this is considered a disgrace among them. Moreover, they practice military marches in formation to the accompaniment of the flute and, under public supervision and at public expense, they perform dances each year in the theaters where the young adults show themselves to their fellow citizens. These practices, it seems, were introduced by our ancient ancestors not for the sake of cultivating a luxurious and extravagant way of life, but because they had observed the harsh Arcadian lifestyle and the austere national character which result from the coldness and gloominess of the climate in their country. All peoples must cope with climate, and it is climate, and climate alone, which explains why peoples dwelling in diverse regions differ considerably in character, appearance, skin color and habits. Thus, wanting to soften and temper the stubbornness and harshness of nature, our ancestors instituted all the above practices as well as frequent social functions and religious sacrifices which they made compulsory for both men and women; in addition, they instituted dances for both boys and girls and, in general, devised every possible means to tame and civilize our stubborn character by the introduction of these customs.

Justifying Slavery: Aristotle, *Politics*, 1.5.

As in other ancient cultures, slavery played an important role in the economic and social life of Greece. Most slaves worked at tasks involving only physical labor, but there were many who functioned as artisans, physicians, tutors, business managers and in other capacities requiring special skill.

In his *Politics* Aristotle maintained that slavery was necessary for the well-being of the household and the state, describing slaves as "animate instruments." In the fifth chapter of Book 1, which appears below, he offered an argument justifying the institution. Simply put, Aristotle claimed that nature intends some entities to rule and others to be ruled. Thus, the human soul rules the body, for it possesses reason while the body is equipped to act on the dictates of reason. Similarly, some human beings have been furnished by nature with the mental ability to direct, while others have only the physical ability to carry out directions. Both benefit by accepting the function assigned to them by nature (which, for Aristotle, is organized according to a rational plan in which everything has a special purpose or *telos*).

His statement that nature does not always distinguish clearly between free men and slaves leads us to suspect that Aristotle saw the weakness of his argument. He offered another defense of slavery in the following chapter.

We must next inquire as to whether or not there are people who by their nature are of such a kind [*i.e.*, slaves]; in other words, are there people for whom the condition of slavery is better than any other, and also just, or is all slavery contrary to nature? This is not a difficult issue, whether we contemplate it in a theoretical mode or consider it on the basis of empirical evidence. That some should rule and others should be ruled is not only necessary but expedient; indeed, from the very moment of birth some are set apart to obey and others to command. There are many kinds of rulers and of those who are ruled and it is always true that that form of rule is better which is exercised over better subjects—for example, to rule a man is better than to rule over an animal; the reason for this is that a function is a better function when the parties involved in its execution are better, and where one party rules and another is ruled we may say that a function involving them is being performed.

In every composite thing, where a plurality of parts, whether contiguous or separate, unite to form a common whole, the ruler-ruled relationship appears. This relationship occurs in living things as a consequence of the way in which the whole of nature is organized, for even in inanimate things there is some sort of ruling principle—as, for example, in musical harmony. This last consideration, however, probably lies outside the scope of our inquiry. Let us confine ourselves to the living creature which, in the first place, is composed of soul and body, the first of which is by nature the ruler, and the second the ruled. In considering what is natural it is necessary to focus on things which are in their natural state rather than on things which have been corrupted. It follows, then, that in studying man we must consider the man who is in the best possible condition with respect both to his body and his soul, the man in whom the rule of the soul over the body is evident; for in men who are bad or in a bad condition it appears that the body often rules the soul because of their unseemly and unnatural condition. In any case, it is in a living creature, as we have said, that it first becomes possible to observe the rule both of master and of statesman. For the soul rules the body with the authority of a master, whereas the mind rules over the appetites with the authority of a statesman or a king. And it is clear that the rule of the body by the soul, and the rule of the passionate part by the rational, is in accordance with nature and beneficial; but for the two parts to have equal influence, or their roles reversed, is always harmful. The same holds true with respect to the relationship between man and the animals: domesticated animals are by nature superior to wild ones, and they are always better off when they are ruled by man, for man provides them with security. Further, in the case of the sexes the male is superior and the female inferior, and so the male rules and the female is ruled. This principle necessarily applies to all mankind. Therefore, men who differ as greatly as the soul does from the body and the human being from the animal (and this is the condition of those whose function is to use the body and from whom physical labor is the most that can be expected)—these [*i.e.*, the inferior sort] are by nature slaves, and it is best for them, as it is for all the inferior things I have already mentioned, to be ruled.

He is by nature a slave who is capable of belonging to another (and therefore *does* belong to another) and who has access to reason in that he senses and understands it but does not possess it. The other animals do not even understand reason, but simply follow their instincts. And indeed the advantages provided by slaves differ little from those provided by animals, for from the bodily services of both of them, slaves and domestic animals alike, we acquire the necessities of life. It is therefore the intention of nature also to make a distinction between the bodies of free men and those of slaves; the latter are strong for the performance of necessary tasks, while the former are erect and useless for such tasks but useful for the life of a citizen (and this last involves usefulness in both war and peace). And yet the very opposite frequently happens, so that slaves have the bodies of free men and free men have the right kind of soul, but not the right body. But this much is certainly clear: if men were born who were as distinguished in physique as are the statues of the gods, then everyone would say that their inferiors deserved to be their slaves. And if this is true in relation to the body, it would be even more just to make the same kind of distinction in the case of the soul. But it is not as easy to see the beauty of the soul as it is to see the beauty of the body. And so it is clear that some are free by nature, and others slaves, and that for the latter slavery is advantageous and just.

"For the Greater Glory of Zeus"—The Ancient Olympics: Pausanias, *Description of Greece*, 5.8.1–11 and 5.21.2–14.

The ancient Olympic games, held "for the greater glory of Zeus" once every four years, were founded in 776 B.C. and lasted until 426 A.D., when they were abolished by the Christian Emperor Theodosius I. The games retained their vitality throughout antiquity and a list of Olympic victors dating from the first Olympiad to the year 217 A.D. was compiled by the Christian philosopher and scholar Julius Africanus and preserved in the *Chronicle* of Eusebius. The passages given here are from Pausanias, a second century A.D. Greek geographer and writer of guidebooks who was fond of describing religious and historical sites and artistic monuments. His sketchy but informative account of the development of the Olympic games and his accurate description of the monuments of Olympia help us understand one of the most fascinating expressions of the Greek genius, athletic competition, with all of its shortcomings.

It is said that about fifty years after the flood of Deucalion in Greece Clymenes, the son of Cotys, a descendant of the Idaean Hercules, came from Crete to Olympia and established games there. He also built and dedicated an altar to the other Curetes, and to his own forefather Hercules, whom he designated as Hercules Parastates. But Endymion, the son of Aëthlius, robbed Clymenes of his realm and then challenged his sons to race at Olympia, offering their father's kingdom as the prize of victory.

A generation later Pelops elevated the games for Olympian Zeus to a higher state of renown than they had ever enjoyed before. However, when the sons of Pelops were dispersed from Elis to all parts of the Peloponnese Amythaon, the son of Cretheus and the nephew of Endymion on his father's side . . . celebrated the Olympic games which, in subsequent years, were jointly sponsored by Pelias and Neleus.

The Olympic games were also sponsored by Augeas and by Hercules, the son of Amphitryon, after he had taken possession of Elis. Hercules awarded the crown of victory to many athletes. One of them was Iolaus, who won his race with the horses of Hercules, for in those days it was a common practice for a contestant to race with a horse belonging to another man. In fact, we are told by Homer that once Menelaus raced Aetha, the horse of Agamemnon, along with one of his own horses. Moreover, Iolaus had once been the charioteer of Hercules. Thus, he was victorious in the chariot race while Isius the Arcadian was the winner in the race on horseback. The sons of Tyndareus also won victories, one of them in the footrace and the other, Polydeuces, in boxing. We are also told that in the same games Hercules won victories in wrestling and in the *pancratium* [a combination of boxing and wrestling].

Oxylus, too, sponsored the games, but after his reign the Olympics were suspended until the reign of Iphitus, who reestablished them. The memory of the earlier games had been lost by then, yet people gradually recalled them and added to the new games everything they remembered about the old ones. There is one undisputed fact connected with the beginning of these new Olympics [established in 776 B.C.], namely that the first event of the games was the footrace, which was won by Coroebus of Elis. Although no statue of Coroebus exists at Olympia his grave can be found on the frontier of his country. Another race of double the distance run by Coroebus was instituted in the fourteenth Olympiad in which Hypenus of Pisa won the olive crown of victory; in the fifteenth Olympiad Acanthus was the victor in this race.

It was in the eighteenth Olympiad that the pentathlon and wrestling events were again introduced into the games; two Lacedaemonians won these contests, Lampis being victorious in the pentathlon and Eurybatus in wrestling. Boxing was revived in the twenty-third Olympiad; the victor in this event was Onomastus of Smyrna, a city which had already been founded in Ionia. Horse racing became a part of the games in the twenty-fifth Olympiad when Pagondas of Thebes won the victory with his chariot.

Eight Olympiads after this the riding race and the *pancratium* were instituted. The horse race was won by Crauxidas of Crannon, while Lygdamis the Syracusan prevailed in the *pancratium*; a statue of this man can be found in Syracuse near the quarries. The Syracusans claim that Lygdamis was as big a man as the Theban Hercules, but I do not know if this is true.

The people of Elis claim that the introduction of boys' contests in the Olympics was their own idea and, in fact, no earlier references to these events exist. Boxing matches and running races for boys took place in the thirty-seventh Olympiad. In these games Hipposthenes the Lacedaemonian was the victor in wrestling and Polyneices of Elis won the footrace. In the forty-first Olympiad boxing matches for boys were held in which Philetas of Sybaris emerged victorious.

In the sixty-fifth Olympiad races of armed men were introduced because, in my opinion, they were considered good war exercises. The victor in the first race of men armed with shields was Demaretus of Heraea. In the ninety-third Olympiad a race with a pair of horses known as the *synoris* was introduced; Evagoras of Elis won this race. In the ninety-ninth Olympiad races of chariots drawn by colts were held; the Lacedaemonian Sybariades with his colts and chariot was declared the winner in this race.

After this races of chariots drawn by pairs of colts and races of men riding colts became part of the games. It is said that Belistiche, a Macedonian woman from the seacoast, won the chariot race and that Tlepolemus, a Lycian, was victorious in the colt riding race. The latter event took place in the one hundred and thirty-first Olympiad; Belistiche's race with her two colts occurred in the third Olympiad before Tlempolemus' victory. A *pancratium* contest for boys was instituted in the forty-fifth Olympiad; an Aeolian from Troas, Phaedimus, was the winner. . . .

On the left side of the road leading from the Metroüm to the stadium, in the direction of the foot of Mt. Cronus, there is a stone foundation near the mountain which has steps which take you up through it. Along the side of this foundation a number of bronze statues of Zeus have been dedicated. The local people call these statues *Zanes* [statues of Zeus]; they were erected with money paid as fines by athletes who cheated in the games.

The first six statues were erected in the ninety-eighth Olympiad. At that time Eupolus of Thessaly paid bribes to Agestor the Arcadian and to Prytanis of Cyzicus who were competing in boxing; he also bribed a winner of the preceding Olympiad, Phormio of Halicarnassus. It is said that this was the first time in the history of the Olympic games that an athlete cheated. They also say that Eupolus and the athletes he paid off were the first people convicted by the Eleans and required to pay monetary fines. Two of the statues are the work of Cleon of Sicyon, but the artists who made the rest are not known. With the exception of the third and fourth, all other statues bear verse inscriptions: the first one aims to show that physical strength and swift feet, not money, should be the means by which one should achieve victory in the Olympic games; the second announces that the piety of the people of Elis has erected the statue in honor of Zeus with the aim of inspiring fear in athletes who resort to cheating in the games; the fifth inscription bestows praises on the Eleans for many things, particularly for imposing fines on the dishonest boxers; the sixth proclaims that these statues of Zeus should serve as reminders to the Greeks never to attempt to buy an Olympic victory with money.

It is also said that after the time of Eupolus, in the one hundred and twelfth Olympiad, an Athenian pentathlon contestant named Callipus bribed his opponents; but when the Eleans fined Callipus and the other contestants the Athenians dispatched Hypereides to Elis with instructions to persuade the Eleans to cancel the fine. The Eleans turned down the request and the Athenians became so disgusted that they not only refused to pay the fine, but boycotted the games. They returned, however, when the god of Delphi made a proclamation to the effect that he would not give any oracles to the Athenian people until they had paid their fine to the Eleans. The Athenians paid the money and again, in this case, six statues were set up which bore verse inscriptions that were by no means better than the inscriptions associated with the fine of Eupolus. The first informs us that the statues were erected as a tribute to the god for his role in supporting the decision of the Eleans to fine the dishonest pentathlon contestants; the second and third also praise the Eleans for imposing fines on the athletes of the pentathlon who had been bribed.

The fourth inscription purports to demonstrate that valor, not money, is the essence of the Olympics; the fifth offers an explanation for the erection of the statues and the sixth mentions the role of Delphi in pressuring the Athenians to pay the fine.

Next to these there are two other statues which were erected with money collected as fines for violations in wrestling matches; the names of the athletes, however, escaped me and my local Elean guides. . . .

A long time after this, in the two hundred and eighteenth Olympiad [93 A.D.], other athletes were also punished with fines by the Eleans. Among them was a boxer from Alexandria named Apollonius and surnamed Rhantes (it is a common practice in that city to give people surnames). Apollonius was the first Egyptian to be convicted by the Eleans of violating the rules of the games. He was not guilty of offering or receiving bribes, but of another infraction: he came to the games late. He was disqualified by the Eleans, as the regulations provided. He claimed as his defense that he had been detained in the Cyclades by unfavorable winds, but his excuse was rejected after another native of Alexandria, Heracleides by name, revealed that Apollonius had been busy during that time earning money in the Ionian games. Consequently, Apollonius was not allowed to participate in the Olympics and some other boxers who had also arrived late were disqualified as well. Heracleides was then declared the winner without fighting a single opponent. But Apollonius put on his boxing gloves and went after Heracleides, who had already been crowned with an olive wreath and had sought safety among the judges. Apollonius struck him and was severely punished for this foolish behavior.

II
Philosophy

Heraclitus of Ephesus—The Doctrine of Universal Flux: Selected Fragments.

Heraclitus of Ephesus was one of the greatest of the Ionian philosophers of Greece and the author of an important work entitled *On the Whole,* which was divided into three parts: the first was concerned with the universe, the second with politics and ethics and the third with religion. Unfortunately, only 130 fragments of this work have survived. His main philosophic doctrine is expressed in the famous dictum *"panta rhei"* (*"all things change"*) which has become proverbial, for it expresses the concept of the eternal flux of things. The fragments given here are based on Diels' edition of the Presocratics (*Fragmente der Vorsokratiker*) and illustrate this aspect of the thought of Heraclitus.

fr. 91. One cannot step twice into the same river.

fr. 49a. In the same river we step and do not step, we are and we are not.

fr. 52. Time is a child at play, playing a game of draughts. Even kingship is determined by a child's play.

fr. 53. War is the father of all and king of all. He has revealed some as gods, others as men. Some he has made slaves, others free.

fr. 80. It is necessary to know that war is the common condition, that contention is justice, and that all things come about through strife and necessity.

fr. 84a. Things find repose in change.

fr. 126. Cold things become hot, a hot thing becomes cold, the wet dries, the parched becomes moist.

A Conversation with a Sophist:
Plato, *Protagoras*, 317–328.

The Greek term *sophistes* was used at first to designate a wise man or a man with some special expertise, but in the fifth century B.C. it was applied to members of a class of professional teachers who provided, in return for a fee, what the various Greek states did not—higher education. The services of the sophists were required especially by those who sought prominence in civic life, for political influence and recognition came only with a knowledge of the subjects they taught: rhetoric, logic, statesmanship, philosophy and science. The sophists were not philosophers in the classical sense, though they did engage in philosophic argument. Most of them argued against the existence of any reality beyond that which can be grasped by the senses and against the existence of absolute truths. Their subjectivism was seen by some as a threat to traditional beliefs and values and, along with their occasionally irresponsible commercialism, made them unpopular in many quarters.

The greatest of the sophists was Protagoras of Abdera, who earned the respect even of Plato and was credited by Diogenes Laertius with inventing the Socratic method of argument. In his *Protagoras* Plato recorded Socrates' recollection of a conversation (which probably took place in the late 430's B.C.) between himself and the sophist. The *Protagoras* begins with an account of how Socrates was convinced by Hippocrates, a young and impetuous friend, to take him to the home of Callias where he hoped to meet and become a student of Protagoras. In the excerpt given below Protagoras explains that he teaches excellence in civic and private affairs. Socrates expresses his doubt whether such a thing can be taught and adds that Athenian political practices and the apparent inability of virtuous men to transfer their excellence to others seem to confirm this view. Protagoras responds with an admirable argument which, by showing that excellence can indeed be taught, justified his profession.

When we had all taken our seats Protagoras said, "Now that these gentlemen are here, Socrates, tell us about the matter you mentioned to me a moment ago on behalf of this young man."

"I'll begin, Protagoras," I said, "just as I did before, with our reason for coming. Hippocrates here wants to join your circle of associates, and he says that he would like to know just what he'll get out of being your pupil. That is what we wanted to say."

Protagoras answered, "Young man, if you join me the result will be that on the very day you do you will go home a better man, and it will be the same the following day. Each day you will continue to improve."

When I heard this I said, "Protagoras, there is nothing at all extraordinary in what you are saying, but only common sense. Even a man as old and wise as you are would become better if someone taught him something he didn't already happen to know. So don't answer us that way. Give us the kind of answer Hippocrates would get if he changed his mind all of a sudden and decided to study with that young man who has just recently come to town, Zeuxippus of Heraclea. Suppose that he approached him, as he has just now approached you, and heard him say the same thing he heard from you, that each day he spent in his company he would become better and make progress. If he went on to ask, 'But *how* will I be better, and in *what* will I make progress?' Zeuxippus would reply, 'Painting.' And if he went to Orthagoras of Thebes and received the same answer he got from you, and then asked him in what sense he would become better each day as a result of their association, Orthagoras would say, 'In playing the flute.' So please, give this young man and me a precise answer when I ask this question on his behalf: 'If Hippocrates becomes your pupil, Protagoras, and goes home a better man on the very first day, and continues to make similar progress on each succeeding day, then exactly how will he become better and in what will he progress?' "

When Protagoras heard what I had to say he replied, "That's a good question, Socrates, and I enjoy answering those who ask good questions. If Hippocrates comes to me he will not receive the same treatment he would get if he were to attach himself to any other sophist, for the others mistreat the young. They take youths who have abandonded traditional subjects and throw them right back into those same studies, teaching them arithmetic and astronomy and geometry and music (he looked right at Hippias as he said this), but if he comes to me he will learn only what he came to learn. The thing that I teach is good judgment—in personal affairs, so that he may manage his household in the best way, and in matters pertaining to the city, so that what he does and says may have the greatest possible influence."

"I wonder if I really understand you," I said, "for it appears to me that you are talking about the art of politics, and that you promise to make men good citizens."

"Yes, Socrates," he said, "that is precisely what I promise to do."

"What a good and useful skill you have mastered," I said, "if you really *have* mastered it (I would never hide my true thoughts from you). I didn't think, Protagoras, that this was something that could be taught. But you say that you *can* teach it and so I don't see how I can disbelieve you. Still, it is only right that I should tell you why I believe it cannot be taught or given by one man to another. Like the other Greeks, I say that the Athenians are wise. Now, I notice that when they meet in the Assembly and a decision must be made with regard to some sort of construction project they call for the builders to hear their advice about buildings; and if they want to build a ship they bring in the shipwrights; and they do the same in all other matters which they believe are learnable and teachable. But if someone they don't consider to be an expert should attempt to give them advice then, no matter how good-looking or wealthy or well-born he may be, they will not accept him. Instead, they will ridicule him and cause a disturbance until he is shouted down and gives up his attempt, or else the police haul him off or he is ejected on the orders of the *prytaneis* (*i.e.*, the fifty members of the Council of 500 who presided over the Assembly). This is the way in which they take care of matters involving what they consider to be technical skills. But when some matter pertaining to city government is being considered the man who stands up to advise them may be a carpenter or, just as likely, a blacksmith, a shoemaker, a merchant, the owner of a ship, rich or poor, from a noble family or a humble one—and yet nobody rebukes him, as they would those I just mentioned, or admonishes him for trying to give advice when he has never received instruction from any source and has never had a teacher. It is evident that they do not think this is a subject which can be taught. Moreover, this holds true not only in public affairs, but in private life, too, our wisest and best citizens are unable to transfer their excellence to others. For example, Pericles, the father of these young men here, gave them a top-notch education in the subjects for which teachers were to be had, but in those matters in which he himself is wise he neither teaches them himself nor hands them over to others for instruction. And so they wander about aimlessly, like sacred cattle seeking pasture, thinking they might somehow acquire excellence by chance. Or, if you'd like another example, there is Clinias, the younger brother of Alcibiades here. As his guardian, this same Pericles was afraid that he would be corrupted by Alcibiades, and so he took him and placed him in the house of Ariphron to be educated. But Ariphron gave him back before six months had passed because he had been unable to do anything with him. I could tell you about many other men who, despite the fact that they themselves are good, never succeeded in making anyone else better, whether they were related or not. In view of this, Protagoras, I don't believe that excellence can be taught. And yet, when I hear you saying that you *do* teach it I lose my confidence and begin to think you may have a point there. For I consider you to be a man of great experience and profound learning who has come up with original ideas himself. So, if you can clearly demonstrate that excellence can indeed be taught, I ask that you show us. Don't deprive us of the truth."

"No, Socrates," he said, "I will not keep it from you. But shall I show you by means of a story, like an old man talking to youngsters, or by a carefully reasoned argument?"

Many of those who were seated near him answered that he should offer his demonstration in whichever way he wished.

"Well then," he said, "I think a story would be more enjoyable."

"There was once a time when there were gods but no mortal creatures. When the appointed time came for the latter to be created, the gods formed them within the earth from a mixture of earth and fire and all the elements which are produced by combining these two substances. When they were ready to lead them up into the light they enjoined Prometheus and Epimetheus to assign to each one the powers befitting it. Epimetheus asked Prometheus to let him distribute the powers himself. 'And when I have done so,' he said, 'you can inspect them.' After Prometheus had been persuaded to go along with this idea Epimetheus went ahead and distributed the powers. In assigning them he gave some creatures strength, but not speed, which he gave to the weaker ones. Some of them he armed, but for the unarmed he devised some other means of protection. To the small creatures he gave the power of flight or an underground dwelling, while the large creatures received protection in the form of size. He distributed all the other powers and faculties in accordance with this principle of parity, taking care that no species should ever become extinct. When he had provided them with the means of escaping destruction he arranged for their comfort during the seasons ordained by Zeus, clothing them in thick hair and tough hides capable of protecting them from the winter cold, and also against heat, and of serving each species as its own special form of bedding when they went to sleep. He shod some of them with hoofs and others with claws and tough, bloodless hides. Then he supplied different foods to the various species; grasses of the earth for some, fruits from trees for others, and roots for still others. To some he gave other animals for food, but he made these less fertile, while causing the creatures they kill to be exceptionally productive in order to ensure the survival of the species.

Now Epimetheus was not particularly wise, and so he carelessly lavished all of the available powers on the irrational creatures. The result was that humankind was left insufficiently equipped, and he did not know what to do with them. As he stood there in confusion, Prometheus came to inspect the distribution and saw that while all the other animals were well equipped in every way, man was naked, unshod, without any bedding, and unarmed. To make matters worse, the day had already arrived on which man, like the others, was to emerge from the earth and go up into the world of light. Prometheus, perplexed by the problem of finding some means of preservation for man, stole from Hephaestus and Athena their skill in the arts along with fire—for it was useless to acquire or employ that skill if one did not also have fire—and gave these as a gift to man. And so it happened that man received the practical wisdom necessary to sustain life, but he still did not have any skill in the art of politics, since this belonged to Zeus. Prometheus was not about to enter the acropolis which is the home of Zeus—and besides, the guards of Zeus were fearsome—but he crept unobserved into the building which Athena and Hephaestus shared and in which they practiced their crafts, stole Hephaestus' skill in using fire and the other art which was Athena's, and gave them to humankind. And thus it happened that human beings received the resources required for life. The legend also says that Prometheus was later brought to justice on account of what he had done, and all because of Epimetheus.

Man was now a participant in divine things. In the first place, because of his relationship with the gods he was the only one of all the living creatures to revere them, and he set about building them altars and images. Secondly, his skill quickly enabled him to articulate sounds and words, to invent houses and clothes and shoes and bedding, and to procure food from the soil.

Being provided for in these ways, men originally lived in scattered groups, and there were no cities. As a result, they were preyed upon by wild beasts, for they were in all respects weaker than these. And even though their practical skill was sufficient to help supply them with food, it proved to be deficient in their war against the beasts; for they did not possess the art of politics, a part of which is the art of war. And so they sought to join together and save themselves by building cities. But when they gathered together in communities they wronged each other because they did not know the art of living together in a city, and so they began to scatter and be destroyed again. It was then that Zeus, fearing that our race would be entirely eradicated, sent Hermes to bring respect and just law to humankind so that there would be well-ordered governments in the cities and ties of friendship to bring men together. Hermes asked Zeus how he should go about giving these things to man: 'Should I allocate them in the same way that the practical arts were assigned—in other words, in accordance with the principle that one man trained in medicine is sufficient to care for many others who have no such specialized knowledge, and that the same holds true with respect to experts in other fields? Shall I give justice and respect to men in this way, or should I bestow them on all men?'

'To all,' said Zeus. 'Let all men share in them. For there could be no cities if, as is the case with the other arts, only a few men have a share of these. And establish a law in my name that he who is incapable of sharing in respect and justice shall be put to death, for he is like a disease which infects the city.' This, Socrates, is why when there is a debate about some issue involving expertise in the art of carpentry or some other craft the people of other cities as well as the Athenians think it proper for only a few to come forward and offer advice and do not tolerate suggestions from anyone other than these few, as you say—and in my opinion they are correct. But when they consult together on a subject which requires excellence in the art of city government, in which they should be guided at every turn by justice and wisdom, they naturally allow everyone to offer advice, since they believe it is right for all citizens to participate in that kind of excellence; otherwise there could be no cities. This is the reason for it, Socrates.

Now, just so you will not think you are being taken in by smooth talk, here is additional proof that everyone believes each and every citizen shares in the knowledge of justice and in all other aspects of civic virtue. With respect to all other forms of excellence, as you say, if someone claims to be an expert at flute-playing or any other art when he really isn't, people either laugh at him or become irritated, and his relatives come and try to pound some sense into him as if he were mad. But when it comes to justice and civic virtue in general, even if they know that a certain individual is unjust, if he publicly admits the truth they consider his truthfulness to be a sign of insanity, though in the previous case it would be regarded as good sense. They say that everyone should claim to be just whether he is or not, and that anyone who doesn't is crazy; for they believe that a human being must have some sense of justice, or he wouldn't be human at all.

That is all I have to say about my point that men act rightly in accepting the counsel of all citizens in matters pertaining to this particular virtue, for they believe that everyone possesses it to some degree. But now I'd like to prove to you that they do not believe it to be something which occurs naturally and spontaneously, but that it can be taught, and that those who acquire it do so through careful study. With regard to the various evils which people believe are caused by nature or chance, nobody is irritated with those who are afflicted by them, or scolds or teaches or punishes such people in order to change them; they merely pity them. Would anyone be so foolish as to try to do any of these things to the ugly or the puny or the weak? Hardly, for I suspect that everyone knows that such things are due to nature and fortune, both the good and the bad. But it is a different matter with the good qualities which men gain through careful study and practice and instruction. For it is when a man does not possess these, but only their corresponding bad qualities, that people become irritated and punish him and try to put some sense into him. Among these bad qualities are injustice and irreverence and, in short, everything which is contrary to civic excellence. It is when these appear in a man that all the other citizens become upset with him and admonish him, because it is clear that excellence as a citizen is achieved through diligent study and instruction. For if you will only reflect on punishment, Socrates, and the way it influences wrongdoers, you will be convinced that men believe excellence to be something which one person can impart to another. Nobody punishes a wrongdoer just because he did something wrong—not unless he is blindly seeking revenge like some wild animal. No, someone who attempts to punish in a rational manner doesn't do so in retaliation for a past offense—for what is done cannot be undone—but because he is concerned about the future and intends that neither the wrongdoer himself nor anyone who witnesses his punishment will ever do wrong again. And the fact that he has this purpose in mind demonstrates his belief that excellence comes from education; for, at any rate, the punishment is meant to be a deterrent. This is the view accepted by everyone who administers punishment, either as a private citizen or a public official. All men punish and chastise those who they suppose to have done wrong, and the Athenians, your fellow citizens, are no exceptions. On the basis of this argument, then, the Athenians must be counted among those who believe that excellence can be taught and imparted by one man to another. And so, Socrates, I believe that I have now satisfactorily demonstrated to you that your fellow citizens are right in accepting the advice of blacksmiths and shoemakers in matters relating to politics, and that they believe excellence is something which can be furnished to a man through teaching.

Socrates on the Sophists:
Xenophon, *Memorabilia*, I.6.13.

Though his contemporaries often identified him with the sophists, Socrates differed radically from them. His disciple Xenophon wrote the following account of his response to their practice of teaching for pay.

"It is generally acknowledged by us, O Antiphon, that beauty and wisdom alike can be disposed of either morally or immorally. For if a man sells his beauty for silver to someone who desires it he is called a male prostitute, but if anyone makes a friend of another who he knows cares for him in a good and virtuous way, then we say he is prudent and of sound mind. Similarly, those who sell their wisdom for money to anyone who wants to buy it are called sophists, or, as it were, prostitutes [*i.e.*, of wisdom]; but whoever makes a friend of someone whom he knows to be of a good and deserving nature, and teaches him what he knows about that which is good, we recognize this man as one who behaves as a good and honorable citizen."

Socrates on Trial: Plato, *Apology*, 18 and 28–30.

It was in 399 B.C., and in an Athens still shaken by its defeat in the Peloponnesian War, that Socrates was brought to trial on charges of irreverence (specifically, for introducing strange new gods) and corrupting the city's youth. The first accusation has always been something of a mystery; there is no evidence that Socrates was ever a member of any unorthodox sect, though he did claim to have received divine instruction on occasion which determined the course of his career. In any case, it is probably the second charge which reflects the fears which led to his indictment. Many conversative Athenians no doubt held Socrates responsible for the anti-democratic attitudes of young men such as Plato, Alcibiades, Critias and Xenophon—all of them his disciples. But his influence certainly extended far beyond the circle of his close associates, and it was the possible widespread effect of his practice of questioning and criticizing the very foundations of Athenian society that worried his enemies.

The jury which tried Socrates consisted of 501 citizen jurors or *dicasts* chosen by lot from a panel of six thousand. According to Athenian law there were no judges or lawyers and the trial had to be completed in a single day. Socrates' accusers (Meletus, Anytus and Lycon) presented their case first, this being followed by the defense (*apologia*) given by the philosopher himself. Plato, who was present at the trial, wrote down the speech of his teacher as he remembered it at a later date.

". . . Now, therefore, you men of Athens, I do not want to offer my defense on my own behalf, as you might expect, but for your sake, lest by condemning me you sin against the god who gave me to you as a gift. For if you sentence me to death you will have a difficult time finding another like me who, if I may use a rather artless and laughable figure of speech, fastens himself to the city just as a gadfly clings to a large and noble horse which, being slow and lazy because of its great size, needs to be stung into action. It seems to me that the god attached me to the city in a similar way, and so I spend the whole day sitting down next to each of you in every part of the city, never ceasing in my efforts to awaken, persuade and admonish you. You cannot assume that another man like me will come to you, Athenians, and, if you take my advice, you will spare me. But maybe you are irritated, like people who are roused from their sleep, and might slap me and easily kill me, as Anytus is urging you to do. But then, of course, you would go on sleeping for the rest of your lives unless God, out of concern for you, sent someone else to you. Here is the reason why you should recognize that I am indeed a gift to you from the god: I have left all my own affairs uncared for, and all these years I have suffered the consequences of their neglect. Indeed, instead of seeing to my own affairs I am always attending to your interests, approaching each of you like a father or an elder brother and pleading with you to care for virtue. This would make sense, at least by ordinary human standards, if I had made a profit by accepting payment for my exhortations. But now you can see for yourselves that even though my accusers have impudently charged me with everything else, they have not been so insolent as to supply a witness to testify that I ever took or asked for any kind of payment. I have a good witness to the truth of what I say—my poverty. . . .

Perhaps someone might say, 'Why don't you just keep quiet, Socrates, and go to live somewhere else?' Making you understand my answer will be most difficult. For if I tell you that to do this would be to disobey the god, and that for this reason I cannot be silent, you will think I am playing games with you and you won't be persuaded. And you'll be even less apt to believe me if I say that the greatest good for man is to converse every day about virtue and all the other matters about which you hear me questioning myself and others, and that a life without self-examination is unworthy of a human being. But what I am saying is the truth, Athenians, though to convince you is not easy. Moreover, I am not in the habit of expecting any kind of punishment. If I had money I would offer to pay as large a penalty as I could afford, for that would not hurt me. But I have no money with which to pay a fine, unless you charge a sum which I will be able to pay. Perhaps I could pay a mina of silver, and so I propose that that shall be my penalty. But Plato here, and Crito, Cristobulus and Apollodorus, are urging me to offer thirty minas, and they say they are willing to guarantee its payment. This, then, is the penalty I propose, and these men of considerable wealth pledge that it will be paid to you.

(The judges now passed sentence, condemning Socrates to death)

By condemning me, men of Athens, you have gained only a short time during which to be free of me, and you have given those who wish to denounce the city both an opportunity and a reason, since you have condemned Socrates, a wise man. For those who wish to reproach you will say that I am wise, even though I am not. If you had just waited a little while what you desire would have happened automatically, for you see how old I am and that at my advanced age death is near. I am not saying this to all of you, but only to those who condemned me to death. And I have something else to say to them. You might think that I was convicted because I lacked the words which would have persuaded you of my innocence, as if I thought it acceptable to do or say whatever was necessary to escape justice. But this is by no means the case. It is indeed because of a deficiency that I have been convicted, but not a deficiency in words; rather, it was a lack of audacity and shamelessness, of a willingness to say to you the things that would have pleased you most to hear. You wanted me to wail and weep and to do and say many things which are, as I say, beneath my dignity—the sort of things you are used to hearing from others. When I offered my defense I didn't think it proper to do anything unbefitting a free man merely for the sake of escaping danger, and even now I don't regret making my defense as I did. I would much rather die after such a defense than live after offering a dishonorable one. Neither in a court of law nor in a war should I or any other person scheme to avoid death by resorting to any available means. In battles it often becomes clear that a soldier can escape death by dropping his weapons and turning around to beg those who are chasing him for mercy. And there are many other schemes which will enable one to flee from death in all sorts of dangerous circumstances, provided that he has the temerity to do and say anything. But it is not death which is difficult to escape, gentlemen. No, it is far more difficult to escape cowardice, which pursues us more swiftly than death. And now I, slow and old as I am, have been overtaken by death, the slower runner, but those who accuse me, men who are crafty and quick, have been caught by the faster one—wickedness. You have judged me and condemned me to death, and so now I go away. And those who convicted me also go, condemned by the truth of their wickedness and injustice. I accept my penalty. They must accept theirs. Perhaps things were meant to turn out this way, and I suppose it's only right that they should be so.

Now that my fate has been determined I would like to prophesy to you who have condemned me, for I have come to that time when most men foretell the future—when they are awaiting death. I say to you who have sentenced me that as soon as I am dead you will be punished far more severely than you have punished me. For you have done this thing to me in the hope that you might thus avoid having to give an account of your lives, but I tell you that the result will be just the opposite of what you expected. For now there will be many who will call you to account, men whom I have held back, though you were not aware of it. They are young men, and so they will be more severe with you, and you will be even more angry and upset then than you are now.

You are mistaken if you think that by putting men to death you will prevent anyone from chastising you for not living as you should, for it is both impossible and dishonorable to escape in this way. The best and easiest way is not to punish others, but to set about the task of making yourselves as good as you can be. This, then, is the prophecy which I make to you who have condemned me. Now I go away."

The Dualism of Body and Soul:
Plato, *Phaedo*, 63c–68b.

Plato's *Phaedo* is an account of a conversation between Eche-crates of Phlius and Phaedo of Elis in which the latter describes in detail the last day of Socrates' life. The philosopher had spent the month following his condemnation in prison, using the short time left to him to put Aesop's fables into verse and write a hymn to Apollo. His closest friends and disciples often came to visit him, and they were with him on the day he died. Apollodorus of Phalerum, Simmias of Thebes, Cebes of Thebes and Crito of Athens—they were all dis-traught as the hour approached when their teacher was to drink the poison. Only Socrates remained calm. He reminded them that the true philosopher looks forward to death because it is only when it is released from the body that the soul can acquire perfect wisdom. As long as the body and the soul are united the soul is distracted from its true purpose (gaining knowledge of the truth) by the constant de-mands of the body for gratification. The philosopher seeks to mini-mize the interference of the body by ignoring it, keeping it and the soul apart. But if he is a true lover of wisdom—and this is what is meant by the word *philosophos*—he will also welcome the complete separation which leaves the soul free to exist in the world of truth.

"Do we believe that there is such a thing as death?"

"Of course," replied Simmias.

"Is it not the release of the soul from the body? And isn't the condition of being dead that in which the body is separated from the soul and exists by itself, while the soul is separated from the body and exists by itself? Could death be anything other than this?"

"No, it is just what you have described," he said.

"Then, my good man, see if you are in agreement with me about this, for if you are it will sharpen the issue at hand: Does it seem to you that a philosopher would care very much for the things which are commonly called pleasures, things such as eating and drinking?"

"Not at all, Socrates," said Simmias.

"What about the pleasures of love? Should he care much for them?"

"In no way."

"Do you suppose that he would think much of the other ways in which the body is indulged, of things such as expensive clothes and sandals, and other ornaments for the body? Do you think he would hold them in high regard? Or would he scorn them, since they are not really necessary?"

110

"It seems to me that the true philosopher would scorn them," he said.

"So then, you are entirely convinced that a man of this sort would not occupy himself with the body but, to the best of his ability, would let go of it and turn his attention to the enrichment of the soul?"

"I am."

"In the first place, then, it is evident that the philosopher, unlike other men, holds the soul apart from fellowship with the body."

"Yes."

"And I suppose, Simmias, that most people think that to the man who has no interest in bodily pleasures and does not partake of them life is not worth living, and that one who doesn't care about the pleasures of the body might as well be dead."

"What you are saying is entirely true."

"Well, what about the acquisition of knowledge? Is the body an obstacle or a help if it shares in the search for knowledge? What I am really asking is this: Is there any truth whatsoever in the human faculties of sight and hearing, or are the poets right when they constantly tell us that we neither see nor hear accurately? For if these two bodily faculties are not accurate and unerring then the others are probably not either, since they are inferior to them. Isn't that how it seems to you?"

"Yes, by all means."

"Then," he said, "when does the soul grasp the truth? For whenever it attempts to contemplate anything together with the body it is apparently deceived by it."

"What you say is true."

"Then isn't it in rational thought, if at all, that true reality becomes clear to the soul?"

"Yes."

"And the best sort of thinking occurs when the soul is not disturbed by any of these things—not by hearing, or sight, or pain, or pleasure,—when she leaves the body and is alone and, doing her best to avoid any form of contact with it, reaches out to grasp what is truly real."

"It is just as you say."

"And so in this way, too, the soul of the philosopher scorns the body, and flees from it, seeking to be by itself?"

"It would seem so."

"What about these things, Simmias? Do we believe that there is such a thing as absolute justice, or not?"

"By Zeus, we do believe that there is such a thing."

"And what about absolute beauty and absolute good?"

"They certainly exist."

"But have you ever seen any of these things with your eyes?"

"Definitely not," he said.

"Did you ever come into contact with them through any of the other bodily senses? I am talking about all absolutes, about absolute greatness in size, absolute health, absolute strength and, in a word, the essence or true reality which all things possess. Is their most fundamental truth ever perceived by the sensory faculties of the body? Or rather, isn't it the man who carefully prepares himself mentally to come to an intellectual understanding of each of the things he considers who gains the most precise knowledge of their true essences?"

"The latter, definitely."

"And wouldn't the man who does this most effectively be the one who approaches each thing with the intellect only, who never allows sight or any of the other senses to influence the process of intellection, but who makes use of pure reason alone in his search for the pure and particular reality of each thing, who distances himself to the greatest extent possible from eyes and ears and, in short, from the whole body, and who believes that these are things that distract the soul and, when it is in communion with the body, prevent it from acquiring truth and wisdom? Who, if not this man, O Simmias, will come to a knowledge of reality?"

"What you say is profoundly true, Socrates," said Simmias.

"Then," he said, "all these things must suggest to true philosophers an idea which they will express to each other in a way such as this: 'There appears to be a path which leads us and our argument directly to the conclusion that as long as we are in the body, and for as long as the soul is mixed with such a base thing, our thirst for the truth will never be satisfied. For the body hinders us in countless ways simply because of its need for nourishment. Furthermore, if diseases attack us, they, too, obstruct our search for what is real and true. The body fills us with loves and desires and fears, all kinds of fanciful imaginings, and much nonsense, and so, as they say, it actually renders us entirely incapable of thought. The body and its desires are the sole cause of wars, rebellions and battles, for all wars are the result of the desire for money, and we are forced to acquire money for the sake of the body, slavishly attending to its needs. And it is because of all these hindrances that we have no time left for philosophy. Last, and worst of all, even if we do have some free time to direct our attention to the contemplation of some thing, the body is constantly interrupting our search with noise and confusion, so that we become so disturbed that we are unable to see the truth. Experience has shown us that if we are ever going to have a pure knowledge of anything we must be rid of the body and see things by means of the soul alone. It is then that we will gain what we desire and say we love—wisdom. But this, as our reasoning shows, will not occur while we live, but after we die. For if pure knowledge cannot be acquired while we are in the body, then one of the following must be true: either knowledge cannot be obtained at all, or it can be gained only when we are dead; for it is then, and only then, that the soul will be alone and apart from the body. We believe that while we are alive we come closest to knowledge when, aside from what is absolutely necessary, we avoid as much as possible any association or communion with the body, and that, not being filled up with its odious nature, we keep ourselves untainted by it until the time when God himself liberates us. By being rid of the foolishness of the body in this way, and by being pure, we will no doubt be pure ourselves someday, and come to know all that is unalloyed perfection—and I think that this, perhaps, is truth. For it is not possible for the impure to grasp what is pure.' This is the sort of thing, Simmias, that true lovers of knowledge must say to each other, and their thoughts must certainly be the same. Don't you think so?"

"I certainly do, Socrates."

"Well then," said Socrates, "if this is true, my friend, there is good reason to expect that when I arrive at the place for which I am bound I will possess completely that which I have sought most in life. And so it is with high hopes that I set out on this journey which is required of me. And this same hope belongs to every man who believes that his intellect has been prepared and, as it were, purified."

"Very true," said Simmias.

"And, as we said earlier in our conversation, isn't purification the result of separating the soul as much as possible from the body? Doesn't it consist in the soul's habit of collecting itself and drawing itself inward from throughout the body, and dwelling, as much as it can, both now and in time to come, alone unto itself, freed from the bonds of the body?"

"Quite true," he said.

"And isn't this what we call death, the release and separation of the body from the soul?"

"Precisely," he replied.

"Well then, as we say, true philosophers are the only ones who are eager for the release of the soul, and the loosing and separation of the soul from the body is the object of their study, is it not?"

"Apparently."

"Then, as I said when we first began, it would be ridiculous for a man to live a life resembling death as closely as possible, and then be upset when death comes. Wouldn't that be foolish?"

"Of course."

"As a matter of fact, Simmias," he said, "true philosophers practice dying, and to die is less frightening to them than it is to other men. Look at it this way. If they resent the body, preferring that the soul should be alone by itself, wouldn't it be unreasonable for them to be afraid and upset when this very thing comes to pass? Wouldn't it be illogical for them not to be glad to go to that place where, when they arrive, there is a chance of getting what they longed for in life—and what they longed for was wisdom—and to be rid of an unwelcome companion? Many men, when their wives or sons have passed away, have willingly gone to Hades in the hope of seeing and being with those for whom they yearned. Should he, then, who is a true lover of wisdom, and is convinced that it can be found only in the other world, be troubled when he dies? Wouldn't he be happy to go there? Of course he would, my friend, if he is a true philosopher. For he will be absolutely certain that there, and only there, is pure wisdom to be found. And so, as I said before, if this is true it would be ridiculous for him to be afraid of death."

"By Zeus, it would be very foolish indeed," said Simmias.

The Death of Socrates:
Plato, *Phaedo*, 115–118.

> The previous selection, an excerpt from the beginning of Plato's *Phaedo*, described the first part of a conversation between Socrates and his disciples on the day of the philosopher's execution. After reminding them that he had no fear of death and offering three proofs of the immortality of the soul, the time came for him to drink the poison hemlock. The *Phaedo* concludes with an account, given below, of the last hours of Socrates' life.

After that, Crito said, "Socrates, do you have any instructions for us concerning your children or any other matter? Is there anything we can do for you?"

"Just what I always say, Crito," he answered, "nothing new. If you will only be diligent in managing your lives you will do me and mine a great honor, and you will be doing yourselves a favor as well, even if you don't agree to do so just now. But if you have no care for yourselves and will not tread the path we have spoken of now and earlier, then, even if you make many impetuous promises to me now, you will end up achieving nothing at all."

"Well, we are eager to do as you have told us," Crito said. "How would you like us to bury you?"

"In any way you wish," he answered, "provided that you can catch me and that I don't get away from you." He chuckled softly, and as he turned to look at us he said, "Friends, I can't seem to convince Crito here that the real Socrates is he who is now talking and organizing every element of his statements. He thinks that I am the body he will see dead in a little while, and so he asks how to bury me. For quite some time now I have used many arguments to make it clear that after I have drunk the poison I will not remain here with you, but will go to share in the happiness of the blessed—and yet, it appears that these things which I have said to comfort you and myself have made no impression on Crito. And so," he said, "I want you to promise me that you will make yourselves responsible for him now, just as at my trial he made himself responsible for me by vouching for me before the judges. Your promise to me will be the opposite of that which he gave to the court, for he offered security that I would stay in the city, while you must be my pledge to him that I will not remain when I die, but will depart; and thus Crito will be less upset by my death, and will not be distressed when he sees my body burned or buried. Neither will he grieve, thinking that I am suffering terrible things, or say at the funeral that Socrates is being laid out or carried to the grave or buried. Dearest Crito, you may be certain that erroneous statements such as these are not merely evil in themselves, but also have a pernicious influence on our souls. Take heart, and say that you are burying only my body, and bury it in whatever way you think proper."

Having said this he stood up and went into a chamber to take a bath. Crito followed him and told us to stay where we were. We did, talking and thinking about what had been said and about the disaster that had befallen us. For we felt that we were being deprived of a father, and that we would spend the rest of our lives as orphans. When he had finished his bath his children were brought to him—he had two small sons and one who was grown—along with the women of his family. He conversed with them in Crito's presence and gave them directions for things he wanted done. Then, after he had sent the women and children away, he came back to us.

By then it was nearly sunset, for he had spent quite some time within. When he returned from the bath he sat down, but no one said much after this until the servant of the Eleven came in and, standing next to him, said: "Socrates, I know that I will not observe you to be like other men who make trouble and curse me when, on the order of the archons, I announce that the time has come to drink the poison. During the time you have been here I have found you to be the noblest, gentlest and most excellent man who has ever entered this place, and now I am certain that you are not angry with me, for you realize that others are to blame. Now, you know what I have come to say, so farewell, and try to suffer the inevitable as easily as possible." With that he broke down in tears, and turned to leave.

Socrates looked up at him and said, "May you, too, fare well; we will do what you ask." Then he turned back to us and said, "How civil that man is! Throughout my stay here he has been coming to see me and, on occasion, to talk with me. He has been the most worthy of men, and now see how generously he sheds his tears for me. Come, Crito, let us obey him. Have someone bring me the poison if it is ready, and have the man make some if it isn't."

Crito said, "Socrates, I think the sun is still on the mountaintops, and has not yet gone down. Besides, I know that other men have waited until long after the announcement has been made before they drank the poison, and have eaten and drunk, and some have even enjoyed the company of their loved ones. Don't be in such a rush, for you still have time."

"Crito," replied Socrates, "the men you are speaking of act quite reasonably, for they think they have something to gain by delaying, but I believe I have nothing to gain by drinking the poison a little later. No, I would consider myself laughable were I to cling to and try to preserve my life when there is nothing left to be gained by living. Come now, don't argue with me, but do as I ask."

When he heard this, Crito signaled the servant boy who was standing nearby. The boy left and, after being gone for a long time, returned with the man in charge, who carried the prepared poison in a cup. When Socrates saw him, he said, "Well, my friend, you are knowledgeable about these things, what do I have to do?"

"You need only drink the poison," he said, "and walk around until your legs begin to feel heavy. Then lie down, and the poison will do its work." As he spoke he handed the cup to Socrates, who accepted it quite graciously, Echecrates, without trembling or any perceptible change in his facial color or expression. He looked up at the man with those big gentle eyes of his and said: "What do you say about pouring out a libation to some god from this cup? Is such a thing permitted, or not?"

"Socrates," he replied, "we pound only as much of the poison powder as we think is enough."

"I see," he said, "but it must certainly be both lawful and necessary to pray to the gods to ensure that my departure will be attended by good fortune. This is my desire, then—so be it." And as he said this he resolutely put the cup to his lips and calmly and good-naturedly drank it down. Up until then most of us had managed to hold back our tears, but when we saw him drink, and then finish the cup, we could no longer restrain ourselves. In spite of myself, the tears poured down my cheeks, and I covered my face and wept—not for him, but for myself, since it was my lot to lose such a friend. Crito, too, had been unable to keep from weeping. He broke down even before I did, and had left his seat. Apollodorus had been crying all along, but now he burst out in such agonized wails of grief that everyone there fell apart completely except Socrates himself. "What are you doing?" he asked. "Why are you acting so strangely? I sent the women away precisely for this reason, so that they would not carry on this way, for I have heard that a man should die cheerfully. Please, keep quiet and be strong."

When we heard this we were ashamed and we controlled our tears. He walked around a bit and then, when he said that his legs were heavy, he lay down on his back according to directions. The man who had given him the poison bent over him and after a short time examined his feet and legs. He pressed his foot hard and asked if he felt anything. He said he did not. Then he pressed his thighs, and moving his hands up along his body in this way he showed us that he was becoming cold and stiff. Then he touched him again and said that he would pass away when the poison reached his heart. When he had begun to grow cold in the area of his lower abdomen he uncovered his face (which he had earlier covered up) and spoke the words which proved to be his last—"Crito, we owe a cock to Asclepius. Don't forget to pay it."[1]

"I won't," said Crito, "but think, is there anything else you want to say?"

He didn't answer this question, but after a few moments he stirred a bit. The man uncovered him. His eyes were set, and when Crito saw this he closed his mouth and eyes.

1   It was customary to offer a gift to the god of healing when one recovered from an illness.

This, Echecrates, was the end of our friend. We may truly say that of all those of his time whom we have known he was the best, the wisest, and the most just.

The Allegory of the Cave: Plato, *Republic*, VII. 514–521.

In his *Republic* Plato has Socrates describe to four of his companions a conversation in which he had participated the previous day. On that occasion he had joined with a number of others—Glaucon and Adeimantus, the brothers of Plato, Polemarchus, Cephalus and Thrasymachus—in discussing government and, more specifically, the nature of the ideal state. Much of Plato's thought on this subject is based upon his belief that while the physical world in which we live and which we perceive with our senses is one of shadow and illusion, there is a higher world of the intellect, a spiritual realm in which reality and truth can be grasped through the intellectual activity of the soul.

The importance of moving into this realm of eternal and absolute realities is illustrated by the so-called Allegory of the Cave. Socrates describes a cavern in which dwell prisoners who have never seen the light of day. Chained in such a way that they can see only the shadows cast on the wall of their subterranean dwelling, they have no way of knowing that these dim images of things are not the things themselves. But when a prisoner is brought out into the light his vision gradually clears until he is at last able to behold the sun itself. Similarly, the individual who focuses his attention on the realm of Ideas, the true essences or realities of all things, will eventually perceive the unified and ultimate source of all truth—the Idea of the Good. Those few who have witnessed this beatific vision will most likely have little interest in ordinary human affairs but, because they are the only ones who have acquired knowledge of the truth, they must be called upon to serve as rulers of the ideal state.

"Next," I said, "think of our nature with respect to knowledge and ignorance as being similar to the following situation. Imagine human beings living in an underground cavern with a wide entrance which is open to the light across its entire width. In this place are people who have been there since childhood with chains on their legs and necks so that, because their bonds make it impossible to turn their heads, they are able only to look forward. Light comes from a fire which is burning at a distance above and behind them. There is an elevated pathway between the fire and the prisoners, and you can see a low wall alongside it which resembles the low screens which puppeteers put up between themselves and their audiences and above which they show their puppets."

"I see," he said.

"Then imagine, too, men carrying along the wall all kinds of vessels that rise above it, and statues of men and other animals made of stone and wood and material of every kind. Some of the men carrying these things along the wall are talking and some are silent."

"The image and the prisoners you are talking about are strange," he said.

"They're like us," I said. "First of all, do you think that it would ever have been possible for these men to see any part of themselves or of one another aside from the shadows cast by the fire on the wall of the cave which they were facing?"

"How could it have been," he said, "if throughout their lives they had been forced to keep their heads still?"

"And wouldn't this also be true of the things being carried past them?"

"Certainly."

"And, if they were able to talk to each other, don't you suppose that in giving names to the things they saw they would believe they were naming the actual objects going past them?"

"Yes, that would definitely be the case."

"And what if the prison had an echo coming from the wall they were facing? Don't you think that if one of the men walking by chanced to make a noise the prisoners would assume that it was the passing shadow that made it?"

"Yes, by Zeus," he said.

"Well then," I said, "prisoners like these would no doubt believe reality to be nothing other than the shadows of the objects, wouldn't they?"

"They most certainly would," he replied.

"Consider, then," I said, "what would actually happen if the prisoners were set free from their chains and cured of their folly. Take, for example, a prisoner who is released from his chains and suddenly forced to stand up, turn his head around, walk, and look up in the direction of the light. While he does all these things he is in pain and unable to see clearly the things whose shadows he saw earlier because he is blinded by the glare of the light. What do you think he would say if he were told that what he saw before was nonsense and illusion, but now, drawing closer to what is real and being turned toward truly real things, his vision is more accurate? And if someone also pointed out to him each of the things passing by and required him to answer questions about what they were, don't you think that he wouldn't know what to say and that he would believe that what he had seen before was more real than the things now being pointed out to him?"

"Much more real," he said.

"And if he were forced to look directly at the light wouldn't his eyes feel such pain that he would turn away toward the things which he could see clearly, and think they were clearer and more distinct than the things being shown to him?"

"It is just as you say," he said.

"And if," I said, "someone forcibly dragged him from there up the rugged and steep ascent and didn't let him go until he had been dragged out into the sunlight, wouldn't he be upset and irritated at being dragged along? And after he had come out into the light, wouldn't his eyes be so full of the sun's rays that he wouldn't be able to see any of the things which we now say are real?"

"He wouldn't be able to see them right away," he said.

"Then I guess he would have to get used to the light before he could see what was above him. In the beginning it would be easiest for him to see the shadows, then the reflections of men and other objects in water and, finally, the objects themselves. And then he could go on to contemplate the things in heaven and heaven itself, seeing more easily the light of the stars and the moon by night, and then, by day, the sun and the light of the sun."

"Of course."

"Lastly, I imagine he would be able to behold the sun itself and see it as it truly is—not its reflection in water or in some other element, but its real self in its own proper setting."

"This must be so," he said.

"After this he would come to the conclusion that it is the sun which produces the seasons and the years and which is the guardian of all things in the realm of the visible, and that it is also in some way the cause of all the things which he and his fellow prisoners had seen."

"Yes, that's what he would do next," he said.

"What would happen then? Don't you think that, when he remembered his former dwelling place, what was held to be wisdom there, and his fellow prisoners, he would count himself fortunate because of the change and feel sorry for them?"

"Certainly."

"And if there had been honors and praises and prizes among them which they awarded to the man who was quickest at discerning the shadows as they passed by and best at remembering the sequence in which they were usually carried past the prisoners, and so was the most adept at predicting which one would come next—do you think he would want to have these prizes, and that he would be envious of those who were so honored and therefore had authority over the other prisoners? Or, would he share the sentiments of Homer and greatly desire 'to be on the soil, the serf of another man, a man without land' [*Odyssey*, XI, 489–492], and suffer anything rather than share the same opinions and live the same life as these men?"

"Yes," he said, "I think he would prefer to accept every kind of suffering rather than live that kind of life."

"And consider this," I said. "If a man like this one were to go down and take his old seat again, wouldn't the suddenness of his coming in from the sun cause his eyes to be so full of darkness that he would be blind?"

"Very true," he replied.

"Now, if he had to vie once more with these men who had always been prisoners in making judgments about the shadows while his vision was still dim and before his eyes had become used to the dark—and this would take a considerable amount of time—wouldn't he be made a laughingstock, and wouldn't they say that he had gone up only to come back with his eyes ruined, and that making the ascent is not worth the effort? And if they were able to seize and kill the man who attempted to free them and lead them up out of the cave, wouldn't they do just that?"

"Most definitely," he said.

"Then, my dear Glaucon," I said, "let us use this image to illuminate what we said before. Compare the region which we perceive by means of the faculty of sight to the cavernous prison where the prisoners dwell, and the light of the fire in the prison to the sun's power. And, if you compare the prisoner's ascent and contemplation of the things above to the soul's ascent to the intelligible realm, you will not fail to express my own expectation— and that is what you want to hear. But only God knows if my expectation happens to be correct. But, whether I am right or wrong, it appears to me that in the realm of knowledge the last and most difficult thing to be seen is the Idea of the Good. When this is seen, the beholder must necessarily come to the conclusion that it is the ultimate cause of all that is right and beautiful in all things; in the visible world it generated light and the master of light [i.e., the sun]; in the realm of the intelligible, being itself supreme, it produced truth and intelligence. He who would act wisely in private or public affairs must understand this."

"I agree," he said, "as far as I am able."

"Come then," I said, "and agree with me also on this point, and don't be surprised that those who have reached this height want nothing to do with ordinary human affairs, for their souls always yearn for the higher realm above. Indeed, if our allegory has any validity this would have to be expected."

"Yes, quite so," he said.

"And here is something else. Do you think it is at all unusual," I said, "that a man who returns from the contemplation of divine things to merely human affairs should act indecorously and seem completely ridiculous if, while his vision is still dim and before he has adjusted to the darkness all around him, he is required to debate in courts or other places about the shadows of justice or the images that cast the shadows, and to argue heatedly about the way in which these things are conceived by people who have never seen true justice itself?"

"That would not be unusual at all," he replied.

"But," I said, "if a man has any sense he would remember that there are two distinct ways in which the eyes are disturbed, and that these result from two different causes; the first is moving from light into darkness, and the second is moving from darkness into light. Moreover, if he were convinced that the soul can be affected in the same way, then, whenever he saw a soul that was perplexed and unable to perceive anything with clarity, he would not break out into irrational laughter, but would observe whether its vision had been dimmed by its coming down from a brighter life into an unfamiliar darkness or whether, having gone from a deeper ignorance into a more brilliant realm, its power of perception had been overwhelmed by dazzling brightness. He would regard a soul of the former kind as happy because of what it had experienced and on account of its way of life, but he would pity the other soul. And, even if he wanted to laugh at the second soul, his laughter would be less ridiculous in this case than it would be if he were to direct it at the soul which had descended from the light above."

"That sounds quite reasonable," he said.

"Then," I said, "if this is true our point of view in these matters must be that education is not what some people boastfully declare it to be when they say that they can put knowledge into a soul in which no knowledge existed before, as if they were putting vision into blind eyes."

"Indeed, they do say that," he said.

"But our discussion," I said, "demonstrates that this power exists within the soul of every human being and that it is the tool with which each of us learns. The eye is unable to turn from the darkness to the light unless it does so together with the whole body, and in the same way this instrument through which we acquire knowledge must be turned, together with the whole soul, from the realm of things which are *becoming* to the realm of things that *are* until it is able to contemplate what *is* and the most brilliant part of what *is*—and this last we call *the Good*, don't we?"

"Yes."

"And," I said, "there might even be an art of doing this, of turning the soul around in the easiest and most effective manner. It would not be an art of creating the power of vision in the soul but, instead, an art which recognizes that the soul already possesses vision, though it is misdirected and does not look where it should.

"So it would seem," he said.

"It is likely that the other attributes of the soul, the ones which we call its 'virtues,' are somewhat similar to those of the body, for they do not exist in the soul from the beginning but are the results of habit and training. But the virtue of intellect seems to be in some way more divine than any of the others since it never loses its efficacy, though it can be either useful and profitable or useless and harmful, depending on the direction in which it is turned. Haven't you ever thought about those men who are reputed to be wicked but also wise, how sharp is the vision of the mean little soul and how accurately it discerns the things toward which it is turned. And doesn't this suggest that it doesn't have poor vision but, rather, that it is required to serve the purposes of evil, so that the evil it does increases according to the sharpness of its vision?"

"Yes, it does," he said.

"Well," I said, "if this part of the soul's nature were cut away in early childhood along with all its connections with the realm of *becoming* (and these connections are like leaden weights which, in the form of food and similar pleasures, become attached to the soul and force its gaze downward) then, if the soul could be freed from them and turned toward the things which are real, this same part of the same people would see the things of truth very clearly, just as it now clearly sees the base things toward which it is turned."

"That is quite probable," he said.

"Well then," I said, "isn't it likely, and doesn't it also necessarily follow from what we have already said, that men who are uneducated and have not experienced the truth could never be competent rulers of a city, and wouldn't the same be true of those who have been allowed to spend all their time in the pursuit of education—the first sort of men because they have no goal or purpose in life toward which they must direct all their private and public actions, and the latter because they won't be willing to do anything at all, since they are convinced that they have gone to live on the Isles of the Blessed while still alive?"

"That's true," he said.

"Then," I said, "as founders [of the ideal city] our job is to require those citizens with the best natures to reach for that knowledge which we have already said is the greatest of all, and to continue that ascent until they behold the good; and when they have risen to that height and viewed it thoroughly, they must not be permitted to do what is now allowed."

"What is that?"

"To stay there," I replied, "and to refuse to come down once again among the prisoners we were talking about before and take part in their labors and honors, regardless of whether or not these have any value."

"But wouldn't we be doing them an injustice," he asked, "by making them live a life worse than the one of which they are capable?"

"You have forgotten again, my friend," I said, "that the law is not concerned with promoting the welfare of any particular class. Its purpose is to produce happiness throughout the entire city by joining the citizens together through persuasion and compulsion and causing them to share among themselves the things which each contributes to the community. The law does not create such men in the city so that they might be free to do whatever they please, but in order that they might be of use in binding the city together."

"You're right," he said, "I *did* forget."

"Reflect, then Glaucon," I said, "that we will not be treating unfairly the philosophers who happen to be in our city, for we will be able to justify our actions when we require them to take care of and guard the other citizens. We will tell them that men like themselves who reside in other cities cannot reasonably be expected to participate in the work of politics there since they sprang up on their own and without the approval of the government. After all, it is right that the self-made man who is not indebted to anyone for his upbringing should not be intent on paying to anyone the price of that upbringing. But we have brought *you* forth for your own sake and for the sake of the city to be like leaders and king bees in hives, for your education has been far better and more perfect than that of the other citizens and so you are more able to take part in both public life and philosophy. And so each of you must take his turn in going down to where the others live together and accustoming yourselves to seeing the things which are dark and obscure. When you have adjusted you will be able to see them ten thousand times better than the cavern-dwellers, and you will know what each of the images is and of what real thing each one is an image, for you have seen the truth and the reality of the beautiful, the just and the good. And so the ideal city will be governed by us and by you with the vision of men who are awake, and not, as is the case in other cities, by men who see as if they were asleep and who senselessly fight over shadows and conspire against each other in order to take power, as though to rule were some great good. The truth of the matter is this: the city which has the best government and is least troubled by factional dissension is that in which those who are to rule are least eager to do so; but the city which has rulers of the opposite sort will be the opposite of the one which is well-governed and peaceful."

"That is certainly true," he said.

"Do you think that, when they hear this, those whom we raise [to be philosophers] will disobey us and be unwilling to do their part in the work of the city, spending most of their time with one another in the realm of the pure?"

"That would be impossible," he said, "for we will be requiring just men to respond to a command which is just. Each of them will consider the holding of public office as a necessary obligation, and in this respect they will be the opposite of those who are now ruling the other cities."

"Yes, my friend, that is quite true," I said. "The well-governed city is a possibility if you can discover a way of life better than that of a public official for those who are required to rule. For it is only in such a city that the truly rich will rule—not those who are rich in gold, but in happiness, because they are good and wise. On the other hand, the well-governed city is an impossibility if beggars and men who want to accumulate private possessions enter into politics in the hope of grabbing the good for themselves. For when political authority becomes something to be fought over the men who contend for it and the city itself will be destroyed by domestic and civil strife."

"Most true," he said.

Socrates on Civic Obligations:
Plato, *Crito*.

It has been said that the story of the death of Socrates best illustrates the singular greatness of the philosopher. In 399 B.C. Socrates was tried before an Athenian popular jury. The formal indictment read as follows: "Socrates is guilty of rejecting the gods acknowledged by the State and of introducing strange gods; he is also guilty of corrupting the youth." The trial and death of Socrates are dealt with in four Platonic dialogues, *i.e.*, the *Apology, Euthyphro, Crito* and *Phaedo*. Although he was condemned to death, we must remember that the guilty verdict was pronounced by a small majority of only thirty out of the five hundred and one jurors who tried his case. Before the death sentence was carried out, however, Socrates spent a month in prison where he was allowed to receive his friends and family. His last conversations with them have been immortalized in Plato's dialogues, especially the *Crito* and *Phaedo*. Among those who paid him a visit in prison shortly before his death was Crito, a wealthy and devoted friend who had made arrangements for Socrates to escape. The final discourse between Crito and Socrates is the subject of the dialogue given here in its complete form. Crito attempts to persuade Socrates to accept his plan of escaping from prison in defiance of the court's verdict, but Socrates insists that respect for the laws is the first and most sacred duty of a citizen. This dialogue of Plato has been characterized as the noblest defense of the law ever written.

SCENE: The Prison of Socrates

SOCRATES

Why have you come at this hour, Crito? Is it not still early?

CRITO

Very early, indeed.

SOCRATES

What time is it exactly?

CRITO

The dawn is breaking.

SOCRATES

I am surprised that the prison guard would let you in.

CRITO

He knows me, Socrates, because I visit here often. Besides, I gave him a little something.

SOCRATES

And did you just come now, or have you been waiting here long?

CRITO

I have been here for a while.

SOCRATES

Then why didn't you wake me up right away instead of sitting here saying nothing?

CRITO

By Zeus, Socrates, I myself would rather not suffer this condition of sleeplessness and sadness, but I've been marvelling for some time at how peacefully you sleep. I intentionally did not wake you because I wanted you to enjoy your repose. Many times before—in fact, through our entire lives—I have thought you happy in your calm ways, but never more than in the present calamity. How lightly and peacefully you bear it!

SOCRATES

Well, Crito, it would be inappropriate for a man of my age to be disturbed by the thought of dying.

CRITO

Many others, Socrates, as old as you, face similar misfortunes, but their age doesn't prevent them from being vexed by their fate.

SOCRATES

You are right. But you still haven't told me why you have come so early.

CRITO

I am here to bring you sad and painful news, Socrates. Not sad for you, I believe, but for all your friends, and especially heavy for me to bear.

SOCRATES

What news? Has the ship arrived from Delos, which means that I must die?

CRITO

No, the ship hasn't arrived yet, but it will be here today. Some people who came from Sunium have informed me that they left it there. What they told me clearly indicates that it will arrive here today, and so, Socrates, your life must come to an end tomorrow.

SOCRATES

Well, Crito, let it be for the best. If it is the will of the gods, let it be done. I believe, however, that the ship will not come today.

CRITO

How did you reach that conclusion?

SOCRATES

Let me tell you. Am I to die the day after the ship's arrival?

CRITO

That's what the authorities say, at least.

SOCRATES

I do not believe, however, that the ship will arrive today, but tomorrow; this I conclude from a dream I had this last night, just a little while ago. It was fortunate that you didn't wake me.

CRITO

And what kind of dream was it?

SOCRATES

A woman appeared to me, fair and well-formed, clothed in white. She called me and said to me, "O Socrates—

'On the third day you will come to fertile Phthia'."

CRITO

What a peculiar dream, Socrates!

SOCRATES

Yet very clear, I think, Crito.

CRITO

Yes, its meaning seems to be only too clear. But my dear Socrates, let me persuade you even at this late hour to save yourself. For if you die I will suffer more than one misfortune; not only will I be deprived of a friend who is irreplaceable, but people who do not know us will assume that I could have saved your life if only I had been prepared to give money, but didn't care enough to do it. And I cannot think of a worse disgrace for a man than to be thought of as placing a higher value on money than on friendship. For most people will never believe that you refused to escape from prison in spite of our efforts to help you.

SOCRATES

But, my dear Crito, why should we take into consideration the opinion of the many? The most logical people, whose opinions are worth considering, will accept that things happened as they did.

CRITO

But I assume you realize, Socrates, that it is also essential to be concerned with the opinion of the masses. Your present misfortune, at least, clearly indicates that they can cause a man whom they dislike not the smallest, but nearly the greatest evil.

SOCRATES

Crito, I only wish that the many could cause the greatest harm, so that they could also do the greatest good; that would be well. Now, however, they can do neither good nor evil, for they cannot make a man wise or foolish; whatever they do is the result of chance.

CRITO

Let that be as you wish; but tell me this, Socrates. Are you worried about me and your other friends? Are you afraid that if you escape from prison we may have difficulties with the informers who would claim that we stole you away, and lose our property or a great deal of money or even suffer something worse than that? If you fear that these things will happen, there is no need to worry. For it is right for us to face these or even greater dangers if doing so is necessary in order to save your life. Please, accept my arguments and do as I say.

SOCRATES

Naturally, I do have these fears, Crito, and many others besides.

CRITO

Then do not be concerned with these matters. There are certain people who are willing to save you and let you out of prison for a modest amount of money. And don't you see how cheaply these informers can be bought? A small amount of money will suffice. All of my money is at your disposal, and I think it is quite adequate; if, however, you have any scruples about spending all of my fortune, please note that there are some foreigners in Athens who are ready to spend their money in order to save you. In fact, one of them, Simmias the Theban, has brought enough for this purpose; and Cebes and many other people are prepared to contribute their money, too. Therefore, as

I say, do not hesitate to save your life on that account, and do not repeat what you said during your trial, that you wouldn't know what to do with yourself if you were to escape from prison. For people will welcome you in many other lands where you may choose to go. If you would like to go to Thessaly, I have many friends there who will honor and protect you so that no Thessalian will ever bother you. Moreover, Socrates, it seems to me that you are not acting justly in giving up your own life when you can preserve it. You are hastening to do to yourself what your enemies have wanted to accomplish, that is, to destroy you. Besides, it appears to me that you are also betraying your own sons, for you seem to be abandoning them when you might be raising and educating them. Instead of meeting your responsibilities you go away and leave them behind to face whatever fate comes to them. Naturally, theirs will be the usual fate of children who are left as orphans. No man should bring children into the world unless he is willing to shoulder the responsibility of raising and educating them. But in my opinion you have chosen the easy way out; yet, you should be making decisions worthy of a good and brave man, especially since you have been proclaiming all of your life the value of human virtue. I am ashamed, Socrates, not only of you, but also of us, your friends, because this entire affair of yours will be attributed to our cowardice. This case which went to court when it was possible to avoid a trial, the whole course of the legal proceedings, and then, at the end, this, the final mockery, would seem to be due to our lack of courage; for we did not save you, and you did not save yourself when salvation would have been possible if only we had been good for anything at all. Consider then, Socrates, whether these things are bad and dishonorable for both you and us. Decide, for you should have made up your mind by now. There is only one course of action to be taken, for any further delay will make your escape impossible. I implore you, therefore, Socrates, to accept my advice and do as I say.

SOCRATES

My dear Crito, your eagerness to save my life would be worth much if only it were right; otherwise, the greater the zeal, the harder it will be to bear. We ought, therefore, to consider whether to adopt your suggestion or not. For I am, and always have been, one of those people who never accept an argument as truth until it has been given careful consideration. And now, in this day of my misfortune, I cannot reject the arguments that I had advanced before; they appear to me to be as valid as ever, and I will honor and respect them as much now as I did then. Thus, unless we can find more persuasive arguments to substitute for them, be sure that I will not accept your proposal, even if the multitude exercised far greater powers than they do now, and terrorized us like children with threats of confiscation, imprisonment and death. But let us now examine the most appropriate way of dealing with this question. Shall we begin first with your argument about the opinions of men and consider whether we were right in saying that some are worth paying attention to and others should be ignored? Were we correct in holding this view before I was condemned to die, and has the argument now become idle talk for the sake of talking? Is it, in fact, nothing but a game for our amusement? I do wish to consider this point with your help, Crito, and to examine whether, in my present situation, the validity of the argument has been affected or not. Should we discard it or be persuaded by it? The argument of those of us who had always reflected carefully was, I think, what I have just said, namely that the opinions of some men are to be respected while the opinions of others are not. For God's sake, Crito, don't you think we were right? You are not going to die tomorrow, at least not by any human action, and the present calamity will not affect your judgement. So, reflect on this matter! Don't you think it is proper to say that we shouldn't respect all the opinions held by a man, but only some of them, and that we shouldn't honor the opinions of all men, but only those of some? What do you think? Isn't that true?

CRITO

Yes, it is.

SOCRATES

So, we should respect the good opinions, but not the bad ones?

CRITO

Yes.

SOCRATES

And the opinions of the wise are good, while those of the foolish are bad?

CRITO

Naturally.

SOCRATES

But to go on, what did we used to say about this matter? Does an athlete in training pay attention to the praise and blame and opinions expressed by all men, or does he value only the opinion of the one man who happens to be his physician or coach?

CRITO

He values only the opinion of the one man.

SOCRATES

So, he ought to fear the censure and welcome the praise of that one man, not of the multitude?

CRITO

That's obvious.

SOCRATES

And he ought to train, exercise, eat and drink in a way that satisfies the coach, who knows best, rather than all the rest?

CRITO

That is correct.

SOCRATES

Fine. But if he disobeys and disregards the opinions and the praise of the coach, and respects the opinions of the multitude who are without expertise in athletic matters, won't he suffer evil consequences as a result?

CRITO

Of course he will.

SOCRATES

And what are these consequences? In what way, and in what part of himself, will the disobedient person suffer?

CRITO

In his body, obviously. That's what is destroyed.

SOCRATES

Yes. And doesn't this also apply to all the other things which we need not enumerate here? Thus, in the case of the just and the unjust, the honorable and the base, the good and the evil which we are now contemplating, should we follow the opinion of the multitude and fear it, or the opinion of the one man who understands these principles, and fear and respect him more than all other people? For if we ignore his opinion we will corrupt and destroy that part of us which is improved by justice and ruined by injustice. Isn't this so?

CRITO

I agree with you, Socrates.

SOCRATES

Now then, if by following the advice of those who have no understanding we destroy that part of us which is improved by health and damaged by disease, would life be worth living when it has been corrupted? And that part is the body, is it not?

CRITO

Yes.

SOCRATES

Is life worth living, then, with a damaged and corrupted body?

CRITO

By no means.

SOCRATES

And will life be worth preserving when that part of us which is improved by justice and damaged by injustice is corrupt? Do you regard that part of us, whatever it may be, which pertains to justice and injustice to be less important than our body?

CRITO

Not at all.

SOCRATES

More valuable, then?

CRITO

Yes, by far.

SOCRATES

Then, my dear friend, we must not take seriously what the many will say of us; rather, we should consider what the man who understands will say, and what the truth itself will say. Therefore, you are wrong, to begin with, when you propose that we should respect the opinion of the multitude in matters pertaining to what is just, good and honorable, and also their opposites. But then, someone might say that the multitude can kill us.

CRITO

That is obvious. One might say that, Socrates.

SOCRATES

You are right. But, my dear friend, it seems to me that what we have just concluded is no different from the conclusion we had reached before. Now tell me whether we still hold to the principle that living well, not merely living, is to be highly valued?

CRITO

Yes, we do.

SOCRATES

And do we also maintain that a good life is a just and honorable one?

CRITO

Yes, we do.

SOCRATES

Then, on the basis of these premises we must proceed to examine whether or not it is just for me to attempt to escape from prison against the wishes of the Athenians; and if we find it to be just, let us attempt it, but if not, let us abandon the thought of escaping. As for the other considerations you mentioned, that is, those of expense and of reputation and of raising my children, they are only the opinions of the multitude who would thoughtlessly kill people and who would just as easily bring them back to life, if they could. As reason dictates, however, we have nothing else to consider now but the question of whether it is right to give money and thanks to the people who would assist in my escape and if we ourselves should do our part, or whether we would be acting unjustly in implementing this scheme. And if we find that these acts are unjust, we should not allow death or any other calamity which may result from my remaining here influence us, but think only that we would be committing an injustice.

CRITO

I think that you are right, Socrates. But how are we to proceed?

SOCRATES

Let us consider the problem together, my dear friend, and if there is something in my argument that you would like to refute, please proceed and I will be convinced; otherwise, my dear friend, quit telling me over and over again that I ought to escape from prison without permission from the Athenians. For I do want to act with your consent, not against your will. Now, consider the starting point of my position and do your best to answer me.

CRITO

I will do that.

SOCRATES

Are we to say that we ought never to do wrong intentionally? Or, is injustice to be condoned in some instances but not in others? Is injustice always evil and dishonorable, as we have often said before, or have we discarded all our previous conclusions in these last few days? Have we, at our advanced age, somehow failed to realize that we were no different from children all those years when we were seriously discoursing with one another? Is not what we always used to say the truth, in spite of the opinion of the multitude? Isn't injustice always an evil and dishonor to him who acts unjustly, whether it results in a heavier or lighter punishment? Do we agree on that?

CRITO

Yes.

SOCRATES

Then we must never do wrong?

CRITO

Of course not.

SOCRATES

Nor repay injustice with injustice, as the multitude think; for we must never act unjustly?

CRITO

Clearly not.

SOCRATES

Well then, Crito, should we do evil or not?

CRITO

Surely not, Socrates.

SOCRATES

And is doing evil in return for evil just, as the masses claim?

CRITO

Definitely not.

SOCRATES

For doing evil to a man is no different from acting unjustly?

CRITO

That's true.

SOCRATES

Then we should not retaliate or do harm to any man, regardless of what sufferings he may have caused us. And consider, Crito, whether you truly mean what you are saying. For I realize that only a few people hold or will ever hold this opinion; and those who espouse it and those who reject it have no common ground, but can only feel contempt for each other's views. Think carefully, then, and tell me whether you accept my belief and agree with me that neither injustice, nor the repayment of injustice with injustice, nor the retaliation against those who cause us harm is ever justified. Or, do you disagree with me and do not share my premise? I myself have maintained it for a long time and still believe in it today. If, however, you are of another opinion, let me know what it is and teach me. But if you still accept our previous agreements, pay attention to my next point.

CRITO

I do accept them and agree with you. Please continue.

SOCRATES

My next point, or rather my next question, is this: Do you think a person ought to do what is admittedly just or should he betray what is just?

CRITO

He should do what is just.

SOCRATES

Then consider the following question: In escaping from prison against the wishes of the Athenians, would I wrong those who are least deserving of being wronged by me, or not? And would I be maintaining those principles which we had agreed were just, or not?

CRITO

I cannot answer your questions, Socrates, for I don't know what you mean.

SOCRATES

Then look at this matter in this way. Suppose I were about to escape, or whatever you want to call this action, and the laws and the constitution of the city came and stood before me and asked: "Tell us, Socrates, what are you planning to do? By attempting to escape from prison do you intend to accomplish anything else but to destroy us, the laws and the whole state, as far as you are able? Or, do you think that a state can survive and not be overthrown when the decisions of its courts are not enforced, but are rendered invalid and undermined by private individuals?" How are we to answer these and other questions similar to them? One could say a great deal, especially an orator, about the evil of violating the law which makes the decisions of the courts supreme. Or, are we to reply to them that the state committed an act of injustice against us and did not decide the case properly? Shall we say that, or what?

CRITO

By Zeus, that's what we will say, Socrates.

SOCRATES

But what if the laws were to say: "Socrates, was that our agreement with you, or were you to accept whatever sentence the state gave you?" And if I were to express surprise at the question, the laws would perhaps say: "Socrates, don't be astonished, but answer the question, since you yourself are used to the practice of asking and answering questions. Proceed, then, and tell us what grievances you have against us and the state that justify your efforts to destroy us? First of all, didn't we give you birth? Didn't your father marry your mother through us, so that you could be born? Tell us, then, those of us who are laws that regulate marriage: do you find anything wrong with us?" "I do not," would be my reply. "Then, what about the body of laws that regulate the rearing and education of children under which you yourself were educated? Or, weren't those laws correct in commanding your father to train you in music and athletics?" "They were correct," I would say. "Fine then. And since you were born, nurtured and educated by us, can you say, first of all, that you, and your forefathers before you, are not our children and slaves? And if that is true, do you think that your rights and our rights are equal, and that you have the right to repay us for what we are doing to you? Do you think that you had equal rights in dealing with your father or your master, if you had one, so that you might retaliate if they abused you or scolded you or struck you or made you suffer some other evil? Now, as far as your country and its laws are concerned, do you think you have the right to retaliate if they should attempt to destroy you because they think it right? And can you claim that this action would be just, you who are so interested in virtue? Or, are you so wise that you have failed to realize that your country should receive a place of honor above father and mother and all your ancestors, for it is holier and more sacred and held in higher regard by both the gods and men of understanding; and when your country is angry, you ought to reverence and obey and soothe it even more so that you would your father when he is angry. You ought either to persuade it of your innocence or obey its commands, and to endure silently whatever punishment it administers, whether it is flogging or imprisonment. And if it sends you to war to suffer wounds and die, you should still comply. This is what justice is: not to yield or retreat or leave your post; whether in war or in a court of law or anywhere else, you must either do what your city and country order or convince them of the justice of your cause. To use violence against a father or a mother is unholy, but it is much more unholy to use violence against your country." How do we respond to that, Crito? Do the laws speak the truth or not?

CRITO

It seems to me that they do.

SOCRATES

Then the laws perhaps would say: "Consider, Socrates, whether we are right in saying that what you are now attempting to do will do us an injustice. For we gave you birth, we nurtured you, we educated you and granted you and all other citizens a share of every blessing that we could give. Still, we further proclaim that if an Athenian so desires he may take his possessions and go anywhere he wants if, when he has come of age, he discovers in the laws of the government of the state things he doesn't like. If you do not like this and the city and want to go to a colony or emigrate to any other land there is no law that will hinder you and forbid you to take your belongings and go wherever you want. However, to him who remains here after seeing how we conduct justice and administer the affairs of the state, we say that by choosing to stay he has consented to do as we tell him. And we maintain that he who disobeys us is wrong in three ways: first, because we are his parents, and yet he has defied us; secondly, because we nurtured him, and yet he disobeys us; and third, because he had agreed to respect us, but neither obeys us nor convinces us that we are doing something wrong. Yet we did not rudely order him to do as we told him, but gave him the choice of either persuading us that we were wrong or obeying us; but he does neither. These are the transgressions for which, we say, you will be responsible if you implement what you are now scheming to do; and you are not to be blamed the least, but the most, among the Athenians." If I were to ask "Why is that?" they might justifiably respond by saying that I, more than any other Athenian, happened to have accepted this agreement. They might say: "Socrates, we have many proofs that we and the city were not offensive to you. For you wouldn't have spent more time in the city than any other Athenian unless you loved it dearly. In fact, you never left Athens either to attend a festival, except once at the Isthmus, or to go anywhere else, if we discount your military service. You never traveled anywhere, as other people do. You never had the desire to know other cities and their laws, for we and our city were enough for you. You were so sure of your decision in choosing us and in agreeing to live as a citizen under our rule that you had children in this city; that's how much you liked us. Besides, even at your trial you could have chosen exile as a penalty if you wanted to, and would thereby have accomplished legally that which you now attempt to do against the wishes of the city. At that time, however, you made a fine display of the pretension that you preferred death to exile and that you were not disturbed by the thought of dying. And now you disgrace those words and disrespect us, the laws, for you are attempting to destroy us. You are acting the way the most miserable slave would act, trying to escape and ignoring the contracts and agreements you made with us in order to live as a citizen. First of all, then, answer this question: Are we telling the truth when we say that you had agreed by your actions rather than by mere words to live as a citizen under our rule, or are we lying?" How are we to answer this question, Crito? Should we disagree?

CRITO

That is necessary, Socrates.

SOCRATES

But then they would say, "Are you not violating your contracts and agreements with us? You did not make these agreements under duress, and you were not deceived or compelled to make up your mind in a short period of time. You had seventy years to test their worth, during which time you could have left the city if you did not like us or if your agreements appeared to you to be unjust. But you chose neither Sparta nor Crete, states which you often claimed to be ruled by good laws, or any other Greek or barbarian city. In fact, you left Athens to go abroad less frequently than the lame, the blind and the other invalids. It is obvious, then, that you, more than all other Athenians, liked the city and also us, its laws; for who would like a city without laws? And now won't you uphold our agreements? If we persuade you, Socrates, you will honor them and avoid making yourself ridiculous by leaving the city.

Consider, too, what good you will accomplish, either for yourself or for your friends, if you transgress and violate this agreement. That your friends will be in danger of facing exile and loss of citizenship, or the confiscation of their estates, is almost certain. You, yourself, to begin with, if you were to go to one of our neighboring cities, Thebes or Megara for example—for both of them are ruled by just laws—will come to them as an enemy of their polity; and those who care for their own cities will view you with scorn as a corruptor of laws. Moreover, you will confirm the opinion of your judges and give the impression that their verdict was justly rendered. For he who is a corruptor of the laws may certainly be considered a corruptor of the young and the foolish as well. Are you prepared, then, to flee from well-governed cities and the society of decent men? And, if you do that, will your life be worth living? Or, will you approach these people and engage them in conversation without any sense of shame—but to discuss what, Socrates? Are you going to repeat the discussions you held here in Athens about virtue and justice and institutions and the laws being the most worthy things in life? Don't you think that this would be an indecent thing for you to do? Surely you must think so. But if you leave these civilized places and go to Crito's friends in Thessaly, where the highest degree of disorder and license prevails, they will, most likely, be pleased to hear the ridiculous account of your escape from prison, how you disguised yourself dressing as a peasant or runaway slave, and changed your appearance. But don't you realize that there will be someone to point out that you, an old man with probably only a little time left to live, have manifested such a miserable desire to stay alive a bit longer that you violated the highest laws? Perhaps not, if you do not provoke them. Otherwise, Socrates, you will hear many degrading things said about you. In fact, you will live your life as a flatterer and slave of all men. And what will you be doing in Thessaly besides eating and drinking? It will be as if you went there to get a free meal. And where will your old arguments about justice and virtue be then? But you claim that you want to live for the sake of your children, so that you may raise and educate them. What for? Will you take them to Thessaly to raise and educate them as foreigners? Will you bestow on them, too, the benefit of exile and alienation from their country? Or, if you leave them in Athens, will they be raised and educated better if you are alive, but not with them? Yes, for your friends will take care of them. Do you really believe that your friends will look after them if you flee to Thessaly, but will neglect them if you go to Hades? You cannot believe that, if those you call your friends are truly friends.

So, Socrates, listen to us who have raised you. Do not place life or children or anything else above justice, so that when you go to Hades you may offer a good defense to those who rule there. For it seems that neither you nor any of those who are with you will be more virtuous or more just or more holy in this world, or happier in the world of the dead, if you do this thing. Now you leave this world, if you leave, a victim of injustice at the hands of men, not of the laws. But if you escape, repaying so shamefully injustice with injustice and evil with evil, violating the compacts and agreements you made with us, and doing wrong to those whom you ought to hurt least, namely yourself, your friends, your country and us, the laws, we shall be unkindly disposed towards you while you live, and when you go to the underworld, our brothers, the laws of Hades, will not offer you a friendly welcome there, knowing that you had done your best to destroy us. So, don't let Crito persuade you to do as he bids, but do as we say."

These are the things I seem to hear, my dear friend Crito, as the Corybants in their passion seem to hear the music of the flute; and the sound of these words buzzes in my ears and prevents me from hearing anything else. And I know well that if you speak against my present beliefs, you will be wasting your time. But if you still think that you can accomplish anything more, please speak.

CRITO

I have nothing more to say, Socrates.

SOCRATES

Then let us do as I say, Crito, since that is the will of God.

The Megalopsychos—A Man of Great Soul: Aristotle, *Nicomachean Ethics*, 1124a.5–1125a.18.

Aristotle's great work known as the *Nicomachean Ethics* is considered to be the earliest treatise on ethics in general and rational ethics in particular. It is divided into ten books and deals with various topics such as "the good for man," moral virtues, intellectual virtues, continence and incontinence, pleasure, friendship and happiness. Aristotle concludes that the highest good can be found only in *theoria*, *i.e.*, in a life of contemplation. The excerpt below describes the *megalopsychos*, the "man of great soul."

. . . The megalopsychos, then, is chiefly concerned with honors and dishonors. When worthy persons bestow great honors on him he is only mildly pleased, for he knows that he is only receiving what is his due, or even less, since no honor can possibly match the worth of perfect virtue. Nevertheless, he will accept these honors since they have nothing greater to bestow on him. But honors conferred by the common people and for no significant reason he will entirely disregard, since they are unworthy of him. Similarly, he will disregard dishonor, for no dishonor can be justly attributed to him. As has been said, then, the megalopsychos is chiefly concerned with honors; but he will also behave moderately with regard to wealth and power and all forms of good or bad fortune, whatever his lot in life may be. He will not be exceedingly glad when good fortune befalls him, nor exceedingly sorrowful when plagued by ill fortune. For not even in matters relating to honor does he behave as if these were things of the greatest importance (for power and wealth are desirable for the sake of honor; at least, those who possess them wish to be honored through them). To the person for whom honor is of little importance, other things must also be unimportant. This is why men of great soul are considered to be haughty. . . .

It is also characteristic of the megalopsychos not to ask for anything, or to do so only with reluctance, but to serve readily and to be haughty towards men of high position and good fortune while behaving in a courteous manner towards people of no great distinction; for it is a difficult and a lofty thing to be superior to the great, but easy to be superior to the lowly. A haughty attitude towards the powerful is not indicative of ill-breeding, but when directed towards the humble people it is as vulgar as a display of strength against the feeble. And he will not be ambitious for the things which common people desire or involve himself in matters in which others take the first place; he will be slow to take action, and idle, except where great honors or great works are at stake; he will not always be active, but only when important and noble deeds are to be performed. It is also necessary for him to be open in his loves and hates, since he will regard the concealment of his feelings as cowardice. He will be more interested in the truth than in what people think, and will speak and act openly. For he enjoys freedom of speech because he is contemptuous of others; and he will be in the habit of telling the truth except when he talks ironically to the common people. He will not center his own life around that of another unless that man is a friend; for this is servile, and thus it follows that all flatterers are servile and all lowly people are flatterers. Nor is he one to admire others, for to him nothing is so great as to be worthy of his admiration. He does not bear grudges, for it is not characteristic of the megalopsychos to have a long memory where wrongs committed against him are concerned, but rather to overlook them. He is not a gossip; for he will not talk about himself or about others since he is not interested in being praised or in others being blamed. Neither is he given to praise; likewise, he does not speak evil, even about his enemies, except from haughtiness. When it comes to the necessities of life or other insignificant matters, he is the man least apt to resort to lamentation or begging. For he who takes these matters seriously should conduct himself seriously where they are concerned. Moreover, such a man will possess beautiful and useless objects rather than profitable and useful ones, for this is more befitting a man of self-sufficient character. A slow gait, a deep voice and carefully considered speech are considered proper characteristics of the megalopsychos. For he who is interested only in a few important things is not hurried, nor is he who thinks nothing great easily excited; but a shrill voice and a speedy gait are caused by hurry and excitement. Such, then, is the megalopsychos; the person who lacks these qualities is micropsychos [unduly humble or a man of small soul], while the person who possesses them to too great a degree is vain.

Character Sketches: Theophrastus, *Characters*, 12 and 16.

Born *ca*. 370 B.C. at Eresus in Lesbos, the birthplace of Sappho, Theophrastus was Aristotle's successor as head of the Lyceum. He wrote scientific, literary and philosophical works, but is best known for his *Characters*, thirty short studies of character types which evince both his wit and psychological insight. This work has been admired and imitated by later writers, particularly seventeenth-century authors such as La Bruyère in France and Joseph Hall and Samuel Butler in England, and its merits are still recognized today. The selections below describe tactless and superstitious people.

12

Tactlessness is bad timing, timing so bad that it is painful. Your tactless man will accost a busy friend and ask him for advice, or serenade his girlfriend when she is in bed with a fever. He will approach someone who has posted bail and lost it and ask him to post bail for him, and will guarantee for the court the correctness of his earlier testimony only after the verdict is given. Invite him to a wedding and he will badmouth women. Return from a long journey and he will invite you out for a walk. He will bring you a second party willing to pay a higher price when you have just struck a deal with the first and will rise from his seat to tell once again a story that everyone present has heard a hundred times before. He eagerly commits you to doing what you don't want to do but cannot graciously decline. On the day you make a sacrifice of a victim you could barely afford he drops by to ask for the money you owe him. He stands there, while you flog your servant, and tells you that one of his own servants hanged himself after just such a flogging. At an arbitration he sets at odds the parties who were on the verge of reconciliation, and when he wants to dance he grabs a partner who is not yet drunk.

16

Superstitiousness, it goes without saying, appears to be a kind of cowardness with respect to the divine. Your superstitious man will not so much as walk out of his front door in the morning until he has washed his hands and sprinkled himself at the Nine Springs and put a piece of bay leaf from a temple into his mouth. If a cat crosses his path he will go no further until someone else has gone by or he has thrown three stones across the street. If he notices a red snake in his house he will pray to Sabazius, if it is a sacred snake he will build a temple then and there. When he comes upon one of the smooth stones set up at crossroads he anoints it with oil from his flask and will not continue his journey until he has gone down on his knees and worshiped it. If a mouse gnaws a hole in his pouch of barley cakes he will go to a seer and ask what he should do; if the answer is "have the shoemaker patch it," he will ignore the advice and free himself from contamination by performing the rites of aversion. He is constantly purifying his house, explaining that Hecate has been there. If owls hoot while he is abroad he is greatly upset and will not go a step further until he has shouted "Athena, protect me!" He will not set foot on a grave or go near a corpse or a woman in childbirth lest he be polluted. On the fourth and seventh days of each month he serves mulled wine to his household and goes out shopping for myrtle branches, frankincense and holy pictures; when he returns he spends the entire day offering sacrifices to the Hermaphrodites and placing garlands around them. He has never had a dream that he has not taken to an interpreter, prophet or augur to ask which god or goddess he should appease, and when he is preparing to be inducted into the sacred order of Orpheus he visits the priests each month with his wife or, if she does not have the time, with his children and their nurse. He always seems to be on his way to the seashore to sprinkle himself, and whenever he sees one of those garlic-wreathed images of Hecate at the crossroads he runs home to wash his head and call the priestesses who purify him by walking around him with a squill or a puppy. If he catches sight of a madman or an epileptic he shudders and spits on his chest.

Diogenes the Cynic and the Simple Life:
Diogenes Laertius, *Lives of Eminent Philosophers*, 6.20–78.

The Cynic school of philosophy was founded by Antisthenes, one of Socrates' pupils, but the most famous of the ancient Cynics was Diogenes (400–325 B.C.), known as *ho kyon* [the dog], a nickname from which the name of the sect is derived. An exile from Sinope, he came to Athens where he lived in extreme poverty. He had been influenced by the philosophy of Antisthenes and shared many of his doctrines; but Diogenes is better known for the practical application of Cynic tenets in his everyday life than for his theories. In fact, he is considered by many to have been an ancient saint or guru who tried to live the simple life by rejecting all conventions and despising all worldliness.

When he came to Athens (from Sinope) he approached Antisthenes, and though he was turned away by him because he did not accept pupils, Diogenes eventually managed to force the issue by persisting. Once, when Antisthenes raised his staff against him, he offered his head and said, "Strike, for you will never find a piece of wood hard enough to keep me away from you as long as it appears to me that you have something important to say." After that he became his pupil and, being an exile, began to practice a simple life.

Theophrastus tells us in his Megarean dialogue that, having observed a mouse running here and there, neither searching for a place to lie down nor fearing the dark or desiring any of the things people consider enjoyable, he found a way to cope with his environment.

According to some authorities he was the first man to fold his cloak, for he had to sleep in it as well as wear it; he carried with him a wallet in which he kept his victuals; and he used any place for any function, for eating breakfast, for sleeping or for conversation.

Sometimes, pointing to the porch of Zeus and the Hall of Processions, he would say that the Athenians had furnished him with places to live. He leaned upon a staff only when he grew infirm; he carried it everywhere, not only in the city, but also on the road, along with his wallet.

Once he had written to someone asking him to try to provide him with a small house, but when the man was slow to respond he took as his residence the tub in the Metroüm, as he himself makes clear in his letters. And he would roll in hot sand in the summer and in the winter he would embrace snow-covered statues, making every effort to accustom himself to hardship.

He was skillful in ridiculing other people. The *schole* [school] of Euclides he called *chole* [bile] and Plato's *diatribe* [lecture] he called *katatribe* [waste of time]. He characterized the performances of the Dionysia as great marvels for fools and the demagogues as servants of the mob. He would also say that when he saw steersmen and physicians and philosophers at work, he thought man to be the most intelligent of the animals; on the other hand, when he saw interpreters of dreams and seers and those who paid attention to them, or those who were swelled with conceit and wealth, he considered no animal to be more foolish. And he always used to say that to prepare for life one needs either reason or a halter. . . .

When he was asked in what part of Greece he saw good men he said, "men nowhere, but boys in Sparta." Once, when he was discussing important matters and nobody was paying attention to him, he began to whistle; as people gathered around him he reproached them for being so quickly drawn to nonsense, and so slowly attracted by important issues. He used to say that men try hard and undergo all sorts of preparations in order to excel in athletic contests, but nobody tries hard to become a truly good man.

He was amazed that scholars should investigate the shortcomings of Odysseus while ignoring their own. And he marveled that musicians should tune the strings of their lyres while leaving the temper of their souls in disarray; also that mathematicians should observe the sun and the moon, while overlooking matters of everyday life.

To those who told him, "You are old, take it easy," he replied, "What? If I were competing in the long distance course at the stadium ought I to slow down at the end of the race? Shouldn't I rather put on speed?"

Once, when he saw a child drinking out of his hands, he threw away the cup from his wallet saying, "A child has given me a lesson in plain living." Likewise, he discarded his bowl when he observed a child who, having broken his plate, picked up his lentils with the hollow part of a piece of bread. He would also reason as follows: "All things are of the gods. The wise are friends of the gods, and friends hold things in common. Therefore, everything belongs to the wise."

Once he saw a woman kneeling before the gods in an unseemly fashion and, wanting to take away her superstition, he approached her and said, according to Zoilus of Perga, "Don't you fear, woman, that some god may be standing behind you—for everything is filled with his presence—and that you may thus be disgraced?"

But he was loved by the Athenians. When a child once broke up his tub, they punished him with a flogging and furnished Diogenes with another tub. After the battle of Chaeronea, as Dionysius the Stoic says, he was arrested and brought before Philip; and when he was asked who he was, he replied, "A spy on your greed." He was admired for his reply, and was released.

There was a husky harp player who was criticized by all and praised only by Diogenes. When he was asked why, Diogenes said, "Because, although he is of such enormous size, he plays his harp and doesn't rob people."

When he was asked why athletes are so senseless he replied, "Because they are built up of the flesh of pigs and oxen." Once he was begging aloud from a statue, and when he was asked why he replied, "I am learning how to accept failure."

He considered good men to be images of the gods, and love the pastime of the idle. Being asked what is wretched in life, he said, "An old man without means of support."

When someone asked him, "In your opinion, what kind of man is Diogenes?" he replied, "A Socrates gone mad." When asked what was the best time to marry, he said, "If you are a young man, not yet, if an old man, never at all."

Once he saw a youngster blushing. "Courage," he said, "this is the color of virtue."

On being asked what kind of wine he enjoyed drinking, he replied, "The kind for which others pay." When he was asked why people give money to beggars but not to philosophers, he said, "Because they fear that they may become lame or blind someday, but they never expect to become philosophers." He was begging of a miser once, and when the latter was slow to oblige him, he said, "My good man, I am asking you for food, not for burial expenses."

Seeing the son of a prostitute throw stones at a mob, he said, "Careful now, don't hit your father."

When he was asked what benefits he had gained from philosophy, he said, "If nothing else, how to be prepared for any eventuality." When asked where he had come from, he replied, "I am a *cosmopolites* [citizen of the world]."

When he was asked if death is a bad thing, he said, "Why should death be bad when we are not aware of its presence?" When Alexander stood in front of him and asked, "Don't you fear me?" he said, "What are you, a good or an evil force?" "Good," Alexander replied. "Who, then, fears the good?" said Diogenes. "Education," he proclaimed, "is a moderating influence on the young, a consolation to the old, wealth to the poor, and an embellishment to the rich."

It is said that Diogenes died when he was nearly ninety years old. There are several versions of his death. Some say that he ate a raw octopus and was afflicted with colic, which caused his death. Others, however, say that he held his breath and died voluntarily. His pupils erected a pillar over his grave and placed a statue of a dog made of Parian marble on top of it. Afterward, the citizens also honored him with bronze statues on which they inscribed the following:

> Even bronze ages with time,
> but your glory, Diogenes,
> defies all eternity.
> For you alone showed to mortals
> the glory of self-sufficiency
> and the easiest way of life.

Epicurus' Letter to Menoeceus:
Diogenes Laertius, *Lives of Eminent Philosophers*, 10.122–235.

Much of what we know about the famous Athenian philosopher Epicurus (342–270 B.C.) has been preserved in the tenth book of Diogenes Laertius, who has transmitted to us forty of the philosopher's ethical aphorisms and three letters to his disciples, Herodotus, Pythocles and Menoeceus respectively. The first letter gives us a brief summary of Epicurus' natural philosophy, the second a review of his meteorology and the letter to Menoeceus, which was probably meant for the general reader, a good account of Epicurean ethics. Specifically, it deals with such issues as the fear of death, good and bad desires, and the nature of pleasure. Interestingly, the letter suggests that Epicurus was not an atheist, as his detractors claimed, but a believer in a God who exists not in the skies, but in the hearts and souls of human beings.

Epicurus to Menoeceus, greetings:

No one should postpone the study of philosophy while he is young or become tired of it when he is old. For it is never too early or too late to cultivate the health of one's soul. He who claims that the time to philosophize has not yet come, or that it has already passed, is like the person who says that it is too early or too late to be happy.

Thus, young and old alike should pursue philosophy so that, in the case of the young, they may still be youthful in good things when they grow old through their recollection of pleasant experiences in the past and, in the case of the old, that they may be simultaneously young and old by virtue of their lack of fear of the future. it is good for us to consider the things which bring happiness, since in the presence of happiness we have everything, while in its absence we do all we can to attain it.

Put into action and exercise diligently all those teachings which I have communicated to you, for I believe they are the elements of the good life. First, believe that God is a living being, blessed and eternal, as the theology common to all humanity asserts, and do not add to your conception of him anything that is alien to his immortal nature or to his blessedness; believe, rather, that he is endowed with all the means that can preserve his eternal blessedness. For the gods do indeed exist, and it is obvious that they can be known. But they are not as people commonly conceive them to be, for popular notions of the gods do not agree with the respect people accord them. The man who rejects the gods believed in by the masses is not impious; rather, it is those who attach to the gods the beliefs of the many about them who are impious. For the views of the many concerning the gods are not mere superstitions, but false opinions. And it is because of these that the gravest injuries that afflict the wicked and the benefits bestowed on the good are thought to be the work of the gods; for people attribute to the gods their own human ideas about virtue and think that all things alien to their own human nature must be incompatible with the gods as well.

Accustom yourself to the idea that death is nothing to be feared, for all good and evil is in sensation, and death is the loss of sensation; therefore, the clear understanding of the fact that death is not a cause of concern makes the finite nature of life something pleasant for us, not by making our lifespan infinite, but by relieving us of the desire for immortality. Life is not a terror to a man who has a clear comprehension of the fact that there is nothing for him to fear in dying; therefore, that man is illogical who says that he fears death not because it will cause him pain when it comes, but because the prospect of its coming distresses him. For it is absurd that that which does not distress a man when it is present should afflict him when it is not present. And so death, the most horrible of evils, is nothing to us; for when we are alive it is nothing to us, and when it is present we no longer exist. Death, then, should not be feared by either the living or the dead, since in the case of the former it has no existence and, in the case of the latter, they no longer exist. The common people sometimes seek to avoid death as the greatest of all evils, but at other times they welcome it as a relief from the miseries of life. The wise man, however, neither disparages life nor fears death. The idea of being alive is not a problem for him, nor does he consider dying an evil, for just as he chooses not the greatest amount of food, but the tastiest, he likewise prefers to enjoy time on the basis of quality rather than length. Moreover, he who advises the young to live nobly and the old to come to a good death is foolish, not merely because life is sweet, but because living well and dying well require the same diligent care. Worse yet is he [the poet Theognis of Megara] who said:

> It is best not to be born, but once born
> to pass quickly through the gates of Hades,

for if he was truly convinced of the truth of his statement, why didn't he die? This would have been easy for him to do, if he truly meant what he said. On the other hand, if he was joking he was speaking foolishly about a matter that should not be taken lightly.

Let us keep in mind that the future is neither entirely ours nor entirely not ours, so that we should never be certain of its coming, nor fall into a state of despair as if we were certain it would never come. We must also realize that some of our desires are natural while others are empty, and that of the natural ones some are necessary and some merely natural. And we must remember that of the natural desires some are essential for the attainment of happiness, some for the comfort of the body and others for the mere assurance that life will go on. The person who clearly understands these truths will make every effort, by avoiding certain actions and choosing others, to cultivate the health of the body and the serenity of the soul, since this is the fulfillment of a happy life. For all of our actions have but one goal, namely the avoidance of pain and fear. Once we have achieved this the disturbance of the soul is removed, since the living creature does not have seek something that is missing or look for something else by which the good of the soul and the body may be perfected. It is only when we suffer that we feel the need for pleasure; when we do not suffer we are no longer in need of it. For this reason we call pleasure the beginning and the end of a happy life. We recognize pleasure as the greatest good and one that is connate with us; we begin, in fact, our every choice and avoidance with pleasure as a basic consideration and return to it since we have established feeling as the standard by which every good thing is evaluated. As pleasure, then, is the first good and connate with our humanity, we do not choose to enjoy every pleasure, but many times avoid those that result in causing us serious difficulties; and sometimes we consider many pains as preferable to pleasures, when the endurance of a temporary pain, or even of a long duration, is followed by a greater pleasure. Every pleasure, then, is good because it is agreeable with our nature, and yet not all pleasures should be pursued for the same reason that, even though all pain is evil, not all of its forms should be avoided. It is wise, however, to evaluate all these things by measuring one against another and discovering what is beneficial and what is harmful. For sometimes we consider good to be evil and also the opposite, that is, we view evil as good. Likewise, we regard self-sufficiency as a great good, not for the purpose of always using little, but rather with the objective that, in case we do not have much, we can be satisfied with little, being honestly convinced that luxury is enjoyed most by those who need it least; we also believe that all natural needs are easily satisfied while all things that are not essential are hard to procure. A simple diet can be enjoyed as much as gourmet foods when the pain of want has been removed, while bread and water give the greatest pleasure when they are brought to someone who is really hungry. To accustom yourself, then, to a simple and non-luxurious diet not only contributes to good health, but also prepares you to face without fear the requirements of life; moreover, it enables you to cope better with the luxurious life when you encounter it on certain occasions and makes you fearless in dealing with the whims of fortune.

When we say, then, that pleasure is the greatest good, we are not referring to the pleasures of debauchery or those that consist of sensual gratification, as some people claim because of their ignorance, disagreement with our views or deliberate falsification of our teachings; what we mean, rather, is the freedom of the body from pain and of the soul from torment. It is not an endless round of drinking and revelry, the enjoyment of all kinds of sexuality, or the feasting on fish and other exquisite foods offered on a luxurious table that make life pleasurable; instead, it is sound contemplation, a careful examination of every choice and avoidance and the expulsion of those beliefs which cause the greatest disturbance to the soul that make life happy. The basis of all these things, and the greatest good, is prudence; therefore, prudence is ever more valuable than philosophy, since all other virtues spring from it. It teaches us that the good life is also a prudent, honorable and just life, and that it is impossible to live prudently, honorably and justly without living a life of pleasure. For the virtues go hand in hand with pleasant living, and the good life cannot be divorced from them.

For who, in your view, is better than the man who maintains holy beliefs regarding the gods, who is totally unafraid of death and has carefully contemplated the purposes of nature, who comprehends that the limit of good things may be easily reached and that the chronological duration and intensity of evil is brief, who ridicules destiny, considered by some the mistress of all things, who attributes some things to necessity, others to chance and others to our own actions, because he sees destiny as a force without responsibility and views chance as inconsistent, whereas our own actions are free. Thus, it is to our own actions that we must attribute praise or blame. It would be better to espouse the myths about the gods than to become slaves to the doctrines of destiny that the natural philosophers have invented, for the myths preserve some hope of escaping the punishment of the gods if we honor them, while the destiny of the philosophers offers no escape. He does not consider chance to be a god, as most people do, since disorderly acts cannot be the work of a god; neither does he see god as an unreliable cause, for he does not believe that good or evil is granted by chance to men so as to make them live a happy life; rather, he believes that chance provides men with the beginnings of great goods and great evils. Thus, he considers the misfortune of the wise to be preferable to the good fortune of the fool. It is better, then, that those actions which are well considered not be the result of chance but reason.

Diligently study, then, these and other similar precepts day and night, reflecting on them when alone and in the company of others of the same bent of mind and you will never be troubled either when sleeping or waking, but will live as a god among men; for a man living in the midst of immortal blessings no longer appears to be mortal!

A Late Greek Stoic of the Roman Empire—Epictetus of Hierapolis:
Selected Fragments.

Epictetus of Hierapolis in Phrygia served in important offices under the Roman Emperors Nero and Domitian. He taught philosophy in Rome and, after his banishment by Domitian in 89 A.D., came to Nicopolis in Epirus where he continued teaching until his death *ca.* 135 A.D. His philosophic works, which manifest a great interest in theology, were posthumously published by Arrian and exerted a considerable influence on the thought of the Stoic philosopher Marcus Aurelius. Numerous fragments attributed to Epictetus have also been preserved, most of them in the anthology of Stobaeus. It appears, however, that only a few are genuine. Of the rest, some may be based on the sayings of Epictetus while others may be of Pythagorean origin. The fragments given here express, nevertheless, the profound religiosity of Epictetus and the true spirit of his brand of late Stoicism.

1

A human life at the mercy of Fortune resembles a torrent: it is turbulent and muddy, difficult to cross, moody, noisy and short.

2

When a soul resides with Virtue it resembles a spring that flows forever. It is like a pure, clear and wholesome drink—sweet, rich and plentiful—that causes neither injury nor destruction.

3

It is a disgrace that people who sweeten their drinks with honey, the gift of the bee, should also embitter Reason, the gift of God, with vice.

4

The eyes of the dead are picked out by ravens only when the dead no longer need them. Flatterers, on the other hand, injure the soul of the living and blind the soul's eyes.

5

Do not carry a sharp knife or an undisciplined, loose tongue.

6

Man has been endowed by Nature with two ears but only one tongue so that he may listen to others twice before he speaks once.

7

Do not pronounce judgement in any court before you have been judged yourself in the tribunal of Justice.

8

It is a disgrace for a judge to be judged by laymen.

9

The shorter and nobler life is in every way preferable to a life which is longer, but less noble and devoid of accomplishments.

10

The name of virtue is freedom, that of vice, slavery. No person whose acts are free is really a slave!

11

Pleasures enjoyed most infrequently give the greatest satisfaction.

12

Act in excess and the greatest pleasures become the least pleasurable.

13

An ape's wrath and a flatterer's threat should be treated with equal consideration.

14

Control your passions, for they will avenge themselves on you.

15

Free is the man who is a master of himself.

16

A ship should not rely on one anchor nor a human life on a single hope.

17

Strengthen yourself with self-satisfaction, for it is an unconquerable defense.

18

A person who loves money, pleasure and glory cannot also love humanity; only those who love things fair and good are lovers of humanity.

19

The thought of God should come to you more frequently than breath.

20

One should adopt the noblest way of life, for custom can make it pleasurable to those who follow it.

21

Daily renewal of your talk of God should take precedence over the renewal of your supply of meat and drink.

22

As the Sun needs no prayers and songs to rise in the sky, but sends forth its warmth and brightness and is beloved by all, so you also should not need applause and loud praise to perform your duty. Do good of your own volition and you will be loved like the Sun.

23

No one can be loved by someone incapable of loving.

24

If only you could remember that God is standing near you to observe and evaluate all of your deeds, bodily or spiritual, you would certainly abstain from all errors in prayer or action, and God would be with you.

III
Religion

The Origin of the Gods: Hesiod, *Theogony* 116–225.

With a date of ca. 700 B.C., Hesiod is among the oldest of Greek poets. We know something of his life from his works, in which he tells us that his family settled in the region of Boeotia where, while tending sheep on Mt. Helicon, he one day heard the Muses calling him to sing of the gods (*Theogony* 22–35). His work as a poet apparently won him praise in his own lifetime, for he tells us that he won the prize for a song at a funeral contest in Chalcis (*Works and Days* 650–60). According to tradition, his tomb was shown to visitors to Orchomenus, a city in northwestern Boeotia.

As its name suggests, Hesiod's *Theogony* deals with the origin and genealogies of the gods. According to this account, the first cosmic powers were Chaos, Earth and Eros. From Chaos and Earth, in two separate lines, sprang three hundred gods. Among the earliest of these was Cronus, who overthrew his father, Heaven (Ouranus), and was in turn displaced by his own children led by Zeus.

In the beginning Chaos came into existence; then broad-breasted Earth, the eternally secure seat of all the immortals who dwell upon the peak of snowy Olympus; and dark Tartarus in the depths of the broad-pathed Earth; and Eros, fairest of the deathless gods, who loosens limbs and overcomes good sense and wise counsel within the hearts of all men and gods.

From Chaos came Erebus and black Night, and Night bore Aether and Day from her union in love with Erebus. Earth gave birth first to starry Heaven, equal to herself, so that he might cover her everywhere and be forever a secure home for the blessed gods. She then bore long Hills, the pleasant haunts of the Nymphs, those goddesses who dwell in the upland glens. She also bore the barren sea with its angry swell, Pontus, without the delight of love. But then she lay with Heaven and bore deep-swirling Ocean, Coeus, Crius, Hyperion, Iapetus, Theia, Rhea, Themis, Mnemosyne, gold-crowned Phoebe and lovely Tethys. After these she gave birth to crafty Cronus, the youngest and most terrible of her children, who hated his lusty father.

Earth also bore the mighty-hearted Cyclopes—Brontes, Steropes, and strong-minded Arges—who gave thunder to Zeus and forged the thunderbolt. They resembled the gods in all ways but for the single eye in the center of their foreheads, and it was from this round eye that they received the name Cyclopes (Round-eyes). Strength and might were in all they did.

Three other sons came from the union of Earth and Heaven whose greatness and power are beyond description. These were the arrogant Cottus, Briareos and Gyes. From their shoulders grew a hundred arms and each had on his shoulders fifty heads set upon strong necks, so that the strength in their huge bodies was irresistible.

The offspring of Earth and Heaven were the most terrible of children and they were hated by their own father from the very beginning. Heaven hid them within the Earth as soon as each was born. He would not allow them to come up into the light, and rejoiced in the evil he had done. But vast Earth groaned, for she was filled to bursting, and she devised a treacherous and evil plan. She quickly created a kind of hard gray stone and made from it a huge sickle. Then she told her plan to her dear sons, and as she encouraged them her anger burned deep in her heart:

"My children, children of a wicked father, if you do as I ask we will punish your father for his crimes, for he was the first to plot evil deeds."

So she spoke, but they were stricken with fear and could not speak. Then great and crafty Cronus found courage and said:

"Mother, I promise to do this thing. I have no love for our evil father, for he was the first to plot evil deeds."

So he spoke, and vast Earth rejoiced. She hid him in an ambush, gave him the sharp sickle and revealed to him all the details of her plan.

Great Heaven came, bringing the night and longing for love. He lay upon Earth, covering her everywhere. Then his son from his ambush stretched out his left hand and, grasping the long sharp-toothed blade in his right, he eagerly severed his father's genitals and threw them behind him. But they did not leave his hand without effect, for Earth absorbed all the drops of blood that were spilled on her and in the course of a year bore the strong Erinyes and the huge giants, wearers of bright armor who hold long spears in their hands, and those of the Nymphs called Meliae throughout the world.

As soon as Cronus had cut off his father's members with his stone blade he threw them from the land into the surging sea, where they floated for a long time. A white foam appeared around the immortal flesh and within it there grew a young woman. At first she drifted to holy Cythera, then to the island of Cyprus where she emerged from the sea as a worthy and beautiful goddess and where grass grew around her and beneath her delicate feet. Men and gods call her Aphrodite; Aphrogenea ["Foam-born"], because she grew within the foam; well-crowned Cythera, because she came to Cythera; Cyprogenes, because she was born in wave-washed Cyprus; and Philommedes ["Member-loving"], because she sprang from Heaven's members. Eros accompanied her, and lovely Desire was with her at her birth and as she joined the assembly of the gods. This honor was hers from the beginning, and the fate assigned to her among the undying gods and men was to be spoken of by maidens and to be the cause of smiles, seductions, sweet delights, love and kindness.

But great Heaven scornfully called his sons Titans ["Stretchers"], for he said that they had reached beyond their limits and committed a terrible deed for which they would one day be punished.

And Night gave birth to hateful Doom, black Fate and Death, and she bore Sleep and the tribe of Dreams. Though the goddess lay with no one, dark Night bore Blame, painful Distress and the Hesperides, who care for the golden apples and fruit-bearing trees beyond the glorious Ocean. She also bore the Destinies and the ruthless, punishing Fates—Clotho, Lachesis and Atropos—who give both good and bad to mortals when they are born and prosecute the transgressions of gods and men. The fearsome anger of these goddesses is never assuaged until they have inflicted a severe punishment upon the sinner. Deadly Night also gave birth to Nemesis to bring misery to mortals and, later, to Deceit, Friendship, deadly Age and strong-hearted Strife.

The Five Ages: Hesiod, *Works and Days* 106–201.

Hesiod's *Works and Days* is a varied work which combines practical advice on agriculture and proper social and religious conduct with the poet's exhortation to a life of honesty and hard work. Although addressed to Hesiod's brother Perses, who is said to have cheated him out of part of his inheritance, it was clearly intended for a wide audience. The poem includes a number of myths, including the famous stories of Prometheus, Pandora and the Five Ages. The latter appears below.

If you like, I will summarize another tale for you, well and skilfully—so be sure to take it to heart—about gods and men and how they came from a single source.

The first men made by the immortal gods who dwell on Olympus were a race of gold. They lived at the time when Cronus reigned in heaven and they lived like gods, without sorrow in their hearts and free from toil and misery. Untouched by miserable old age, their arms and legs remained strong. They delighted in feasts and, living beyond all evils, when they died it was as though they were overcome by sleep. All good things were theirs, for the fertile earth yielded its fruits in abundance and without stinting, and they lived lives of contentment and peace upon their lands, rich in flocks and beloved by the blessed gods. Ever since the earth covered this race they have been known as kindly, sacred spirits who live upon the earth, warding off evil and watching over mortals. Roaming the earth cloaked in mist, they watch over judgments and cruelties, and they grant wealth to men. This is the royal honor they have received.

After this the Olympian gods fashioned a much less noble race made of silver. They resembled the race of gold neither in body nor in mind. Children were cared for by their mothers for a hundred years, playing childishly all the while in their own homes. Once they had grown and reached their prime they lived for only a little while—and in suffering, because of their foolishness. They could not help offending each other, and they would not serve the immortal gods or offer sacrifices on the holy altars of the blessed ones as is right for men to do no matter where they dwell. Angered because they would not honor the blessed gods who live on Olympus, Zeus the son of Cronus put them away. Since the time when this race was covered by the earth they have been known as the blessed spirits who dwell beneath the earth. They are second in rank, but they are honored nonetheless.

Then Zeus made a third race of mortals, this one of bronze, forming them from ash trees. They were in no way the equal of the silver race. Terrible and strong, they cared only for the wretched works of Ares and for acts of violence. No eaters of bread, their hearts were hard and stony. Though they were misshapen, they had great strength and invincible arms which grew from their shoulders atop their powerful bodies. Their armor was of bronze, their homes were of bronze and the tools with which they worked were of bronze, for there was as yet no black iron. In the end they destroyed themselves and descended to cold Hades, leaving no names behind them. They were fearsome, but black Death took them and they left the bright light of the sun.

When this race had also been covered, Zeus the son of Cronus created a fourth one upon the nourishing earth. Nobler and more righteous than those who came before them, these were the godlike heroes who are called demigods. They were the last race before our own on the boundless earth. Vile war and dread battle destroyed them, some at Thebes of the seven gates in Cadmus' country when they fought for Oedipus' flocks, others at Troy across the wide expanse of the sea where they had been led in ships to fight for the honor of lovely-haired Helen. There death enshrouded a part of them, bringing their end, but to others father Zeus, son of Cronus, granted life and a place to live apart from men at the ends of the earth. Free from cares, they live in the Isles of the Blessed beside deep-swirling Ocean, fortunate heroes for whom the bountiful earth bears honey-sweet grain thrice a year, far from the immortal gods. Cronus rules over them, for the father of gods and men released them from his bonds, and they have an equal share of honor and glory.

Then keen-eyed Zeus created a fifth race of men upon the abundant earth. How I wish that I were not among them, but had either died before or been born after them! For this is a race of iron. For them there will be no end of toil and misery either by day or by night, though there will be some good mixed with the harsh troubles sent by the gods. But when they are born gray about their temples, Zeus will destroy this race also. In those days fathers will be in conflict with their children, and children with their fathers. Guests will be at odds with their hosts, and friends with friends. Brothers will not hold each other dear as they did in former times. Ignorant of what it means to revere the gods, men will dishonor their aging parents, attacking them with bitter words. They will not recognize the debt they owe for their nurture. Their justice will be the power of fists; one man will sack another's city, and there will be no thanks for the man who keeps his promise, or for the righteous man or the good one. Praise will belong instead to the evil and the violent. Justice will be in the power of fists; decency will no longer exist. The wicked man will deceive the good with lies and swear an oath upon them. Scowling, foul-mouthed Envy will dog the steps of miserable men everywhere. Then Decency and Righteous Indignation, their fair forms cloaked in white robes, will abandon humanity, leaving the wide-pathed earth to join the immortal gods upon Olympus. Dark troubles will be left for mortals, and there will be no help for them against evil.

The Homeric Hymn to Gaia, Mother of All:
Allen-Halliday-Sikes, eds., *The Homeric Hymns*, no. 30.

The Homeric Hymns are invocations to various gods written in dactylic hexameter by members of the Homeric school in the seventh and sixth centuries B.C. The hymn below is one of the most interesting hymns of the entire collection. Its precise date is unknown, though it is certainly quite late, and it resembles the older hymn to Demeter, which has obviously influenced its author. Both hymns are dedicated to *Gaia*, the Earth, whom the poets recognize as the archetypal mother and the giver of birth and sustenance to all living creatures. *Gaia* is not seen here as an anthropomorphic deity, as were the Olympian gods, but rather as the primeval mother whose power and immensity defy representation in terms of the human form.

I shall sing of solid Earth,
mother of all, most ancient,
nourisher of all that exists:
all beings that walk the land,
all that swim the seas,
all that fly the skies—
all these her richness sustains!
From you, O mighty one,
fair children and rich harvests spring,
and life you give or withhold from mortals.
Happy is he whom your heart favors,
for he possesses all things abundantly!
For him the land abounds in crops,
in his fields his flocks increase
and his house is filled with riches!
Such a man governs with justice
a city of fair women
and great fortune and opulence attend him;
his sons shine with the joyful vigor of youth,
and his daughters, with contented hearts,
play in the flower dances
and romp among the tender blossoms of the field.
Such is the man you honor,
august goddess, spirit of plenty.

Hail, mother of the gods,
wife of the starry sky.
For this hymn grant me a life
that pleases my heart
and I shall remember you
in yet another song!

The First Philosophic Theologian—Xenophanes of Colophon: Selected Fragments.

Little is known of the life of Xenophanes of Colophon other than the few biographical data furnished to us by Diogenes Laertius. It seems certain, however, that he lived in the sixth century B.C. and that he taught the famous philosopher Parmenides of Elea, the founder of metaphysical monism. Xenophanes is widely admired both for his scientific observations, which have led some to call him the first geologist and paleontologist, and for his religious ideas, which are monotheistic. He has been characterized as the first critical or philosophic theologian of Greece and also as a modernist for his rejection of anthropomorphism and his espousal of the belief that in matters of religion investigation is more reliable than divine revelation. Some of the religious doctrines of Xenophanes are revealed in the fragments given here, which are drawn from Diels' classic edition of the Presocratics (*Fragmente der Vorsokratiker*).

11. Homer and Hesiod have attributed to the gods things which are considered disgraceful and worthy of censure by humankind, namely theft, adultery and deceiving one another.

14. But mortals suppose that their gods were created by birth, that they have the garb, voice and form of men.

15. If oxen or horses or lions possessed hands or the ability to draw and create the works of art that men are capable of creating, and painted or sculpted the images of their gods, then they would give them their own forms; horses the form of horses, oxen the form of oxen, each species portraying its own kind.

16. The Ethiopians say that their gods are dark-skinned and snub-nosed, while the Thracians claim theirs are blue-eyed and red-haired.

18. The gods have not revealed to humankind all things from the beginning; it is by seeking that humans eventually discover what is better.

23. There is one God, greatest among gods and men, different from mortals in bodily form and in mind.

24. As a whole God sees, as a whole he thinks and as a whole he hears.

25. God effortlessly sets everything in motion by the thought of his mind.

26. God always stays in the same place, never moving; nor is it appropriate for him to occupy different positions at different times.

27. For all things come from the earth and reach their end by going back to the earth again.

34. As for plain truth, no man has seen it, nor will there ever be one who knows about the gods and all the things I have discussed. Even if someone accidentally happened to say what is true, he himself would not be aware of it. But they all think they know.

Euhemerus of Messene and the Human Origin of the Gods: Diodorus, *Historical Library*, 6.1–11.

Euhemerus of Messene is one of the most interesting religious writers of the Hellenistic Age. He appears to be the author of a novel of travel entitled *Sacred History* which dealt with the origins of the pagan gods. An authentic fragment of this work has survived in the sixth book of Diodorus, who was in the habit of including his source materials within the general scheme of his chronological compendium without noticeable revision or modification. Euhemerus claimed to have journeyed into the Indian Ocean and to have visited the island of Panchaea and the Temple of Zeus Triphylius where he discovered a golden column which revealed to him the truth about the gods. According to the theory of Euhemerus, the pagan gods had originally been humans who had governed and served humanity and had then been deified by their grateful subjects *post mortem*.

"Concerning the gods, the ancients have handed down to the people of more recent times two distinct ideas. The first is that some of the gods are everlasting and indestructible, such as the sun and the moon and the stars in the sky, and also the winds and other forces endowed with a similar nature; for each of these has a perpetual genesis and duration. The second is that the other gods were once human beings who achieved immortal honor and glory because they performed deeds which were beneficial to mankind, as is the case with Hercules, Dionysus, Aristaeus and others like them. Many different accounts have been preserved by historians and writers of myths about these gods. Among the historians, Euhemerus, the author of the *Sacred History*, has composed a special work on them, while the mythographers, Homer, Hesiod, Orpheus and others of similar bent, have fabricated hideous stories about the gods. We shall attempt to examine briefly the accounts written by both groups, making it our aim to maintain a proper balance in our discussion.

Euhemerus, who was a friend of King Cassander and was obliged to perform certain royal services for him and to undertake long journeys abroad, says that he traveled southward to the ocean. Sailing out of Arabia the Blessed, he voyaged for many days across the ocean and came to some islands in the sea, among which was one named Panchaea. There he observed the inhabitants of that island, men of exceptional piety who honor the gods with the most magnificent sacrifices and with remarkable offerings of silver and gold. The island is sacred to the gods and there are several objects on it which astonish us because of their antiquity and the excellence of their workmanship; we have written about these things in our previous books. On this island, on a certain hill which is exceptionally high, there is also a temple of Zeus Triphylius founded by the god when he ruled as king over all the earth and was still among men. There is a golden stele in this temple which bears an inscription, in Panchaean letters, recording the most important achievements of Uranus and Cronus and Zeus. After describing these things, Euhemerus says that Uranus became the first king and that he was an honorable and benevolent man, learned in the movement of the stars, who was also the first to honor the heavenly gods with sacrifices; for this reason he was called Uranus [Heaven]. By his wife Hestia he had two sons, Titan and Cronus, and two daughters, Rhea and Demeter. After Uranus, Cronus became king, married Rhea and had three children by her: Zeus, Hera and Poseidon. Zeus inherited the kingship, married Hera, Demeter and Themis and begat the Curetes by the first, Persephone by the second and Athena by the third. And, coming to Babylon, he was hospitably received by Belos and afterwards went to the island of Panchaea which lies in the ocean and established an altar of Uranus, his own forefather. From there he came through Syria to Casius, who ruled that region in those days and after whom Mt. Casius was named. Then, coming to Cilicia, he defeated in battle the local governor, Cilix, and visited very many other nations where he was honored and proclaimed a god by all."

Empedocles on Reincarnation:
Selected Fragments.

Empedocles of Acragas (*ca.* 493–433 B.C.) was the most versatile of the Presocratics. He was not only a philosopher, but also a poet, scientist, physician, social reformer, seer, miracle worker and healer. Empedocles wrote three books on nature (in verse), a poem on medicine and a number of purification songs, now lost. Extensive fragments of his works have survived, however, which allow us to form some idea of his philosophy and scientific thought. He is best known for postulating the existence of four physical roots, *rhizomata* as he called them—fire, air, earth and water—which constitute the four elements of popular cosmology. As a scientist, he undertook many experiments and managed to prove, among other things, the corporeality of air. His work as an anatomist and physician was also impressive. The fragments selected here, however, reveal another aspect of the thought of this remarkable man, namely his mystical belief in the transmigration of the soul. They are taken from Diels' classic edition of the Presocratics (*Fragmente der Vorsokratiker*).

115. There is a matter of Necessity, an old decree of the gods, eternal and secured with broad oaths, that when one of the *daemons* [divine spirits] endowed with a long life sinfully defiles his body with blood, or as a result of hate has broken a sacred oath, he must wander for thrice ten thousand seasons, cut off from the company of the blessed, being reborn during this period in all kinds of mortal forms, exchanging one kind of a painful life for another. For the force of the air chases him into the sea, the sea spits him out on to dry land, the earth chases him toward the rays of the blazing sun, and the sun hurls him again into the eddies of air. One element seizes him from the other, and all abhor him. I am one of these spirits now, a fugitive from the gods and a wanderer, relying on raging strife.

117. Already I have been born a boy, a girl, a bush, a bird and a mute fish of the sea.

118. I wept and lamented when I saw this unfamiliar land.

119. From what great honors and deep happiness have I fallen to this mortal state on earth?

120. We have come into this roofed cavern.

125. For he took them and changed their forms from living creatures to dead ones.

126. A female spirit wraps them in the unfamiliar garment of flesh.

127. As reincarnated animals they become lions that make their lair in the mountains and sleep in the ground; or they become laurels with beautiful foliage.

Dionysus, God of Wine:
Diodorus, *Historical Library*, 4.2.5–3.4.

The cult of Dionysus has long been a subject of controversy among scholars since ancient accounts of it are often contradictory. We can be certain, however, of the association of the god's cult with the beginnings of Greek tragedy and of the fact that Dionysus, though widely regarded as the god of the vine, was also associated with grain, figs and various trees. He ultimately came to be known as the god of wine. In fact, we are told by Diodorus, Pliny and Pausanias that in several of the temples of Dionysus in Greece—at Corinth, Andros, Teos and Elis—wine miraculously sprang from the earth during celebrations of the god's festivals.

They say that after he had been reared by the nymphs in Nysa, Dionysus invented wine and taught human beings how to cultivate the vine. They also say that he traveled throughout the inhabited world bringing many lands under cultivation, something for which he was greatly honored by all peoples. Dionysus invented the drink made from barley which some call beer, a beverage whose aroma is not much inferior to that of wine, and he taught the art of brewing it to those peoples who lived in lands where vines will not grow. It is also said that he went about the countryside with an army of men and women punishing people who were unjust and profane. And, paying homage to his fatherland, he freed all the cities in Boeotia and founded a city named after autonomy which he called Eleuthernae [City of Freedom].

After this Dionysus campaigned in India. He returned to Boeotia after three years, bringing with him considerable booty and celebrating a triumph on an Indian elephant, thus becoming the first ever to do so. To commemorate the Indian campaign the other Greeks and Thracians have established the practice of performing sacrifices every three years, and they believe that on these occasions the god manifests himself to human beings. This is why in many Greek cities there are assemblies of Dionysus' female devotees. On such occasions it is proper for the young maidens to carry the *thrysus* [a wand wreathed in ivy and vine leaves with a pine cone at the top] and to inspire each other with cries of *"Euai!"* as they honor the god. The older women offer sacrifices in groups as they celebrate his feast and honor his presence with their hymns. In doing so they imitate the Maenads who in the olden days were the god's escorts, as history tells us . . . .

Since the invention of wine and the gift that he made of it to humanity were so very pleasing, both because of the enjoyment that comes from drinking it and the increased strength it gives to the bodies of those who consume it, they say that during a meal, when undiluted wine is offered, one should propose a toast with the words "to the Good Deity." However, when wine mixed with water is served after a meal one should say "to Zeus the Savior." This is because the consumption of unmixed wine produces a kind of madness, while wine mixed with the rain Zeus sends produces pleasure, but no harmful aftereffects. Generally speaking, the myths tell us that people give the greatest praise to those gods who have excelled in benefiting humanity by the discovery of good things, that is, Dionysus and Demeter; for the one invented the most enjoyable of drinks and the other gave human beings the best of all solid foods [wheat]!

The Sanctuary of Asclepius at Epidaurus:
Pausanias, *Description of Greece*, 2.27. 1–7.

The sanctuary of the god of healing, Asclepius, at Epidaurus on the coast of the Argolid in the Peloponnese, was one of the most important centers of religious worship in the Greek world. Although the cult of Asclepius probably originated at Tricca in Thessaly, Epidaurus had become the main center of his worship by the fourth century B.C. Many other shrines were founded by the Epidaurians throughout the Greek world, *e.g.* at Athens, Pergamum, Balagrae in Cyrene, Lebena in Crete, and at Rome. The description of the sanctuary with its buildings, theater and other monuments given here is taken from Pausanias, a traveler and guidebook writer who lived in the second century A.D. when some of the original buildings had already collapsed. People from all parts of the Greek world came to Epidaurus seeking relief from various diseases, and many were cured. A record of these cures was kept in the sanctuary and parts of it have survived in the inscriptions found in the area.

The sacred grove of Asclepius is contained by boundaries on all sides, and no men die or women give birth within its confines, as is also the custom on the island of Delos. The victims, whether sacrificed by one of the Epidaurians or by a foreigner, must be consumed within the grove itself. I know that the same thing is done also at Titane. The statue of Asclepius is half the size of that of the Olympian Zeus in Athens and is made of ivory and gold. An epigram proclaims that the artist who made it was Thrasymedes, the son of Arignotus, a Parian. The god is seated on a throne holding a staff in one hand and the other over the head of a serpent. A dog lies beside the god. On the throne are inscribed the great deeds of the heroes of Argos, namely Bellerophon's killing of Chimaera and Perseus' decapitation of Medusa. Beyond the temple is the area where the suppliants of the god sleep. Nearby there is a round building worth seeing which is constructed of white marble and called the Tholos. In this building there is a painting by Pausias which shows Eros taking up a lyre after having discarded his bow and arrows. There is also another work of Pausias here, a painting of Methé [Drunkeness] drinking from a glass bowl. You can actually see in the picture the glass bowl and the woman's face through it. Within the enclosed area stand tablets of which there were many in ancient times, though now only six remain there. On these tablets were recorded the names of men and women healed by Asclepius as well as the illnesses which afflicted them and the ways in which they were cured. These writings were composed in the Doric tongue. Separate from the rest stands an ancient tablet which states that Hippolytus dedicated twenty horses to the god. The Aricians relate a story which is in agreement with this tablet. They say that after Hippolytus died as a result of the curses of Theseus, Asclepius resurrected him. When he came to life again he did not consider his father worthy of forgiveness, but ignored his pleas and came to Italy to settle among the Aricians. There he reigned as king and dedicated a temple to Artemis in which, up until my own time, contests of single combat have been held after which the winner is made a priest of the goddess. No free man has ever been allowed to take part in such contests, but only slaves who escaped from their masters. In the sanctuary of Epidaurus there is a theater which, it seems to me, is especially worth seeing. Now, the theaters of the Romans are by far superior to all others throughout the world, and the theater of Megalopolis in Arcadia is superior to all in size. But with regard to harmonious symmetry and beauty, what architect can compete with Polyclitus? For it was Polyclitus who designed this theater, and the rotund building as well. Within the confines of the grove there is a temple of Artemis and a statue of Epione and sanctuaries of Aphrodite and Themis as well as a stadium formed, like most Greek stadiums, by banks of earth. There is also a fountain remarkable for its roof and its overall beauty. The structures built in our days by the senator Antoninus are a bath of Asclepius and a temple of the gods which they call Bountiful. He also constructed a temple to Hygeia [health] and to Asclepius and Apollo, surnamed the "Egyptians." And there was a colonnaded porch named after Cotys; but after the roof collapsed the entire building was destroyed because it had been constructed of unbaked brick. He rebuilt this as well. The Epidaurians in the vicinity of the sanctuary were greatly distressed since their women could not give birth to their children under a roof and their sick were dying in the open air. To correct this situation, he constructed a building in which it was not a sin for a man to die or a woman to give birth to her child. There are mountains above the grove, one named Mt. Titthium and another called Cynortium, where the temple of Apollo Maleatas is found. This is one of the ancient structures; but the rest of the buildings around the temple of Maleatas and the cistern of the fountain in which the holy water of the god is collected, these, too, Antoninus built for the Epidaurians!

The Cures of Asclepius at Epidaurus:
Inscriptiones Graecae, IV^2, 1, nos. 121–122.

The inscriptions from the sanctuary of Asclepius at Epidaurus which record the cures of the god are very important to students of ancient medicine and religion. Asclepius, the god of healing and patron of physicians, restored the health of believers who came to sleep in his temple by appearing to them in dreams. Epidaurus may, in fact, be called the Lourdes of antiquity, where the workings of faith often accomplished miraculous cures. The selected cases given here are drawn from an inscription of the second half of the fourth century B.C. and are typical of the thaumaturgy of Asclepius at Epidaurus. It must be emphasized, however, that these miraculous cures were by no means the only ones practiced at the various *Asclepieia*, as the temples of the god were called. More scientific therapeutic methods, such as diet, exercise, hot baths, etc., were often employed, especially at Cos and Pergamum in Asia.

21. Arata of Laconia, a woman with dropsy. For her cure, while she was in Lacedaemon, her mother slept in the temple and had a dream. It seemed to her that the god cut off the head of her daughter and hung up her body with the throat pointing downwards. When much fluid came out of it, he took the body down and placed the head on the neck again. After seeing this dream she departed for Lacedaemon and found her daughter cured. The daughter had the same dream.

22. Hermon of Thasos. A blind man, he was cured by Asclepius. But since, after his healing, he did not bring his thank-offering, the god caused him to be blind again. When he returned, however, and slept again in the temple, Asclepius restored his sight.

23. Aristagora of Troezen. Having tapeworm in her intestines, she had a dream while sleeping in the temple of Asclepius at Troezen. It seemed to her that the sons of Asclepius, while the god was away in Epidaurus, cut off her head. Then, when they were unable to put it back on her body, they sent someone to Asclepius requesting his return. In the meantime daylight came and the priest clearly saw her head detached from her body. With the coming of night Aristagora had another vision. It seemed to her that the god, having returned from Epidaurus, placed her head on her neck again and then cut open her belly, removed the tapeworm, and sewed her up. Her health was restored after that.

24. The boy Aristocritus of Halieis. A rock fell on him. After diving into the ocean and swimming away he came to a dry hiding place which was encircled by rocks, but he got lost and could not find his way out. Afterwards his father, who searched everywhere but could not find him, came to Asclepius and slept in the temple for the sake of his son. There he had a dream. It seemed to him that the god led him to a certain spot and showed him that his son was there. And, leaving the temple, he searched the rocks and found the boy on the seventh day.

26. A dog healed an Aeginetan boy who had a growth on his neck. When he came to the god one of the sacred dogs cured him by licking him with his tongue while he was awake, and made him healthy.

27. A man who had an ulcer in his abdomen. While he was sleeping in the temple he had a dream. It seemed to him that the god commanded the servants who were escorting him to get a tight hold on him so that he could make an incision in his abdomen. He tried to escape, but they grabbed him and tied him to the knocker of a door. After that, Asclepius cut open his belly, removed the ulcer, sewed him up again and released him from the ties which had held him. The result was that he left the temple a healthy man, though the floor of the temple was stained with blood.

28. Cleinatas the Theban, who was infested with lice. Having a vast multitude of lice on his body, he came and slept in the temple and had a dream. It appeared to him that the god took off his clothes and made him stand up naked; then he swept the lice off his body with a broom. The next morning he left the temple in good health.

29. Hagestratus, who had headaches. He could not sleep because of his headaches. When he came to the temple he went to sleep and had a dream. It seemed to him that the god took away his headaches and, after making him stand up naked, taught him the lunge position employed in the *pancratium* [a contest combining wrestling and boxing]. The next day he left healthy, and shortly thereafter he won the *pancratium* at the Nemean games.

30. Gorgias of Heracleia, who suffered from pus. He had been wounded in battle by an arrow which pierced his lung, and for a year and a half his condition was so bad that he filled sixty-seven basins with pus. It seemed to him that the god removed the point of the arrow from his lung. In the morning he left the temple healthy, holding the arrowhead in his hands.

31. Andromache of Epirus, who hoped to have children. While sleeping in the temple she had a dream. It seemed to her that a handsome youth removed her covers and that the god later touched her with his hands. As a result, Andromache had a son by Arrybas.

32. Anticrates of Cnidus. He was struck by a spear in battle and was blinded in both eyes. He carried the point of the spear embedded in his face.

While sleeping in the temple he saw a vision. It seemed to him that the god extracted the projectile and then put the so-called pupils back into his eyes. The next day he left the temple cured.

35. [   ] of Epidaurus, who was lame. He came to the sanctuary as a suppliant on a litter. While sleeping he saw a vision. It seemed to him that the god broke his crutch and told him to bring a ladder and to climb to the highest point of the sanctuary. He tried, but then he lost his nerve and halted on the cornice; eventually he abandoned his effort and slowly came down the ladder. At first Asclepius was displeased with his behavior, but then laughed at him for his lack of courage. When daytime came he dared to try it again, and he walked out unscathed.

37. Cleimenes of Argos, who was a paralytic. He came and slept in the temple and saw a vision. It seemed to him that the god wrapped his body with a red woolen cloth and led him to take a bath in a lake of exceptionally cold water which was located a short distance from the temple. When he hesitated, Asclepius said that he would not heal men who were so afraid of cold water, but only those who came to his temple confident that he would not do them any harm, but would send them away in good health. When he awoke he bathed and left the place healthy.

39. Agameda of Ceos. She slept in the temple hoping for children and had a dream. It seemed to her in her sleep that a serpent lay on her belly. She gave birth to five children after that.

42. Nicasibula of Messene, who hoped for children. She slept in the temple and had a dream. It seemed to her that the god came to her with a serpent crawling behind him and that she had intercourse with the serpent. Within a year she gave birth to two sons.

43. [   ] of Cos, who had gout. While awake, he approached a goose who bit his feet and caused him to bleed, thus making him healthy.

The Hymn of the Curetes to Zeus Cretagenes:
Inscriptiones Creticae, III, ii, 2.

One of the most interesting religious hymns of antiquity is that of the Curetes, which was discovered in 1904 by British archaeologists at Palaikastro in the Eteocretan district of Crete. The hymn was meant to be sung before the altar of Zeus Cretagenes [Cretanborn] at an annual festival held on Mt. Ida. It is a hymn of invocation which was chanted by armed dancers who appeared as Curetes, *i.e.*, the attendant spirits who had protected the infant Zeus and recounted the story of his abduction from Mt. Dicte. The Curetes enumerated the blessings bestowed upon the world by the god and asked for his continued benevolence.

O hail, Kouros most Great, Kronian;
O welcome, Lord of Radiance, now among us with thy attendant spirits;
Move on to Dicte for the year and rejoice in this dance and song
that we make to thee on strings of harps, blending it with the sound of pipes,
and chanting as we stand round thy well-fenced altar.
O hail, Kouros most Great, Kronian;
O welcome, Lord of Radiance, now among us with thy attendant spirits;
Move on to Dicte for the year and rejoice in this dance and song.
For here, immortal child, the shield-bearing Curetes,
taking you from Rhea, hid you away with circlings of feet.
O hail, Kouros most Great, Kronian;
O welcome Lord of Radiance, now among us with thy attendant spirits;
Move on to Dicte for the year and rejoice in this dance and song.
And the Seasons began to be fruitful from year to year, and Justice to possess
    humankind,
and Peace, the wealth-loving, now attended all living creatures.
O hail, Kouros most Great, Kronian;
O welcome, Lord of Radiance, now among us with thy attendant spirits;
Move on to Dicte for the year and rejoice in this dance and song.
Leap for us, then, for cattle herds and fleecy flocks,
and leap for fields of corn and fruitful households.
O hail, Kouros most Great, Kronian;
O welcome, Lord of Radiance, now among us with thy attendant spirits;
Move on to Dicte for the year and rejoice in this dance and song.
Leap for our cities, leap for our sea-borne ships,

and leap for our youthful citizens and for renowned Themis.
O hail, Kouros most Great, Kronian;
O welcome, Lord of Radiance, now among us with thy attendant spirits;
Move on to Dicte for the year and rejoice in this dance and song!

Stoic Pantheism—Cleanthes' Hymn to Zeus: A. C. Pearson, *The Fragments of Zeno and Cleanthes*, fr. 48.

Cleanthes of Assus was a disciple of Zeno of Citium and the second head of the Stoa in Athens from 263 to 232 B.C. He was interested in theology and added a religious tone to Stoic philosophy. Cleanthes viewed the universe as a living being whose soul was god and whose heart was the sun. His most famous work, a hymn or prayer to Zeus, expresses Stoic pantheism in a religious language that approaches sublimity. Here, Zeus is identified with fire, the highest principle of Stoicism, which pervades and animates the universe. The hymm was preserved by Stobaeus, a fifth century A.D. editor of an anthology of excerpts from more than five hundred poets and prose writers which he collected for the benefit of his son.

Greatest glory of the gods, Almighty forever,
Lord of many names, may you be blessed!
It is proper that all men should call on you,
for we are your offspring,
favored recipients of the gift of speech—
we alone among all things
that live on earth and walk upon its surface.
So my hymn is of you, and I sing of your power forever.
The vast universe follows you, its Guide and Ruler,
as it rolls forever round the earth.
Your unswerving hands hold a powerful instrument,
the double-edged, flaming, eternal thunderbolt
whose blows cause all Nature to shudder!
You guide the universal Word—
the Word that directs all things in the World,
mingling with the great and lesser Lights—
which, as befits its great birth, is the highest king of all.
Without you, nothing is done on earth
or in the sea, or the sacred heights of heaven,
save the sinful deeds of the wicked.
And yet, you can make wrong things right
and create order out of chaos.
In your sight worthless things become worthy;
for you have so fitted together things good and evil

that supreme Reason reigns eternal over all.
To this the hearts of the wicked are closed,
wretched men who, though longing to grasp things good,
see not and hear not God's universal law
which, if we but wisely obey it, assures the noble life.
But they hastily flee here and there, heedless of right,
some consumed by zeal in their thirst for honor,
some recklessly pursuing personal gains,
others turning to lust and bodily pleasures.
But you, O Zeus, giver of all things good,
you, who reside in the dark cloud,
you, who wield the thunderbolt,
save men from their grievous ignorance!
Scatter it, Lord, from their souls
and grant them to know the wisdom
with which you rule justly and govern all things,
so that we, being honored by you,
may return to you our honor,
praising your works forever;
for there is no higher duty for man or god
than to extol forever your universal law!

The Homeric Hymn to Ares:
Allen-Halliday-Sikes, eds., *The Homeric Hymns*, no. 8.

This interesting hymn to the war god Ares has been assigned to the Homeric collection for unknown reasons. Its tone, style and astrological character indicate that it was composed in the Hellenistic age or even later. Some scholars, however, classify it among the Orphic poems. It is interesting to note that Ares is viewed not only as the master of war, but also as the giver of peace.

Ares most powerful, golden-helmeted, rider of chariots,
strong-minded, shield-bearing, brazen-armored, protector of cities,
strong of hand, untiring, mighty with the spear, rampart of Olympus,
father of happy Victory, supporter of Justice—
you subdue the adversary and attend the most just of men.
O sceptered lord of manhood, you make your fiery-bright chariot wheel through
the seven-pathed constellations of the ether,
where flamboyant steeds carry you ever above the third orbit.
Hear my prayer, helper of mortals, dispenser of courageous youth,
pour down from above your brightness on my life and on my martial strength,
that I may be powerful enough to throw off shameful cowardice from my
head, to reduce in me the beguiling impetuosity of my soul and to contain
the sharp ardor of my heart when it incites me to enter the chilling din of
battle.
O blessed god, give me a fearless heart and grant that I may remain under the
inviolable laws of peace,
escaping the enemy in combat and the fate of violent death!

A Shrine in the Fields: Bacchylides, *Anthologia Palatina*, VI. 53.

Bacchylides of Iulis in Ceos flourished in the early part of the fifth century B.C. He was the nephew of the poet Simonides and spent part of his life with his uncle in the court of Hieron in Syracuse.

Eudemus dedicates this shrine in his field to Zephyrus,
that most generous of winds,
for he heard his prayer and came to help him
quickly winnow the corn from the ripened ears.

On the Folly of Humanity:
Rhianos of Bene, in Powell,
Collectanea Alexandrina, 9–10.

Rhianos of Bene in Crete was an epic poet and epigrammatist of the third century B.C. He was influenced by Homer, Hesiod and Theognis of Megara, as the few surviving verses of his work indicate. The following poem is based on his longest extant fragment, twenty-one hexameters on the folly of mankind which are preserved in Stobaeus. Some historians believe that, in dismissing as foolish and impious man's attempts to climb Olympus and share the blessings of the gods, Rhianos openly condemned the deification of his contemporary Hellenistic monarchs.

Truly, we humans have minds that err
and senselessly endure the uneven distribution
of the gods' gifts:
the poor man who wanders here and there,
filled with bitterness, cursing the Immortals,
respects not his honor and his spirit.
He has no courage to speak or act;
terror strikes him down in the presence
of the wealthy landlords,
and his heart is eaten away by dejection and misery.
And the wealthy man,
to whom god grants riches
and power over many,
forgets that his feet touch the earth
and that he is the offspring of mortals.
Full of presumption and of sinful mind,
he thunders like Zeus
and raises his head with pride,
though he is just a puny man.
He takes Athena as his bride,
She with the beautiful arms,
and seeks the path to Olympus,
there to revel in the company of the gods.
But behind him Ate, invisible and unexpected,
follows with light feet above his head,
either as a young girl

catching up with the old sins,
or as an old woman,
reaching the new ones
for the sake of Zeus,
greatest of the gods, and Dike.

A Dedication to Pan and the Nymphs:
Anyte of Tegea, *Anthologia Palatina*.

Anyte of Tegea was recognized as a talented writer of epigrams but, despite her fame, we have no precise dates for her. She probably belongs to the early third century B.C.

To bushy-haired Pan and the Nymphs of the sheepfold
Theodotus the shepherd left this gift beneath his lonely look-out place;
for during the scorching summer they alleviated his great suffering,
reaching out to him with honey-like water in their hands.

A Prayer for Healing: Moero, *Anthologia Palatina*, VI. 189.

Moero of Byzantium, the daughter of the tragedian Homerus, is said to have flourished *ca.* 250 B.C. She was regarded as a great poet but, unfortunately, little of her work survives. The selection below is a dedication to the nymphs of the river Anigrus on the borders of Elis and Triphylia. Pausanias tells us that persons suffering from skin diseases came to the cave of the nymphs on the banks of the river to offer prayer and sacrifice. They then swam across the waters (which had a reddish tinge and smelled of sulfur) and emerged cured.

Nymphs of Anigrus, daughters of the river, who forever tread
these ambrosial depths with rosy feet, greetings!
Preserve Cleonymus, who put up these fair wooden statues for
you, goddesses, beneath the pines.

IV
The Greeks at War

Spartan War Songs: Tyrtaeus, *Elegies*, 6–7.

The man who expresses most clearly the military spirit of the Spartans was Tyrtaeus, an elegiac poet of the seventh century B.C. who wrote marching songs sung by the Spartan soldiers as they attacked the enemy. The two fragments of his elegies given here constitute a single poem in which Tyrtaeus urged his young countrymen to fight and die for their country. The poem echoes a Homeric passage in the *Iliad* (22, 71–6) in which Priam expresses similar thoughts on the glory of dying young.

It is a noble thing for a good man to die
fighting in the front lines for his country;
but to abandon his city and fertile fields,
to be reduced to poverty,
this is the most grievous of things—
for then a man wanders from place to place
with his beloved mother and elderly father,
his small children and lawful wife.
He shall be hated by those to whom he comes
in need and wretched poverty;
he brings shame to his race,
disgraces his noble beauty,
and every evil and dishonor attends him.
And so, since such a wanderer receives no recognition,
neither honor nor respect nor mercy,
let us fight with all our might for this land
and die for our children,
never caring to spare our lives.
Stand together and fight, then, O young men;
take no step in shameful flight.
Be not overcome by fear,
but let your hearts be great and strong within your chests,
and never flinch when you face the enemy.
Flee not, leaving behind, fallen on the ground,
the elders whose knees are no longer nimble.
For it is a disgrace when an older man,
his hair already white and gray of beard,
falls in the front line
and lies before a younger one,
his brave soul expiring in the dust,

while he holds his bloodied genitals
 and his flesh is naked—
a shameful sight to behold,
and one which forebodes much evil.
But all things are seemly for a young man
as long as he possesses the noble flower of lovely youth.
While he lives he is admired by men
and desired by women;
and he is fair, too, when he has fallen in the front lines.
So let every man bite his lip
and, with both feet firmly on the ground,
take his place for battle.

The Spartan Army: Plutarch, *Lycurgus*, 22.3–23.

The legendary Spartan army, which constituted the best fighting force in classical Greece, was made up of all adult citizens of the state. These men fought as *hoplites, i.e.*, heavily armed infantrymen. The cavalry of the Spartans was small and not very effective. The Spartan *perioeci* also served in the army; originally they were used as support troops, but eventually they were incorporated into the regular ranks. In later years, beginning with the Peloponnesian War, the Spartans were forced to use even helots for service and garrison duty abroad. As a result of the serious decline in the number of their citizens, the Spartans also used mercenary soldiers in the fourth and later centuries. With its own elite force as a nucleus and with the contingents furnished by their allies in the Peloponnesian League, which had been established in the last years of the sixth century B.C., the Spartans could raise an army of about fifty thousand men. This made them by far the leading military power in Greece in the fifth century B.C. Plutarch's description of the Spartan army, given here, is of a much later period, but it reflects the admiration the ancients felt for the Spartans even after the latter had ceased to exist as a proud and independent people.

When the young Spartans were on the battlefield their training exercises were less severe, their life easier, their discipline less strict; in fact, they were the only people in this world to whom war offered some relief from training. When their forces were lined up in battle formation, with the enemy in view, the king sacrificed a young goat, ordered his soldiers to adorn their heads with garlands, and commanded the pipers to sound the tune of the hymn to Castor; at the same time he personally began to sing the paean of attack. Seeing them march to the sound of their flutes while maintaining a perfect order in their ranks, full of self-control and confidence, with unflinching expressions as they moved calmly and cheerfully with the beat of music to the deadly encounter, was both a magnificent and terrifying spectacle. In this condition it was unlikely that the men would be possessed by fear or reckless fury. Instead, they displayed the studied valor of hope and certainty, as if some divine force had taken charge and was guiding them.

The king always marched against the enemy accompanied by a man who had been crowned in the Olympic games. It is said, in connection with this custom, that a Spartan once refused a valuable present offered to him on the condition that he abstain from competing in the games. When, after defeating his opponent with a great effort, some of the spectators asked him, "Spartan, what have you now gained with your victory?" he replied with a smile, "I shall fight at the side of the king."

When the Spartans forced an enemy to retreat they pushed him only until they were completely assured of their victory; then they halted, for they considered it ignoble and unworthy of a Greek people to annihilate men who had given up their fight and ceased to resist.

This treatment of their enemies was not only noble and magnanimous, but politically sound as well: being aware that the Spartans destroyed only those who resisted them, and spared the rest, their enemies found it more advantageous to flee than to hold their position and perish.

Archilochus on War and Generals.

Archilochus of Paros occupies a leading position in the lyric poetry of the seventh century B.C., which expressed the individualism of the times. He is to lyric poetry what Homer is to epic poetry. The character of Archilochus' poetry was determined by his personal experiences, which were varied and painful. In search of a better life and fortune, he left his native island of Paros and came with other colonists to Thasos, but found no happiness there. It appears that Archilochus fought with other citizens of Thasos in the conquest of the coast of Thrace and that he also served as a mercenary and died in battle. His pragmatic approach to war and his comments on generals given here are quite remarkable and express a new spirit in the attitude of the Greeks towards war. The first poem was preserved in Plutarch (*Spartan Institutions*) and the second in Dio Chrysostom (*Orations*, 2.456).

1.

Today my shield belongs to some proud Seian;
for, despite my good intentions,
I dropped it by a convenient bush
as I fled the battlefield.
But my life was spared:
why should I care for an old shield?
I can get another that's just as good
when again I take the field!

2.

I have no love for big, pompous generals,
nor those who take pride in their hair
or shave their upper lips.
I prefer a small one with bowed legs,
firmly set on his feet, and full of heart.

The Death of the Brave—Epitaph of Tettichus: Kaibel, *Epigrammata Graeca*, 1.

This Attic inscription of the sixth century B.C., one of the earliest epitaphs known to us from ancient Greece, is characteristically simple and restrained in its praise of a young man of Athens who died in war.

Whether you are a man from the city
or a stranger from another land,
have pity for Tettichus,
a brave man, as you go by.
He died in war, his youthful vigor extinguished.
Mourn him, then, and go on to great deeds.

On a Dead Soldier: Anacreon, *Anthologia Palatina*, VII. 160.

This epigram is usually attributed to Anacreon (563–478 B.C.), a native of Teos in Ionia. Some believe it was written as an epitaph for a certain Timocritus who, like Anacreon, was forced to flee from Teos when it was captured by the Persians (544 B.C.) and who died heroically in a battle against the Thracians.

> This is the tomb of Timocritus,
> a man brave in battle;
> for Ares spares the coward,
> not the brave.

The Battle of Marathon: Herodotus, *Histories*, VI. 105–107.

In the last years of the sixth century B.C. the Persians seized
Greek cities in Ionia and, under Darius I, invaded Thrace and
Scythia. Alarmed by the power and proximity of the Persians,
Athens and Eretria subsidized a revolt of the Ionian cities. The
effort was unsuccessful, however, and the Persians retaliated by
sending a punitive expedition against the Athenians and Eretrians
in 490 B.C. After capturing and burning Eretria, they landed at
Marathon on the coast of Attica. The site may have been chosen by
Hippias, the deposed Athenian tyrant who had fled to Persia and
offered to rule Attica for Darius in the event of a Persian victory.
His argument that fighting on the plain of Marathon would work
to the advantage of the Persians proved false, for the tiny Greek
force composed of Athenians and Plataeans routed the Persians in
a victory which astonished the Greek world and allowed the new
democracy at Athens to take root.

First, while they were still in the city, the generals sent a messenger to
Sparta. He was an Athenian named Phidippides who had trained as a long
distance runner. This man later announced to the Athenians that he had come
across Pan as he was running near Mount Parthenium above Tegea. Pan, he
said, had called him by name and had wanted him to say to the people of
Athens, "Why don't you care for me, for I am kindly disposed toward you,
have often helped you in the past, and will be helpful to you in the future?"
The Athenians believed this story and later, when their affairs had once again
been set in order, they built a temple for Pan below the Acropolis and
established annual sacrifices and torch-races.

It was on the day after he had been sent by the generals and on which
Pan had appeared to him that Phidippides arrived at Sparta. He went before
the magistrates of the city and said, "O Lacedaemonians, the Athenians
urge you to come to their aid and so prevent one of the most ancient cities
of Greece from being enslaved by barbarians. Greece has already been
weakened by the loss of an important city, for even as I speak Eretria has
been reduced to slavery." This is how Phidippides delivered the message
which had been entrusted to him. The Lacedaemonians decided to help the
Athenians but, since they did not want to violate their law, they would not
come to their aid right away. It was the ninth day of the month, and they
said they could not leave on the ninth when the lunar cycle had not been

completed.[1] And so the Lacedaemonians waited for the full moon. Meanwhile, Hippias the son of Pisistratus was leading the barbarians to Marathon. While asleep the previous night he had seen a vision in which he had intercourse with his own mother, and he had interpreted the dream as a sign that he would return to Athens, regain his power, and die in his own land as an old man. That is how he interpreted his dream. Then, as the Persians' guide, he took the captives taken at Eretria to an island known as Aeglea which belongs to the Styreans. He was also the one who guided the ships to Marathon, showed them where to drop anchor, and arranged the barbarians in proper order when they had disembarked. While he was engaged in these tasks he began to sneeze and cough much more violently than he usually did. Now Hippias was an old man and most of his teeth were loose, and so it happened that the intensity of his coughing blew one of his teeth out of his mouth and into the sand. He tried his best to find it but, since it didn't appear, he said regretfully to the men who were standing nearby, "This is not our land, and we will never be able to bring it under our control. My share of it is only that occupied by my tooth." Hippias considered this to be the fulfillment of his dream.

The Athenians were deployed in the order of battle in the precinct of Heracles when the Plataeans came to help them with their entire army. The Plataeans had previously placed themselves under the protection of the Athenians, who had already undertaken many tasks on their behalf. This is how the Plataeans had given themselves over to the Athenians: Once, when they were threatened by the Thebans, they had offered themselves to those who happened at that time to be in the area—Cleomenes, the son of Anaxandrides, and the Lacedaemonians. But the Lacedaemonians refused their offer and said, "We live far away from you, and the military support we could give you would not be of much use since you might be carried off into slavery many times before any of us heard about it. Our advice is that you offer yourselves to your neighbors, the Athenians, who are able to defend you adequately."

In giving this advice the Lacedaemonians were motivated more by a desire to cause trouble for the Athenians by pitting them against the Boeotians than by goodwill towards the Plataeans. Still, when they had heard the counsel of the Lacedaemonians the Plataeans did not hesitate, but came and sat around the altar as suppliants while the Athenians were sacrificing to the twelve Olympian gods, and so gave themselves over to them. When the Thebans heard of this they marched against the Plataeans and the Athenians responded by coming to the Plataeans' aid. But when the battle was about to begin the Corinthians, who chanced to be in that region, would not allow the two armies to fight. With the consent of both sides they brought about a reconciliation and established a boundary between the two states with the understanding that the Thebans would not interfere with those Boeotians

1   The reference here is to a celebration in honor of Apollo, during which an expedition of this sort would have been in violation of religious custom.

who did not want to be regarded as members of the Boeotian community. When they had settled this matter the Corinthians departed. The Athenians also set off for home, but while they were on their way they were attacked by the Boeotians, who were defeated in the ensuing battle. The Athenians then established a new border beyond the one which the Corinthians had made for the Plataeans, making the Asopus river itself the boundary between the territory of the Thebans and that of the Plataeans and the Hysians. These were the circumstances under which the Plataeans had come to be under the protection of the Athenians; and now they had come to help them at Marathon.

But the Athenian generals were split in their opinions. Some of them argued that they should not fight, for they thought that there were too few of them to take on an army as large as that of the Medes; others, including Miltiades, advised that they should fight. There was an eleventh man who was entitled to vote, and this was the polemarch [*i.e.*, war magistrate] whom the Athenians had chosen by lot (for according to an old Athenian custom the polemarch voted with the generals). The polemarch at that time was Callimachus of Aphidnae, and when the generals were divided and it looked as if the worse opinion would ultimately prevail, Miltiades went to this man and said, "Callimachus, it is up to you to decide either to enslave Athens or, by freeing her, to leave to all posterity a memorial greater even than that left by Harmodius and Aristogeiton [*i.e.*, the men who had killed Hipparchus, the son of Pisistratus]. Athens has never faced as great a danger as that which threatens her now. If the Athenians submit to the Medes their suffering is guaranteed, for they will be handed over to Hippias. But if the city survives this danger she may well become the foremost city in Greece. I will now explain to you how these things can occur and how it happens that the decision regarding them is yours to make. We ten generals have reached an impasse, for some of us wish to fight and some do not. I fear that if we do not fight a great quarrel among these factions within the city itself will so shake the will of the Athenians that they will lose their resolve and yield to the Medes. But if we go to battle before such decay sets in, and if the gods will only be fair with us, then we may well show ourselves to be the superior power in the fray. It is your decision. Everything depends upon you. If you side with me the land of our fathers will be free and your city will be the first city in Greece, but if you decide to join with those who so eagerly seek to prevent a battle, you will bring about the exact opposite of these good things."

By speaking these words Miltiades won Callimachus over to his side, and the polemarch's vote resulted in the decision to fight. After this the generals who had been in favor of fighting handed over to Miltiades the right to command the army on those days when it would normally have been theirs.[2] He accepted their offers of the command, but was unwilling to begin the battle until the day came when it was his turn to lead.

---

2   The command of the army was rotated among the generals on a daily basis.

When that day arrived the Athenians were drawn up for battle in the following order: Callimachus the polemarch led the right wing, for at that time the law of Athens prescribed that the right wing should be led by that magistrate. With him as the commander there, the remaining tribes lined up according to the numbers assigned to each tribe. Last of all came the Plataeans, who formed the left wing. Ever since the day of this battle it has been a tradition during the sacrifices offered at the quinquennial festival for the Athenian herald to pray for the welfare of the Plataeans as well as the Athenians. When the Athenians at Marathon were forming themselves into the order of battle they made their line the same length as that of the Medes. The center was only a few ranks in depth, and so it was the weakest part of the line, but the wings were strong because they were many ranks deep.

Then, as soon as the army was properly arrayed and the sacrificial victims had provided good omens, the Athenians launched their attack, charging the Persians at a run. The distance between the two armies was just about a mile. When the Persians saw them running they made ready to meet them, and yet it seemed to them that the Athenians had lost their minds and were bent on destroying themselves, for what they saw was only a few men running toward them who had no support from cavalry or archers. That is how it looked to the Persians at that moment. But when the Athenians clashed with the Persians they fought in a manner worth remembering, for to the best of my knowledge they were the first Greeks to charge the enemy at a run. They were also the first to stand fast at the sight of Median clothes and men clothed in that style. Up until that time merely hearing the name "Mede" had terrorized the Greeks.

The fighting at Marathon went on for a long time. The barbarians overwhelmed the center of the Greek line, against which the Persians themselves and the Sacae were positioned, and when they had broken through they pursued the Greeks inland. But the Athenian and Plataean wings were victorious. They put to flight the barbarians whom they had defeated and then, joining the two wings together, they fought and defeated the others who had burst through the center of their line. As the Persians fled the Greeks followed them, cutting them down until they reached the sea. Then they called for fire and seized the ships.

It was while he was engaged in this task that Callimachus the polemarch was killed after fighting bravely. Stesilaus son of Thrasylaus, one of the generals, also perished. Cynegirus the son of Euphorion had his hand cut off with an ax as he grabbed an ornament on the stern of an enemy ship, and so he died, as did many other noble Athenians.

The Athenians seized seven ships in this way. As for the Persians, they pushed off from shore in the remaining ships, and taking with them the Eretrian captives from the island where they had left them they sailed around Cape Sunium in the hope of capturing the city before the Athenians arrived. At Athens it was charged that this was a plot contrived by the Alcmaeonids, who were said to have made a pact with the Persians and held up a shield as a signal to them, when they were on board their ships, that the city was undefended.

And so the Persians sailed around Cape Sunium. But the Athenians rushed back as quickly as possible to defend the city and arrived there before the enemy. And just as at Marathon they had camped in a precinct of Heracles, now they camped in another precinct of Heracles at Cynosarges. The Persian fleet dropped anchor near Phalerum, which at that time was an Athenian naval station, but after they had been there for some time they sailed back to Asia.

Six thousand four hundred barbarians were killed at the battle of Marathon, and one hundred and ninety-two Athenians. These are the numbers of the slain on both sides. It also chanced that a wondrous thing happened during the battle. Epizelus the son of Cuphagoras, an Athenian, was fighting bravely in the thick of the battle when he lost his sight. This happened even though he had not been struck or shot, and he remained blind for the rest of his life. I heard that he gave this account of the incident: a huge foot-soldier came up against him whose beard was so large that it covered his entire shield; but this phantom passed by him and killed the man standing next to him. I understand that this is the story which Epizelus told.

On the Eretrian Exiles in Persia: Plato, *Anthologia Palatina*, VII. 256 and 257.

In 490 B.C. the Persians launched a campaign by sea against the Greek cities of Eretria and Athens. Eretria was taken by treachery, but the invaders met with defeat at Marathon. The surviving population of Eretria was deported en masse to Persia, where the Eretrians are said to have established a colony in which they clung fiercely to their own language and customs. Both of the following epigrams have been attributed to Plato, although one tradition holds that the first was seen on a tombstone at Ardericca, the site of the Eretrian settlement.

We who once left behind the loud-roaring swells
of the Aegean lie here in the midst of
Ecbatana's plain:
farewell famous Eretria, our lost fatherland;
farewell Athens, bordering on Euboea;
farewell beloved sea.

We are Eretrians of Euboea by birth,
but we lie here, near Susa—
alas! so far from our own country.

Xerxes and Demaratus: Herodotus, *Histories*, VII. 101–105.

In 480 B.C., ten years after their defeat at Marathon, the Persians again invaded Greece. This time they were led by Xerxes, their king, who had organized both land and sea expeditions. Herodotus tells us that the Persian host numbered in excess of 2,500,000 (not counting engineers, provisioners and slaves) and that whole rivers dried up when it slaked its thirst; added to these, he said, was a fleet of 1,207 triremes and transport ships. These exaggerated figures must be modified, perhaps to about 160,000 soldiers and cavalry and roughly 900 ships. Still, even the lowest estimates of its size describe a Persian force far superior to any that could have been mustered even by a united Greece.

Eager to learn more about his enemy, Xerxes called upon Demaratus, a deposed Spartan king (reigned 510–491 B.C.), to answer his questions. Demaratus' response, which appears below, was a warning that the fiercely independent Greeks, and especially the Spartans, would not easily surrender their freedom.

After Xerxes had sailed past the fleet and disembarked he called for Demaratus the son of Ariston, who was accompanying him on his march against Greece, and questioned him as follows: "Demaratus, I would like to ask you about some things I wish to know. You are a Greek and, as I have learned from you and the other Greeks with whom I speak, a citizen of not the smallest or weakest city in Greece. So tell me, will the Greeks stand firm and raise a hand against me? It seems to me that even if all the Greeks and all the others who dwell in the West were gathered together in a single army they still would not be able to resist my attack, for there is no real unity among them. But I would like to hear what you have to say about them."

To this question Demaratus replied: "O King, do you desire the truth, or do you want to hear an answer that will please you?"

Xerxes urged him to speak the truth, and said that by doing so he would not fall out of favor.

When Demaratus heard this he spoke as follows: "O King, since you ask me to tell you the whole truth, and not what will one day prove to be untrue, here is my answer. In Greece poverty has always been a familiar companion to us, but courage is something we have had to win by wisdom and strict laws. It is by the constant exercise of courage that Greece defends herself from poverty and despotism. I speak in praise of all the Greeks who dwell in those regions which are Dorian, but what I will say now does not concern all of them, but only the Lacedaemonians. First, they will never accept any settlement from you which would mean the enslavement of Greece. Second, they will fight you even if the rest of the Greeks ally themselves with you. But do not ask about the number who will do as I have said; for it may be a thousand men who march out against you, or more, or less—but they will fight you regardless of their number.

When he heard this Xerxes laughed and said, "That is really quite a rash statement, Demaratus, that a thousand men would fight a powerful army like mine. You say you were once the king of these men. Come now, tell me: are you willing at this moment to fight ten men? For if the entire citizen body of your state is as you have described, you, as their king, and according to your laws, ought to be prepared to fight twice that number. For if each of the Greeks is able to take on ten soldiers from my army, then I can expect you to be a match for twenty. In this way you would demonstrate the truth of what you have said; but if the Greeks who make such great claims about themselves are similar in size and other qualities to you, Demaratus, and the other Greeks with whom I am familiar, then beware, lest what you have said turns out to have been nothing more than senseless boasting. Come now, let us look at this matter reasonably: how could a thousand men or ten thousand, or even fifty thousand, if each one is as free as the next and they are not under the command of a single ruler, resist an army as powerful as mine? Even if the Greeks should have five thousand men we would still have a thousand to every one of theirs. If, as is our custom, they were under the rule of one man, their fear of him might cause them to be extraordinarily brave, and under the lash they might be compelled to go against a more numerous enemy. But they would do neither of these if each man were left free to follow his own will. My opinion is that even if the Greeks had to fight only the Persians, and both sides were numerically equal, they would still have a hard time of it. It is we alone who have men of the caliber of which you speak, and yet even we do not have many, but only a few. For example, some of my Persian spearmen would be quite willing to fight three Greeks at once. But you are ignorant of this, and your talk is mere nonsense."

To this Demaratus answered, "O King, from the very beginning I knew that you would not be pleased by my speaking the truth. But since you required me to answer with complete honesty, I told you how things stand with the Spartans. You are surely very much aware of the kind of love I have for these men at the present time, men who robbed me of my honorable rank and the hereditary prerogatives of my family; an exile without a city, your father received me and gave me life and a home. Is it likely that a man of sound mind will reject the goodwill shown to him, and not be satisfied with it? As for myself, I do not promise that I can fight with ten men, or two; and given the choice I would not fight even with one. But if I were forced to do so, or if there were some great cause to urge me on, I would gladly fight with one of those men who say they are a worthy match for three Greeks. It is the same with the Lacedaemonians; when fighting singly they are as good as any man, and when they fight together they are the best warriors of all. They are free, but not completely free; for law is their master, and they fear it much more than your men fear you. They do whatever it commands, and it always commands the same thing: they must never flee from battle, no matter how many are their enemies; they are to hold their ground, and there they are required either to conquer or to die. If what I am saying seems foolish to you, then from this moment on I will keep silent. It is at your command that I have spoken. Let it be according to your will, O King!"

This being the answer of Demaratus, Xerxes displayed no anger, but only laughed and calmly sent him away. After this conversation, and after appointing Mascames the son of Megadostes lieutenant-governor of Doriscus, thereby deposing the man placed in that office by Darius, Xerxes set out with his army through Thrace and down upon Greece.

The Athenians Abandon Their City—The Themistocles Decree: Meiggs and Lewis, *A Selection of Greek Historical Inscriptions*, no. 23.

Themistocles' order for the evacuation of Athens before the battle of Salamis has survived by an odd chance in an interesting and controversial document known as the Themistocles Decree. Its discovery occurred only recently and its authenticity is still a matter of dispute among scholars. In 1932 a Greek peasant found a stone step for his garden in an abandoned graveyard, but since the stone bore an inscription it was eventually taken to the one-room Museum of Troezen. There it was seen in 1958 by a visiting American classicist, Professor Jameson of the University of Pennsylvania, who read it and recognized its significance. The inscription, which is dated in the third century B.C., may well record what actually happened in Athens as the Persians moved towards the city, or it may be a late reconstruction based on literary sources, as some scholars claim.

The Gods,

Resolved by the Boule and the People on the proposal of Themistocles the son of Neocles of the deme Phrearrhioi: to entrust the city to the Guardian of Athens, Athena, and to all the other gods to protect it and defend it against the barbarian.

All Athenians and the resident aliens of Athens shall remove their families to Troezen. . . . The older people and the movable possessions shall be transported to Salamis for safekeeping.

The treasures and the priests shall remain on the Acropolis to protect the property of the gods. All other Athenians and aliens who are of military age shall embark on the two hundred ships that lie ready for service, to repel the barbarian in defense of their freedom and the freedom of the other Greeks, in common cause with the Spartans, the Corinthians, the Aeginetans and all the rest who desire to share the danger. Beginning tomorrow, the generals shall appoint from among those who have legitimate children and own land and homes in Athens two hundred trierarchs, one for each ship. To these men, who may not be older than fifty, the ships will be assigned by lot. The generals shall also assign ten marines to each ship, men between twenty and thirty years of age, and four archers. They shall also assign by lot the petty officers for each ship when they allot the trierarchs. Moreover, the generals shall make a list of the rest of the crew, ship by ship, on whiteboards, drawing the names of the Athenians from the lexiarchic records and those of the aliens from the registers of the polemarch. They shall list them, after dividing them into two hundred units, each containing one hundred men, and they shall record for each division the name of the ship and the names of the trierarch and the petty officers, so that they will know which ship each unit shall board. When all the divisions have been assigned and allotted to the ships, the Boule and the generals shall proceed to man all of the two hundred ships after performing sacrifices to appease Zeus the Almighty and Athena and Victory and Poseidon the Securer.

When the manning of the ships is completed, they shall dispatch one hundred of them to Artemisium in Euboea, while the remaining one hundred shall be kept around Salamis and the rest of Attica for the protection of the country. In order to ensure that all Athenians may be united in warding off the barbarian, those who have been ostracized for ten years shall go to Salamis and stay there until the People reach a decision about them. . . .

The Speech of Archidamus: Thucydides, *History of the Peloponnesian War*, 79–85.

In 432 B.C. the Spartans, at the insistence of some of their Peloponnesian allies, met with them to consider what action they should
take to protect themselves against an increasingly powerful and
aggressive Athens. In the previous year the Athenians had intervened
in a dispute between Corinth and its colony Corcyra, coming away
from the conflict with the latter as a new and powerful ally. For this
and other reasons the Corinthians called for war, arguing that Athenian imperialism demanded decisive action on the part of those it
threatened. They were supported by the Megarians, who had been
subjected to severe economic hardship when the Athenians issued the
Megarian Decree (432), which prohibited them from trading with
cities belonging to the Athenian empire. An Athenian embassy which
happened to be in Lacedaemon at the time addressed the Spartan
assembly, warning it to use caution in making its decision. It was then
that Archidamus, a Spartan king, delivered the speech which appears
below. He advised delay, but the majority of the Spartans favored
immediate action. The Peloponnesian War broke out in 431.

When the Lacedaemonians had heard the complaints of their allies
against the Athenians and the Athenian response they ordered everyone to
depart and discussed the issue among themselves. Most were of the opinion
that the Athenians were in the wrong and that war should be declared upon
them immediately. But Archidamus, their king, a man who was considered
to be both intelligent and prudent, stepped forward and addressed them as
follows:

"Lacedaemonians! I have been through many wars in my lifetime, and I
see some among you who are just as old as I am who will not yearn for war
as do many who have no experience of its severity or who think it is a good
or safe course of action. Anyone who prudently reflects on the matter will
conclude that the war which you are now considering would not be a minor
one. When we come into conflict with our Peloponnesian neighbors our kind
of military strength is much the same as theirs, and we can quickly march
upon each and every one of them. But a war against men whose land is far
away, who have extensive experience on the sea and are well prepared in
every other way—in private and public wealth, ships, horses, heavily armed
foot soldiers, a population larger than any other region of Greece, and, finally,
numerous allies who pay them tribute—how can it be right for us to throw
ourselves into such a war carelessly and ill-prepared? In what do we place

our trust? In our navy? There we are inferior, and it would take time to drill and prepare ourselves sufficiently. In our money? There our shortcoming is greater still, for we have nothing in the way of public funds, and no one is willing to contribute any of his own.

There may be some among you who are heartened by our superior equipment and manpower, which will make it possible for us regularly to go and devastate their land. But the Athenians rule many territories besides their own and they can import whatever they need by sea. We could try to incite rebellions among their allies, but the rebels would require the assistance of our fleet since most of them are island-dwellers. How, then, shall we wage our war? Unless we either defeat their navy or rob them of the revenues which sustain it, we will suffer greatly. Moreover, once we have gone this far we will not be able to make an honorable end to the conflict, especially if it is thought that we were responsible for starting it. We must not allow ourselves to be carried away by the hope that a quick end can be made to the war by the destruction of their country. No, I fear that we would then bequeath the quarrel to our children, for it is unlikely that the high-spirited Athenians will ever compromise their freedom to spare their land, or that they will be terror-stricken in war like untried soldiers.

I am not urging you to be so insensitive as to turn a blind eye to the injuries they inflict on our allies or to cease exposing their schemes. But do not take up your weapons just yet. Let us first go and lodge our protests with them, without giving any indication of whether or not we plan to fight, and in the meantime we can better prepare ourselves. We may seek to augment our forces with either Greek or barbarian allies, it makes no difference which, provided that they are able to help us with ships and money (for no one can blame us, objects of Athenian conspiracies that we are, if in the interest of self-defense we do not distinguish between Greeks and barbarians). And, at the same time, we must also provide for ourselves out of our own resources. If they listen to our ambassadors, that would be best; but, if they do not, it would seem that after two or three years have passed we will be better fortified against them and in a better position to attack them if we wish. When they see that we are making preparations for war, and that we intend to back up our words with action, perhaps then, while their land is still unravaged and their possessions are not yet destroyed, they will more carefully consider their position. You must not think of their land in any way other than as your hostage, one whose value increases in proportion to the extent that it is better cultivated. You should spare it for as long as possible, and not bring them to such a state of despair that they become more stubborn and unruly. For if the complaints of our allies cause us to destroy the land before we are sufficiently prepared, then we will have to be careful lest we bring shame and great difficulties upon the Peloponnese. When cities or private citizens bring charges against each other it is possible to arrange a satisfactory disposition; but when a confederacy, in order to protect its own interests, enters into a war whose course cannot be predicted it is not easy to bring about an honorable settlement.

Let no one consider it unmanly for so many to hesitate before they attack only one. For the Athenians have no fewer tributary allies than we do, and war is less a matter of weapons than it is a matter of money, which makes it possible to use weapons and which is of paramount importance when a land power goes to war against a sea power. Let us first raise the necessary funds, and not permit ourselves to be roused by the words of our allies until then. Since we will be held largely responsible for the outcome of the war, whether good or bad, we ought calmly to consider the possibilities beforehand.

Do not be ashamed of that for which they most criticize us—the slow and deliberate way in which we act. For if we begin the war too hastily our lack of preparation will serve only to delay its conclusion. Keep in mind that we have always lived in a free and most glorious city, and that this has been made possible because of our moderation and prudence, qualities for which we are criticized. It is because of these that we alone do not become arrogant when things go well for us, or yield in times of misfortune. We are not carried away by the sound of compliments into dangerous situations of which our judgment does not persuade us to approve; accusations do not provoke us, nor can we be persuaded to adopt another's position when we are annoyed. It is our habits of order and discipline which make us both courageous and wise. We are courageous because the greater part of self-control is that sense of shame which is akin to modesty, and such shame gives rise to courage; we are wise because we are not so well-educated that we look down on the laws, and because we are too harshly trained in self-discipline to disobey them. We are not brought up to be adept at acquiring that knowledge of useless matters which makes a man able to do well in finding fault with an enemy's war preparations in theory, but unable to move against him with equal efficiency in reality. No, we expect that the mental acumen of our enemies is similar to our own, and that there is no rational way to eliminate the element of chance. In practice we always go about preparing ourselves with the expectation that the plans of the enemy have been formulated with the benefit of wise counsel. We should not place our trust in the possibility that he will make mistakes, but in the provisions we have made for our security. We should not think that there is any real difference between one man and another, but that the better one is he who is trained in the most rigorous manner.

These are the practices which our fathers handed down to us. We have always benefited by following them, and so we should not abandon them now. Nor must we allow ourselves to be rushed into making a decision in the short space of a single day when the issue involves many lives, much money, many cities, and honor. The decision must be made calmly and unhurriedly. It is our strength which makes this more possible for us than it is for others. And now, send an embassy to the Athenians to speak to them about the matter of Potidaea, and also about the other injustices of which the allies have spoken, especially since they are ready to come to a just settlement, and because the law forbids you to proceed against anyone who offers to submit to arbitration as you would against a criminal. In the meantime, prepare yourselves for war. Your decision to do these things will be the best possible one for you and the most damaging to your enemies.

On the Athenian Dead at Plataea:
Simonides of Ceos, *Anthologia Palatina*, VII.253.

Simonides of Ceos, who was born *ca.* 550 B.C. and died at the age of eighty-nine, is one of the most celebrated lyric poets of Greece, although only about one hundred lines of his work have survived. He is considered to be the undisputed master of the funeral epigram, as the following elegiac hymn to the Athenian dead at the Battle of Plataea in 479 B.C. clearly shows.

If to die nobly is the greatest part of virtue
then to us, of all men, Fortune has granted this fate;
for, hastening to assure the freedom of Greece,
we lie here enjoying ageless glory.

On the Spartan Dead at Plataea:
Simonides of Ceos, *Anthologia Palatina*, VII.251.

This is another classic example of the work of the great master of the funerary epigram, Simonides of Ceos, in honor of the Spartan dead at Plataea.

These men, having crowned their beloved country
with everlasting honor,
were shrouded in the dark cloud of death;
yet, though dead, they have not died,
for their virtue raises them in glory
high above the house of Hades!

The Athenians Honor Their Dead at Potidaea: Kaibel, *Epigrammata Graeca*, 21.

The city of Potidaea on the coast of Macedonia was a Corinthian colony which had originally joined the Delian League but later revolted after its tribute was raised. The Athenians attacked and occupied the city in 430 B.C., but not without casualties. The Athenian soldiers who died before the gates of Potidaea are praised by their compatriots in this moving epigram.

This city and the people of Erechtheus
mourn those sons of the Athenians
who died in the frontlines at Potidaea,
trading their lives for virtue
and bringing glory to their country.

The Theban Sacred Band:
Plutarch, *Pelopidas*, 18.

The Sacred Band was an elite corps of the Theban army formed by Gorgidas in 378 B.C. and used mostly as shock troops. It was largely responsible for the brief period of Theban hegemony in Greece following the battle of Leuctra in 371 B.C. On that occasion it fought under the command of Pelopidas and on the left wing of the army of Epaminondas, which defeated the Spartans and killed their king, Cleombrotus. The Sacred Band had the distinction of never losing a battle until Philip of Macedon demolished the combined armies of Thebes and Athens at Chaeronea in 338 B.C.

According to some authorities, Gorgidas first formed the Sacred Band out of three hundred picked men who were encamped on the citadel and were provided by the city with everything necessary for their maintenance and exercise. They were called the city band, for citadels were once known as cities. Others, however, claim that the band was made up of young men attached to each other by bonds of love, and a witty saying of Pammenes is recorded, that Nestor in Homer was not displaying a great tactical skill when he suggested that the Greeks should rank tribe with tribe and clan with clan "so that tribe may aid tribe, and clan aid clan"—he should have suggested that lovers be ranked with their beloved. This is because kinsmen and members of the same tribe do not care much for each other in times of danger, while a unit of men united by the friendship of lovers is unbreakable and invincible, since a lover is ashamed to display cowardice in front of his beloved and, as a consequence, both face danger willingly in order to protect one another. This is not surprising in view of the fact that they have more regard for the opinions of their absent lovers than for those who are present. This is revealed in the case of a man who, when he was about to be killed, earnestly begged his adversary to cut him through the breast, so that his lover might not be embarrassed by seeing him wounded in the back. Likewise, Iolaus, the man who fought at the side of Hercules and assisted him in his labors, was his lover, according to tradition; in fact, Aristotle has recorded that even in his own time lovers gave pledges of their faith on the tomb of Iolaus. This may well be the reason that this band was called sacred, for Plato calls a lover a divine friend. It is also said that the Sacred Band was never beaten before the battle of Chaeronea and that, after the battle, when Philip examined the corpses of the slain and halted at the place where the three hundred who had fought his phalanx lay, all mingled together, dead, he was astonished, and on realizing that this was the Band of lovers, he shed tears and uttered: "Destroy anyone who suspects these men of doing or suffering anything ignoble."

An Inscription on a Statue of Epaminondas: Pausanias, *Description of Greece*, 9.15.5.

This famous inscription on the statue of Epaminondas has been preserved in the work of Pausanias, a second century A.D. traveler and writer of guidebooks. It records the most important achievements of Epaminondas, the founder of Theban hegemony in Greece, namely his military triumph over Sparta, his creation of an independent Messenia and a free Arcadia, and his emancipation of the Greeks from Spartan oppression.

Because of my counsel Sparta has been shorn of glory,
holy Messene receives her children after many years,
Megalopolis has been crowned with the weapons of Thebes
and all of Greece governs itself in freedom!

Greek Professional Soldiers—The Army of Cyrus II: Xenophon, *Anabasis*, 1.3.14–18.

In the year 401 B.C. the Persian prince Cyrus II conspired to overthrow his brother, King Artaxerxes II, and enlisted Greek mercenary soldiers to fight for him. Xenophon the Athenian, who was a participant in this operation, wrote the *Anabasis* in which he tells us the story of the march of the ten thousand Greek soldiers of Cyrus from Sardis to Babylon and their return to the Black Sea. It was in the early days of this campaign, when the army had camped at Tyriaeum, that Queen Epyaxa, wife of King Syennesis of Cilicia, asked the Persian prince to display his soldiers for her. The following excerpt clearly illustrates the martial spirit and smartness of ancient Greek soldiers.

The Queen of Cilicia is said to have asked Cyrus to show her his army. To satisfy her request he staged on the plain a review both of his Greek and Asian troops. The Greeks were ordered to march in their regular battle array with each of their commanders marshalling his own men. They paraded in units four men deep, Meno and his regiment being on the right wing, Clearchus with his on the left, while the other commanders were placed in the center.

Cyrus began with a review of the Asian soldiers who marched past in columns of cavalry and squadrons of foot soldiers and then proceeded to the inspection of the Greeks, driving by in an open carriage while the Queen drove in a closed one. All the troops paraded in helmets of bronze, wearing purple tunics, and with their shields uncovered. After driving along the entire length of the line, he halted his carriage in front of its center and dispatched his interpreter Pigres to the commanders of the Greeks with orders to present arms and advance along the entire front. The commanders conveyed the orders to their men who, with the sound of the trumpet, presented arms and advanced. But as their pace accelerated and they began to cheer the troops broke into a march at double time toward the camp, a sight which caused such a panic among the Asians that the Queen fled in her carriage. Even the sutlers ran away, leaving their wares behind. By the time they arrived at the camp the Greeks were unable to control their laughter.

The smartness and the discipline of the troops amazed the Queen, while the fear which the Greeks had inspired in the Asians delighted Cyrus.

Alexander at Opis: Arrian, *Anabasis*, VII. 8–12.

In 324 B.C., when nearly all of his conquests had been completed, Alexander arrived at the city of Opis on the Tigris river. There he held an assembly of his Macedonian soldiers and announced that he was discharging those who had been wounded or were too old to fight and would give each of them a large bonus. He had expected his troops to be impressed by his generosity, but was shocked when they angrily called upon him to discharge them all. The rift between the great conqueror and his men had been brought about by a number of factors. His adoption of Persian customs and dress, his public declaration of his own divinity, his increasingly Oriental view of kingship and his favorable treatment of Persians—these had convinced the Macedonians that their king had succumbed to the very people he had conquered and that he no longer had any use for them. Their conduct at Opis verged on mutiny, but in the space of a few days they were reconciled with Alexander. The dramatic account of these events by Arrian, an historian of the second century A.D., appears below.

When Alexander arrived at Opis he assembled the Macedonians and told them that those who were no longer fit for military service due to age or physical disability were to be released from the army and sent home. He also announced that he intended to give each of them a bonus big enough to make them the envy of their friends and to inspire in the other Macedonians a desire to take part themselves in such dangerous missions as they had undertaken. It is likely that he had hoped to win their gratitude, but by this time they had come to believe that Alexander held them in contempt and considered them absolutely worthless for fighting. Thus it was that they were disgusted by Alexander's speech and, as they saw it, with good reason; for throughout the campaign he had irritated them by adopting Persian dress, allowing the barbarian *Epigoni* to use Macedonian equipment and including foreign horsemen in the ranks of the Companions. Being unable to contain their anger and listen to the speech in silence, the soldiers shouted that all of them should be discharged from the army and jeered that he could continue the campaign with his father Ammon instead of them. Now Alexander had become rather temperamental, and he was no longer as open and fair with the Macedonians as he had been before because of the way he had been flattered and fawned on by the barbarians. Jumping down from the rostrum, he pointed his finger at the men most responsible for agitating the assembly and ordered the commanders who were with him to have them arrested. There were thirteen of them, and all were led away to be executed. The rest of the troops stood there in stunned silence as Alexander returned to the rostrum and addressed them as follows:

"Macedonians, my purpose in speaking to you is not to dissuade you from going home. You may go wherever you wish. I won't try to stop you. But if you do decide to go there is something I want you to understand before you leave—how much I have done for you, and how you have responded to my benevolence.

It is only right that I should begin with some mention of Philip, my father. When he became your king you were nothing but poor wanderers, most of you wearing only hides for clothing. You had a few sheep to herd in the hills, but you fought pitifully to protect even these from your neighbors, the Illyrians, Triballians and Thracians. But Philip gave you cloaks to wear instead of hides, and led you down from the hills to live on the plains. He was the one who taught you to fight worthily against the barbaric peoples surrounding your country so that you could rely on your bravery for protection instead of the fortification with which nature provided your villages. It was Philip who taught you how to live in cities and who established good laws and customs. You had been dominated by foreign tribes who plundered your possessions and made you their slaves and subjects, but under Philip you became the masters of those same tribes. He annexed most of Thrace to Macedonia, captured the most strategically located seaports in order to open up the kingdom to trade, and made it possible for you to work in your mines without fear of being attacked. In former times you had been terrified by the Thessalians, but he made you their rulers. By humbling the people of Phocis he made the impassably narrow passage into Greece a wide road easy for you to travel. The Athenians and Thebans had long awaited an opportunity to march against Macedonia, but Philip and I (for by this time I was old enough to fight by his side) struck them down so low that, instead of our paying tribute to Athens as we had before, and obeying the commands of the Thebans, those two cities had to depend on *us* for their security. He also marched down into the Peloponnese to set the affairs of that region in order. And then, when he had announced himself as supreme commander of all the other Greeks for the upcoming campaign against Persia, instead of claiming the glory for himself he declared that it belonged to the whole of Macedonia.

These things which my father did for you are truly impressive when seen on the basis of their own merits, but they are nothing compared to what I have done. Philip left me a few gold and silver drinking cups, less than sixty talents in the treasury, and debts amounting to five hundred talents. But I, after borrowing another eight hundred, launched my campaign from a land that could barely produce enough food for its inhabitants and immediately, despite the fact that the Persians ruled the sea, opened up the Hellespont for your use. Then, as my cavalry vanquished Darius' satraps, I enlarged your empire by the annexation of Ionia, Aeolia, Phrygia and Lydia. I captured Miletus by siege, but all other cities surrendered to me, and I gave them to you to exploit. I took Egypt and Cyrene without a struggle, and now the riches of those countries belong to you. Coele-Syria, Palestine and Mesopotamia are yours. So, too, are Babylon, Bactria and Susa. The treasures of the Lydians and the Persians belong to you, and also the wealth of India and the land beyond the sea. Some of you are satraps, others generals, and still others commanders. What have I kept for myself besides the purple robe and this crown I wear? Nothing. No one can point to any possessions which I have piled up for myself—there are only the treasures which belong to you and the things which I am keeping safe for you. Indeed, why should I keep any of these for myself, since it is my habit to eat the same food and get the same amount of sleep as you do? But then, I suppose I do not eat as well as those of you who live softly, and I know that I get up early, while you are still asleep.

Perhaps you will say that in acquiring these new possessions I did not share in your hard work and troubles. But is there any man here who really thinks he has suffered more for me than I have for him? Come then, if you have been wounded remove your clothes and show your wounds, and I will do the same. Every part of my body—except my back—is scarred, and there is no weapon, whether held in the hand or thrown, that has not left its mark on my flesh. I have been cut by daggers, pierced by arrows, and struck by missiles hurled by engines of war. Time and again I was pounded by stones and cudgels. All my suffering was for your sake, to bring you glory and wealth. I led you through every land and sea, across every river, mountain and plain—and always you were victorious. I married just as you did, and many of you will have children related to my own. When you had debts I paid them for you, never asking how you had incurred them when you were paid so well and had plundered so many cities after sieges. I also gave wreaths of gold to most of you as undying memorials to your courage and tokens of my respect. As for those who have fallen in battle, they died nobly and were given magnificent funerals. The memory of most of them is kept alive back in Macedonia by statues of bronze, and their parents are not only honored, but are no longer required to perform public services or pay taxes. These men and their parents are held in high regard because not one of my soldiers has ever been killed while fleeing from the enemy.

It had been my intention to send those of you who are no longer capable of fighting back to your homes to enjoy the admiration of everyone there. But it appears that all of you want to leave. Go then, all of you! And when you get home tell the Macedonians that your King, Alexander, conqueror of the Persians, Medes, Bactrians and Sacae; victor over the Uxians, Arachosians and Drangae; ruler of Parthia, Chorasmia and Hyrcania to the very shore of the Caspian Sea; the man who traveled the Caucasus on the far side of the Caspian Gates, and who crossed the Oxus and Tanais rivers as well as the Indus, of which no one but Dionysus has seen the far side; who also crossed the rivers Hydaspes, Acesines and Hydraotes, and would also have gone across the Hyphasis if you had not been too frightened to follow; who burst into the great sea [*i.e.*, the Indian Ocean] by both mouths of the Indus river and crossed the Gedrosian desert, where no one had ever taken an army before; who seized Carmania because it happened to be in his path, and the land of the Oreitans too; the man whom you brought back to Susa while his expeditionary fleet was sailing along the coast from India to the Persian Sea—tell the Macedonians that you abandoned this man, leaving him to be guarded by the conquered barbarians. I'm sure that your announcement will win you fame among gods and men. Now go!"

When he had said these things Alexander angrily jumped down from the rostrum and went into the palace. Once there he gave no thought to the needs of his body, and for the rest of that day and throughout the next he remained in seclusion, hidden even from the Companions. On the third day he called a number of outstanding Persians into the palace and made them the commanders of the various divisions of the army. It was also at this time that he refused permission to everyone except his relatives to give him the customary kiss.

Now, Alexander's speech had an immediate effect on the Macedonians, who remained standing dumbfounded before the rostrum after he had left. Indeed, no one had followed the King except his most intimate friends among the Companions and his personal bodyguard. There was nothing the rest of the assembled soldiers could do or say, but they remained there nonetheless. It was not until later, when they heard the news about the Persians and the Medes, that Persian officers had been given commands and that platoons of foreign troops were being enlisted in Macedonian units, that one Persian unit had taken a Macedonian name and that others, composed of Persians and other foreigners, were calling themselves "Infantry Companions," and that there was a unit of Persian "Silver Shields" and another of "Cavalry Companions" which included a royal squadron—when they heard about these they lost their self-control and ran to the palace, throwing down their weapons before its doors in submission to the King and begging to be let inside. They said that they wanted to hand over the men who had caused the trouble and begun the outcry, and that they would stay by the palace doors until Alexander took pity on them.

As soon as he heard of this Alexander went out to them, and when he had seen how ashamed they were and heard them weeping and wailing he, too, broke down in tears. Then, as they continued to beg him for mercy, he prepared to address them; but Callines, an officer of the Cavalry of the Companions distinguished by rank and his many years of service, spoke first: "O King, we Macedonians are distressed because you have accepted some of the Persians as family, and because Persians are called 'kinsmen of Alexander' and are allowed to kiss you while Macedonians are refused this honor." At this point Alexander interrupted: "But I consider all of you my kinsmen, and from now on that is what I shall call you."

When he had said this, Callines went to him and kissed him, and all of the others who wished to do so also kissed him. Then they picked up their weapons and returned to their camp, shouting and singing. As for Alexander, out of gratitude for this happy event he sacrificed to all the gods whom it was his custom to honor. He also gave a public feast at which he sat among the Macedonians and, next to these, the Persians. Beside the Persians sat other foreigners who had earned this privilege on the basis of rank or virtue. As the Greek seers and the Magi were performing the rites which opened the ceremony, Alexander and those around him drank from the same cup and poured the same libations. And he prayed for many blessings, the most important of these being concord and fellowship among the Macedonians and Persians in the empire he had created. It is said that nine thousand men attended the feast, and that all of them poured out this same libation and joined in singing the same triumphal hymn.

When all this had taken place the Macedonians who were no longer able to campaign because of advanced age or injury left for home. There were about ten thousand of them. Each was given the regular wages he had earned, an additional amount to cover the expense of the homeward journey and a bonus of one talent. Those who had children by Asian wives were asked to leave them behind so that there would be no conflict between foreign women and children and those back in Macedonia. Alexander said he would take care of these children and bring them up as Macedonians. He promised that the boys would receive military training and that he himself would bring them to Macedonia and hand them over to their fathers when they had grown up. These promises that he made were rather vague, but he demonstrated the sincerity of his friendship and fondness for them by appointing Craterus, his most trusted associate and a man whose life he valued as much as his own, to be their leader and guardian on their journey. And then, with tears in his eyes and theirs as well, he bade them farewell and sent them home.

The Song of Hybrias the Cretan:
Athenaeus, *Deipnosophists*, 15.695.

This intriguing martial song may have been composed as early as the sixth century B.C.; in its present form, however, it dates back to the third, or perhaps the second century B.C. The Byzantine lexicographer Hesychios considered it to be a Cretan marching song; others suppose its author was a successful soldier of fortune and associate the song with the way of life of the well-known mercenaries of Crete. But it may well be that Hybrias was simply a member of the ruling Doric oligarchy of Crete, whose exploitation of the labor of the Cretan serfs is reflected in this song.

My great wealth is my spear and sword,
and the fine shield that guards my body.
With them I plow, with them I reap,
with them I tread the sweet wine from the vine.
Because of them I am called lord of the serfs.
But those who, for their defense, dare not wield
the spear and the sword and the fine shield,
all cower and kiss my knee,
proclaiming me master and great king.

An Athenian Woman—Victim of War:
Erycius, *Anthologia Palatina*, VII, 368.

Erycius of Cyzicus was a poet who lived in the first century B.C.
This epigram is dedicated to a woman who had been captured and
carried off to Rome by Sulla after the sack of her native Athens in 86
B.C. She finally settled in Cyzicus, where she died.

I am a woman of Athens,
that is my city.
But long ago the Italian Ares
carried me away from my country
and made me a citizen of Rome.
Now I am dead, and Cyzicus,
a city surrounded by the sea,
wraps around my bones.
Farewell, land that nourished me,
you that held me afterwards,
and you that finally received me
in your bosom.

War Between City-States—The Oath of Dreros: *Inscriptiones Creticae*, I, ix, 1.

The endemic wars that plagued the ancient Greek city-states in antiquity were nowhere more intense than on the Doric island of Crete with its hundred cities, large population and limited resources. In spite of the establishment of a loose federation of city-states in the Hellenistic Age known as the "Cretan *Koinon*," the islanders continued their endless rivalries until the Romans conquered and pacified Crete in 67 B.C. Dreros was a small city-state in central Crete which had to contend with Lyttus, one of the most powerful of the Cretan states. For its protection Dreros allied itself with Cnossus in 260 B.C. The alliance was still in force in the early years of the second century B.C., when the oath of the Drerian youth was administered. Loyalty oaths were common throughout the Greek world, but that of Dreros expressed in a singular way the bitterness of inter-city conflicts in ancient Greece.

God. Fortune. With Good Fortune.

At the time when Lydilas, Cephalus, Pylus, Hippias and Bision of the Aithaleis tribe held the office of Kosmoi, and Philippus was secretary, this was the oath sworn by one hundred and eighty young men upon entering the ranks of adults: I swear by the hearth kept in the Prytaneum, by Zeus Agoraeus, by Zeus Tallaeus, by Apollo Delphinius, by Athena Poliouchos, by Pythian Apollo, by Lato, by Artemis, by Ares, by Aphrodite, by Hermes, by the Sun, by Britomartis, by Phoenix, by Amphiona, by the Earth, by Heaven, by the heroes and heroines, by the springs and the rivers, and by all the gods, male and female, that I will never be well-disposed towards the Lyttians in any way whatsoever, neither by day nor by night. I will strive to the best of my ability to do all manner of harm to the city of the Lyttians, without being restricted by any oaths taken in courts of law or other transactions. And I will not betray the city of the Drerians or their fortifications nor those of the Cnossians; I will not betray the Drerians and the Cnossians to the enemy, nor will I start a factional strife. I will be against those who do so. I will not form a conspiracy inside or outside the city, and will not be a part of the conspiracy of others. If I hear that someone is conspiring I will expose him to the majority of the Kosmoi. If I do not honor these commitments, may all the gods and goddesses who hear my oath turn against me, and may I face the worst of ruins, myself and all my belongings, and may the earth not bear crops for me, nor women and flocks give birth in a natural way. But, if I observe my oath, may the gods to whom I swear it be propitious and bestow many blessings on me.

V
Women in Greece

Women in Sparta: Plutarch, *Lycurgus*, 14–15.

The Spartans, always proud of the antiquity and severity of their political and social institutions, attributed most of these to a lawgiver named Lycurgus. Most Greeks believed he was an actual historical figure who had been inspired by the oracle at Delphi and influenced by the laws of Minos. However, modern historians believe he was only a legendary personality since many of the institutions said to have been established by him did not evolve until the sixth century B.C.— much later than the time when he was supposed to have lived.

Leaving aside the question of their origin, the government and social customs of Sparta were intended to maintain Spartan supremacy over the serfs or *helots* who vastly outnumbered the citizens. Thus, Sparta was a state in which all citizens subordinated their own interests to military preparedness. The rigorous training of men and boys is well-known, but the contribution of women to the welfare of the state was just as significant and earned them much greater respect than that enjoyed by their counterparts in other Greek cities. Such practices as eugenics, the sharing of wives and strenuous physical conditioning, described below in an excerpt from Plutarch's *Lycurgus*, will seem strange by our standards, but the Spartans appear to have been content with the system which they believed had made their city the most powerful in Greece.

With regard to education, which he considered to be the greatest and most noble work of a lawgiver, he began at the very beginning by carefully overseeing matters pertaining to marriages and births. For it is not true, as Aristotle says, that he sought to control the women but then gave up his efforts because he was unable to prevail against the great freedom and power which the women had gained due to the many military expeditions of their men. During the campaigns it was necessary for wives to be left alone with complete authority at home, and as a consequence their husbands held them in higher regard than was appropriate, even to the point of addressing them as "Mistress." Lycurgus gave his full attention even to women. He required the girls to exercise their bodies by running, wrestling and throwing the discus and javelin so that their children might have strong roots in strong bodies and better grow and blossom into adulthood and so that they might thus have the strength necessary to endure the pain of childbirth with dignity and ease. He took them away from delicacy and soft living by requiring the girls, along with the boys, to go naked in processions and at certain festivals to dance and sing when the young men were present and watching them. On such occasions the jokes they made at the expense of those youths who had misbehaved were a valuable incentive to good conduct. On the other hand, to those worthy of it they sang songs of praise, and in this way they filled the young men with a great love of honor and a desire to distinguish themselves. A youth who was praised by the maidens for his manly virtue went away elated and with an enhanced reputation because of their praises, but the sting of their playful mocking was just as sharp as that of serious criticisms, because the kings and elders, as well as all the other citizens, attended these events.

There was nothing shameful in this nakedness of the maidens, for it was accompanied by modesty rather than wantonness and produced in them the habits of a simple lifestyle and a zeal for physical health and strength. Instead of inclining women toward base things, it disposed them toward virtue and a love of honor. This is why they spoke and thought like Gorgo, the wife of Leonidas. According to the story, some foreign woman said to her: "You Laconian women are the only ones who rule men." Gorgo replied: "We are the only ones who give birth to men."

Further, these things also served as incentives to marriage. I am speaking here of the processions of the maidens, the stripping off of their clothes, and the athletic contests at which they were observed by the young men who, as Plato says, are influenced more by matters of love than by those of geometry. In addition, Lycurgus attached a certain disgrace to bachelorhood. Unmarried men were excluded from the festival of the Gymnopaedia, and in winter the magistrates ordered them to walk naked around the marketplace and, while walking, to sing a song written about them which stated that their suffering was justified because they had disobeyed the laws. They were also deprived of the honor and respectful attention otherwise paid by the young men to the elders. This is why no one could find anything blameworthy in what was said to Dercyllidas, even though he was a distinguished general. When he entered a social gathering one of the young men there refused to give him his seat, and said: "You have not fathered a son who will offer his seat to me."

Marriage among them was effected by forcibly carrying off the bride. They did not marry small or immature girls, but women who were ripe and in their prime. After the bride had been carried off the bridesmaid took her, cropped her hair close to her head, dressed her in a man's cloak and sandals, and placed her on a mattress, alone and in the dark. Then the bridegroom, not drunk with wine or weakened by revelry, but as sober as always, and after eating at the public dining hall, slipped into the room, removed her girdle, and carried her to the bed. After spending a little time with her he went away calmly and in a well-behaved fashion to sleep where he usually did—with the other young men. From that day on he continued in this way, spending the day with his comrades and sleeping with them at night, but cautiously going on secret visits to his wife, ashamed and fearful lest someone in the house should detect his presence. And his wife, for her part, plotted and conspired to find occasions when they might meet unobserved. This went on for a long time, so that some men even had children before ever seeing their own wives in the light of day. These meetings not only developed their self-control and temperance, but always brought them together when their bodies were full of productive energy and their passion new and fresh, not when their desire had been exhausted and forgotten as a result of unlimited love-making; and afterward there always remained in them a spark of yearning for each other.

After making marriage an honorable and dignified institution, he did away with the vain and womanish passion of jealousy by making it morally acceptable for them, while keeping the estate of marriage free of licentiousness and unworthy conduct, to share with other men of good character in the task of fathering children, and to ridicule those who would not participate in the sharing of wives and were prepared to resort to murder and fighting to protect their rights. It was lawful, for example, for an older man with a young wife, if he approved of some good and honorable young man, to acquaint them and adopt the offspring as his own.

It was also acceptable for a respectable man, if he admired a woman married to someone else for her fine children and moderate behavior, to persuade her husband to permit them to have intercourse; thus he planted his seed, as it were, in a fertile field, and produced healthy sons related by blood to men of noble stock.

Lycurgus did not consider sons to be the property of their fathers, but the property of the state, and for that reason he desired that citizens should not be born of chance, but out of the union of the best parents available. He also observed the great absurdity and vanity in the laws enacted by other peoples regarding these things. When breeding dogs and horses they will pay money or court the favor of the owners of the very best sires and studs in order to procure their services, and yet they lock up their wives and stand watch over them, thinking that they alone are worthy of having children by them, even though they may be foolish, or past their prime, or sickly. Such people behave as if the qualities of children, whether good or bad, are not determined by their parentage, and as if the parents are not the first to be affected by these qualities.

The marital practices of that time were established for the purposes of physical health and political well-being and were quite different from the sexual recklessness later imputed to the women—so much so, in fact, that among them adultery was entirely lacking. There is a story told about a certain Geradas, a Spartan of the very ancient kind, who was asked by a foreigner what punishment they inflicted upon the adulterers in their city. "Stranger," be answered, "we have no adulterers among us." The foreigner replied: "But what if there were one?" Geradas said: "He would have to pay as his penalty a bull so big that it could lean over Mount Taygetus and drink from the river Eurotas." Astonished, the foreigner asked: "How could there be a bull so big?" Geradas laughed and said: "How could there be an adulterer in Sparta?" These are the things which are reported concerning marriage in Sparta.

Women and the Spartan Constitution:
Aristotle, *Politics*, 2.9.5–18.

The position of women in ancient Sparta constitutes one of the most interesting aspects of life in Greece, for it was in this militaristic state that women enjoyed more freedom than anywhere else in the Greek world. In contrast to Athens and the Ionian cities, where the seclusion of women was strictly observed, the women of Sparta were almost privileged; in fact, it seems that women enjoyed more rights in the warlike Doric city-states in general than in the more cultured and "enlightened" Ionian city-states which, in this respect, remind us of their Oriental neighbors. Aristotle, who is generally considered a misogynist, attempts to explain this paradox by pointing out that in a militaristic state where men are always fighting in foreign campaigns, women are given the opportunity to be more active members of the community and to assume men's responsibilities in their absence.

Again, the license of the Spartan women hinders the attainment of the aims of the constitution and the realization of the good of the people. For just as a husband and a wife are each a part of every family, so may the city be regarded as about equally divided between men and women; consequently, in all cities where the condition of women is bad, one half of the city must be viewed as not having proper legislation. And this is exactly what happened in Sparta. There, the lawgiver who had intended to make the entire population strong in character has accomplished his aims with regard to the men, but has neglected the women, who indulge in every kind of luxury and intemperance. A natural consequence of this lifestyle is that wealth is highly valued, particularly in societies where men come to be dominated by their wives, as is the case with many military and warlike peoples, if we except the Celts and a few other races which openly approve of male lovers. In fact, there seems to be some rational justification for the myth of the union of Ares with Aphrodite, since all military peoples are prone to sexual activities with either men or women. This was evident among the Spartans in the days of their supremacy, when much was managed by women. But what is the difference between women ruling, or rulers being ruled by women? The result is the same. Courage is a quality of little use in daily life but necessary in war, and yet even here the influence of the Spartan women has been negative. This was revealed during the Theban invasion of Laconia when the women of Sparta, instead of being of some use like women in other cities, caused more confusion than the enemy. It is not surprising, however, that the license of the women was characteristic of Spartan society from the earliest times, for the men of Sparta were away from home for long periods of time as they fought first against the Argives and then against the Arcadians and the Messenians. When they returned to a peaceful life, having grown accustomed to obedience by military discipline, which has its virtue, they were prepared to submit themselves to the legislation of Lycurgus. But when Lycurgus attempted to subject women to his laws they resisted and he gave up, as tradition says. These, then, are the causes of what happened and thus it is clear that the constitutional shortcoming under discussion must be assigned to them. Our task, however, is not to praise or blame, but to discover what is right or wrong, and the position of women in Sparta, as we have already noted, not only contravenes the spirit of the constitution but contributes greatly to the existing avarice. This problem of greed naturally invites an attack on the lack of equality among the Spartans with regard to the owner-ship of property, for we see that some of them have very small properties while others have very large ones, and that as a result a few people possess most of the land. Here again is another shortcoming in their constitution; for although the lawgiver rightly disapproved of the selling and buying of estates, he permitted anyone who so desired to transfer land through gifts or bequests, with the same result. And nearly two-fifths of all the land is in the possession of women due to the fact that heiresses are numerous and the customary dowries are large. The regulation of dowries by the state would have been a better measure, abolishing them entirely or making them, at any rate, small or moderate. As the law now provides, the heiress may be given in marriage to anyone, and if a man dies without a will, the guardian of his estate has the privilege of giving her away. . . .

Women in the Code of Gortyn:
Inscriptiones Creticae,
IV, no. 72, col. 112–IV54.

The Code of Gortyn, discovered in 1884 by the Italian archaeologist Halbherr, is generally considered to be the most important Greek legal document before the Hellenistic Age. It was recorded on layers of stone in a circular wall and consisted of twelve columns in sequence from right to left. The wall on which it was written was associated with a building dating back to the fifth century B.C. A second Code of the same period has also been found, but only in fragmentary form. The Code, which deals with civil law, is important, among other things, for its comparatively enlightened provisions regarding the traditional victims of ancient societies: slaves and women. In Gortyn, slaves enjoyed definite rights of protection and property and were allowed to marry free women. It is also noteworthy that the legislation of Gortyn was more liberal than that of classical Athens in showing some concern for the rights of women, as the selected passages given here show.

Doric Gortyn was a city-state in Crete which had always challenged and eventually replaced Cnossus as the leading power on the island even before it became the capital of the Roman province of Crete and Cyrene. Besides the Code, many other impressive monuments of antiquity have been found in Gortyn; in fact, its magnificent ruins, including the two thousand fallen statues that he counted during his visit to the island in 1415, prompted the Italian visitor Buondelmonti to compare this ancient city with Florence.

If someone rapes a free man or a free woman, he shall be fined one hundred staters; in the case of an *apetairos* [*i.e.*, socially inferior person), ten; if a slave rapes a free man or a free woman, he shall be fined double that amount. If a free man rapes a male or female serf, five drachmas; if a male serf rapes a male or female serf, five staters. If someone rapes a slave belonging to the house, he shall be fined two staters; in case he rapes one who has already been seduced, he shall be fined one obol if he raped her during the day, but two if the rape occurred during the night; the slave shall testify under oath. If someone attempts to seduce a free woman while she is under the guardianship of a relative, he shall be fined ten staters, if there is a deposition from a witness. If someone is found committing adultery with a free woman in her father's or brother's or husband's house, he shall be fined one hundred staters; if in the house of another, fifty. If he commits adultery with the wife of an *apetairos*, ten; if a slave with a free woman, he shall be fined double that amount; if a slave with a slave, five. In the presence of three witnesses the captor shall proclaim to the relatives of the person caught inside the house that he shall be free within five days after he pays the fine; and to the master of a slave, in the presence of two witnesses. If, however, the accused does not pay the fine, the captor shall have the right to treat him as he wishes. If the arrested person claims he is a victim of guile, a case in which the fine is fifty staters or more, the captor shall swear along with four others, each pronouncing solemn curses upon himself, that he caught him committing adultery and that he is not a victim of guile; in the case of an *apetairos*, he shall swear with two others; in the case of a serf, his master and another person shall take the oath. If a husband and wife divorce, she shall keep her own property, which she brought to her husband, and half of the income, if that derives from her own property; likewise, she will keep half of whatever she has woven, whatever that may be, and five staters, if the husband is responsible for the divorce. If, however, the husband claims he is not responsible, the judge will decide under oath. If a woman carries away anything else from her husband's property, she will pay a fine of five staters and she will return that which she received or purloined. But if she denies that she received anything else, the judge shall rule that she should take an oath of denial in the name of Artemis before the statue of the Archeress at the Amyclaeum. And if anyone takes anything away from her after she has submitted her denial under oath, he shall pay a fine of five staters and the thing itself. And if a stranger helps her carry off anything, he shall pay ten staters and double the value of what the judge, under oath, decrees he carried off. In case the husband dies and leaves children, the woman may marry again if she wishes and she may keep her property and whatever her husband gave her, in accordance with what is written in the presence of three adult free witnesses; if she takes anything belonging to her children, this will be a matter for a trial. But if her husband leaves her without children, she shall keep her own property and half of the things she has woven, and of the family property she shall receive, along with the lawful heirs, her portion and whatever her husband has given her, as it is written. If, however, she takes away anything else, this will be a matter of judicial dispute. If the wife dies childless, the husband shall return her property to her heirs, along with one half of what she has woven and one half of the income, if that derives from her property. If a husband or wife want to make porterage payments, this may be clothing or twelve staters or something worth twelve staters, but no more. If a female serf separates from a male serf, either in life or through death, she will keep her property; if she carries away anything else, that should be a matter for a trial. If a wife bears a child while divorced, the child shall be brought to the husband at his residence in the presence of three witnesses. If, however, he does not accept the child, the mother shall have the right either to raise or expose it. The relatives and the witnesses shall testify under oath as to

234

whether the child was brought to the father. If a female serf gives birth while divorced, the child shall be brought, in the presence of two witnesses, to the master of the man who married her. If, however, he does not accept it, the child shall be placed under the authority of the master of the female serf. But if she marries the same man again before the end of a year, the child shall be placed under the authority of the master of the male serf. The person who brought the child and the witnesses shall testify under oath. If a woman, while divorced, exposes her child before it is brought to the father in accordance with the law, and is convicted, she shall be fined fifty staters for a free child, and twenty-five for a slave child. In the event that the man has no house to which she can bring the child, or if she doesn't see him, she shall not be punished if she exposes the child. If an unmarried female serf conceives and gives birth, the child shall be under the authority of the master of her father. In case, however, her father is dead, the child shall be under the authority of the masters of her brothers. The father shall have in his authority the children and his own property and the mother shall control her property. While they are alive, it is not mandatory to divide it. If, however, one is fined, he shall be given his apportioned share, as it is written. If the father dies his houses in the city and all things contained in his houses in the country in which no serf resides, and all the animals, large and small, that do not belong to a serf, shall belong to the sons. All of the remaining property shall be justly distributed, with the sons, regardless of their number, receiving two parts each, while the daughters, regardless of their number, one part each. And the mother's property shall be distributed, when she dies, exactly as the father's. But if there is no property except the house, the daughters shall receive their share, as it is written. If, however, the father, while still alive, wishes to give property to a married daughter, he may give as the law provides, and no more. The daughter to whom he gave or promised before shall keep these things, but shall not receive anything else from her father's property.

Aspasia of Miletus: Plutarch, *Pericles*, 24.1–12.

A brilliant Ionian woman from Miletus, Aspasia was a *hetaera* (courtesan) who charmed Pericles and became his mistress. Although she was maligned by the politician's many enemies and even tried for impiety at the beginning of the Peloponnesian War, she was admired by the intellectual elite of the city and exerted a considerable influence on Pericles, who presided over Athens during the Golden Age.

After this, a thirty year truce having been concluded between the Athenians and the Lacedaemonians, Pericles ordered by public decree a naval expedition against Samos on the pretext that, when they were ordered to terminate their war against Miletus, the Samians refused to obey. Since these actions against the Samians seem to have been taken by Pericles in order to please Aspasia, this may be the best time to inquire about the woman and whatever art or power she possessed to be able to dominate the most powerful politicians and to inspire philosophers to talk so much and so positively about her.

That she was Milesian by birth, the daughter of Axiochus, is generally recognized. It is said that in wanting to emulate Thargelia, an Ionian woman of earlier times, she attached herself to the most powerful of men. For Thargelia, too, was a beautiful woman who had been endowed with grace and sagacity. She became the mistress of many Greeks and won over to the [Persian] King's side all those who approached her; and through these men, who were great and powerful, she sowed in the cities the beginnings of Median factions. Aspasia, some people say, was courted by Pericles because of her wisdom and skill in politics. Even Socrates and his well-known friends would sometimes visit her, and the men who kept company with her would bring their wives to listen to her, although her profession was neither proper nor respectable, for she kept young girls as courtesans. Aeschines claims that the sheep-dealer Lysicles, a man of vulgar and ignoble nature, came to be the most prominent man in Athens by keeping company with Aspasia after the death of Pericles. And Plato's *Menexenos*, though its first part was not written to be taken seriously, contains this much historical truth, that the woman had a reputation for having received many Athenians as pupils for instruction in the art of public speaking. It appears, however, that Pericles' love for Aspasia was more physical than philosophical. He had a wife, a relative of his, who had previously been married to Hipponicus and had by him a child named Callias, known as "the Rich." She also gave Pericles two sons, Xanthippus and Paralus. Afterwards, since their life together was not pleasant, he gave

236

her up to another man, with her own consent, and he himself took Aspasia and loved her with unusual affection; for every day, they say, when he left home and when he returned from the agora, he embraced her and kissed her. In the comedies she was called "New Omphale," Dianeira and Hera. . . . Cratinus openly calls her a concubine in the following verses: "The goddess of lust gave Aspasia to Pericles as his Hera, the dog-eyed concubine." It seems also that his illegitimate son was her child. Enpolis, in his *Demes*, has Pericles asking: "Is my illegitimate son alive?" and Myrionides answering, "Yes, and he would have long since been a man if he were not embarrassed by being the son of the harlot." They say that Aspasia became so renowned and celebrated that even Cyrus, who fought Artaxerxes for the throne of the Persians, gave the name Aspasia to the concubine he loved most, a woman previously called Milto.

Husbands, Wives and the Household:
Xenophon, *Oeconomicus*, VII.

By compounding the words for house (*oikos*) and law (*nomos*) the Greeks created the term *oikonomia*—the art of household management or "economics." *Oeconomicus*, the word for one who is skilled in this art, is the title of Xenophon's work in which the home is the subject of a discussion between Socrates and Critobulus. The excerpt given below is an account by Socrates of an earlier conversation he had had with Ischomachus, a "fine and good man," in which the latter tells the philosopher how he and his young wife had divided their domestic responsibilities. In accordance with custom, Ischomachus says that he has left all indoor work to his wife and concerns himself with bringing home an income from outside. She has received the better part of her education from him, but this is only in matters pertaining to the home; we must assume that Ischomachus saw no reason to prepare his wife for any pursuit other than the management of her household, the only proper occupation for women at that time. Indeed, it is Ischomachus' belief that the gods have created women for this purpose, and men for theirs, so that the happy and prosperous household is that in which husband and wife faithfully perform the duties appropriate to each of them.

"Seeing him sitting one day in the stoa of Zeus the Liberator, I approached him and sat down next to him, since he seemed to have time on his hands, and said, 'Why are you sitting idly like this, Ischomachus, you who are not used to loitering? I usually see you either doing something, or at least not altogether wasting your time, in the market place.' "

" 'You wouldn't see me lingering now, Socrates,' he said, 'if I had not agreed to wait here for some foreigners.' "

" 'By the gods,' I said, 'where do you spend your time and what do you do when you aren't waiting for someone? I really would like to hear just what it is you do that prompts people to call you a fine and good man. After all, you don't spend your time indoors, and your physical condition certainly doesn't appear to be that of a man who does.' "

"And Ischomachus, laughing because I had asked him what he did to be called a fine and good man, and rather pleased, too, or so it appeared to me, said, 'I don't know whether anyone refers to me as such when discussing me with you. But it is certain that when they call me to an *ántidosis*[1] for the financing of a trireme or a chorus no one seeks "the fine and good man," but they address me instead in a plain fashion and call me by my own name, Ischomachus, and by my patronymic.[2] And in response to your question, Socrates, I definitely do not spend my time at home. As a matter of fact,' he said, 'my wife is entirely capable of managing the household tasks by herself.' "

" 'But Ischomachus,' I said, 'I'd be very pleased if you permitted me to ask you whether you were the one who taught your wife to be what she ought to be, or whether she already knew how to manage the tasks which are appropriate to a woman when you took her from her father and mother.' "

" 'How could she have known about such things, Socrates,' he said, 'since she was only fourteen when she came to my house and had up until that time lived a very sheltered life, so that she might see and hear as little as possible and ask a minimum of questions? Don't you think I should have considered myself lucky if she came to my house able only to take wool and make a cloak, and having seen how the work of woolspinning is divided among the female servants? And as far as gastronomic matters are concerned, Socrates,' he said, 'she came to me very well trained—and it seems to me that this kind of training is of the utmost importance to both men and women.' "

" 'But did you yourself instruct your wife in other matters, Ischomachus,' I asked, 'so that she would be able to handle the responsibilities of a woman?' "

" 'By Zeus,' said Ischomachus, 'not until I had offered a sacrifice and prayers that I would be able to teach and she would be able to learn what would be best for both of us.' "

" 'Didn't your wife join you in sacrificing and praying for these things?' I asked."

" 'She certainly did,' said Ischomachus. 'She made many vows to the gods that she would become what she ought to be and made it clear that she would not disregard the things I taught her.' "

" 'By the gods, Ischomachus,' I said, 'tell me what you taught her when you first began; for I would enjoy hearing you describe this more than if you were to tell me about the best gymnastic or equestrian competitions.' "

"Ischomachus answered, 'Well, Socrates, when she had become comfortable enough with me and life in my household that we could have conversations, I questioned her in the following way. "Tell me, woman, have you ever wondered why I married you, and why your parents gave you to me? I know, and it must be obvious to you, too, that it was not for want of others to sleep

---

1   *Antidosis* means "a giving in return" or an "exchange." There was a law in Athens which permitted a citizen appointed to a public office (such as that of trierarch) to call upon someone wealthier than himself, and therefore better able to accept the financial burden, either to take the office or to exchange properties with him.

2   The Greeks used the patronymic to distinguish individuals; thus, Ischomachus the son of so-and-so.

with. But when I was considering for myself, and your parents for you, whom we should select as the best partner for home life and having children, I selected you, and it appears that your parents preferred me out of all the possible choices for a spouse. If the gods should give us children we will then consult together about them and how to bring them up in the best possible way, for it will be a blessing which both of us can share if they should happen to be the best associates and the best supporters of their parents when we are old. But, for the time being, what we hold in common is this household. I affirm that everything belonging to me is a part of what we own in common, and you have placed everything you brought to our marriage into our common fund. It's not necessary to calculate which of us has contributed more, but we ought to bear in mind that whichever of us contributes the things of greater worth will be the better partner." To these things, Socrates, my wife responded, "What is there that I can do for you? What authority do I have? Everything is in your hands. My mother told me that my business is to be discreet." "By Zeus, woman," I exclaimed, "that's what my father said! But it is the responsibility of discreet people, husbands as well as wives, to maintain their property in the best condition and to add as much as possible to it by honorable and just means." "Then what do you see," my wife asked, "that I can do to augment our household?" "By Zeus," I replied, "just try to do your best at those things for which the gods created you and which the law praises." "What are these things?" she said. "I suppose they are things of no little value," I replied, "unless, of course, the queen bee in the hive also has authority over tasks of little value. For to me, woman," ' he said that he had said, ' "it seems that the gods acted with the greatest care in joining together that pair called male and female, so that they may be of the greatest benefit to each other in the context of a partnership. In the first place, pairs are brought together to produce offspring, so that the various species of living things may not become extinct; and to human beings, at least, it was granted that from this union they should be provided with supporters in their old age. Moreover, human beings do not live out in the open air as cattle do, for they clearly have need of shelter. However, if human beings are going to have something to bring into their homes it is necessary to have someone perform the required tasks outdoors. Plowing the fallow land, sowing, planting and herding animals to pasture are all tasks performed in the open air, and it is from these that the things necessary for life are acquired. But when these things which are required for life have been brought into the house, there must be someone there to take care of them and to do the chores which need to be done under shelter. The rearing of young children requires shelter, and shelter is also necessary for the preparation of food from the fruits of the earth, as well as the making of clothes from wool. And since labor and diligence are required both indoors and outdoors," ' he had said, ' "it seems to me that the god prepared the woman's nature especially for indoor jobs and cares, and the man's nature for outdoor jobs and concerns. He provided the body and the soul of the man with a greater ability to endure cold and

240

heat and journeys by land and military campaigns, and so he commanded him to do the outdoor work. But in making the body of the woman less capable with respect to these things," ' he had said, ' "it seems to me that the god assigned to her the indoor work. But knowing that he had implanted in the woman the means for nourishing newborn children, and that he had given her that task, he also allotted to her a greater measure of fondness for infants than he gave to the man. Since he had also enjoined the woman to guard the things brought into the house, the god, aware that the ability to guard is not at all impaired by a frightened soul, made the woman more prone to fear than the man. But since he knew that the one responsible for the outdoor labors would need to defend himself in the event that someone acted lawlessly, to him he apportioned a greater share of boldness. Since it is necessary for both to give and take, he bestowed memory and attentiveness upon them equally, so that it is not possible to discern which kind has more, the male or the female. He also gave both of them equal measures of self-discipline respecting the necessary things [i.e., probably food and drink], and allowed that whichever of the two is better in this, whether the man or the woman, shall gain more from this good. Because the nature of each has not been created to be naturally adept at all these things, they need each other all the more, and their pairing is of greater advantage to each, for where one is incapable the other is capable. Now, woman," I said, "since we know what the god has assigned to us, we must do our best in trying to accomplish what befits each of us. The law, too," ' he said that he had said, ' "commends these [assignations of characteristics and abilities] by uniting man and woman; for as the god made them partners in their children, so the law establishes them as partners in the household. And the law also shows that the things which the god has made each of them capable of are noble. For it is a better thing for the woman to remain indoors than to spend her time outside, while it is shameful for a man to stay in the house instead of giving his attention to outdoor matters. If anyone acts in a way contrary to that for which the god created him, he will probably not escape the notice of the gods as he leads his disorderly life, and will pay the penalty for neglecting his own tasks or for doing the woman's work. And it seems to me," I said, "that the queen bee also works hard to discharge the duties which the god has assigned to her." My wife asked, "How are the duties of the queen bee like those which I am required to perform?" "She stays in the hive," I said, "and does not allow the bees to be idle, but sends the ones who must work outside to their labors. She takes note of what each of them brings in, receives it, and preserves it until it is needed for consumption. And when the time comes for it to be used, she dispenses to each bee its rightful portion. She also has authority over the weaving of the cells within the honeycomb, so that they may be finely and speedily woven. She attends to the newborn offspring and their upbringing, and when the young bees are grown and able to work she sends them out to form a colony with one of their peers as their leader." My wife asked, "Will I have to do these things?" "It will be necessary for you to stay inside," I said, "and to

241

send the servants whose work is outside to their tasks, and also to be in charge of the servants who have work indoors. You must receive what is brought into the house and distribute whatever part of it must be used up. With regard to the part which is set aside, you must use foresight and guard it so that what was intended to last a year is not used up in a month. When wool is brought to you it will be your responsibility to make sure that clothes are made for those who need them. You must also take care that the dry grain is in good condition and edible. There is one of your duties, however," I said, "that will probably seem rather disagreeable to you, and that is that you will have to take charge of all the servants who become ill so that they may be healed." "By Zeus," said my wife, "that will be most pleasant if those who receive good care appreciate my efforts and have more affection for me than they did before." I admired her answer,' said Ischomachus, 'and said, "Isn't it through just this kind of thoughtful concern for the future that the queen bee so disposes the other bees to her that when she leaves the hive not one of them thinks of staying behind, but all of them follow her?" My wife answered, "I wonder, though, if the duties of the leader are not yours rather than mine. For my protection and distribution of the things inside the house would seem a bit silly, I suppose, if you did not see to it that something was brought in from outside." "On the other hand," I said, "it would seem absurd if I brought something in if no one were there to take care of it. Don't you see," I said, "how people who are said to draw water into a leaking jar are pitied, since their labor is obviously in vain?" "Yes, by Zeus," my wife said, "they certainly are miserable, if that is what they do." "Some of your other responsibilities, woman," I said, "will please you, such as when you take a woman who doesn't know how to spin wool and make her skillful at it, so that she becomes twice as valuable to you; or when you take someone who is ignorant of housekeeping and of the duties of a servant and make her a knowledgeable, faithful and useful servant whose value is priceless; or when it is your right to do good things for those who are temperate in, and beneficial to, your household, and to punish anyone who appears to be wicked. But the most pleasant thing of all will be if you show yourself to be superior to me and make me your servant, for then you will have no reason to fear that as you grow older you will be respected less in your household. You could then be confident that as you get older the better a partner you will be for me, and that the more you become a better guardian of the household for the sake of your children, the more you will be honored by your family. For the fine and good things in life do not accrue to men and women as a natural consequence of youthful beauty, but by the living of a virtuous life." Such were the things which I remember saying to her, Socrates, when we had our first serious conversation.' "

Advice to Newlyweds: Plutarch, Conjugal Precepts.

Among the works which comprise his *Moralia* is Plutarch's *Conjugal Precepts*, a short essay which he gave as a wedding present to Pollianus and Eurydice, a young couple whom he seems to have known well. Though it was written in the latter part of the first century A.D., it is more or less representative of the attitudes toward women and marriage which had prevailed in Greece since the fifth century B.C. One of these is the principle that wives should subordinate themselves to their husbands, an idea deeply-rooted and widespread in antiquity. But Plutarch was no misogynist. This is obvious to anyone who has read the letter he wrote to his grieving wife on the occasion of their daughter's death (*Consolatio ad uxorem*). Plutarch believed that men should take precedence over women and that a woman's life should be spent at home, but he also advised that marriage should be characterized by the cooperation, mutual respect, and spiritual and intellectual companionship of husbands and wives.

3. It is in the beginning that married people should most carefully guard against differences and quarrels, for they see that household articles which are made of sections fitted together can, at first, be easily torn apart by any accident of chance, but after a time, when the joints have firmly set, they cannot be separated by fire or steel.

4. Just as fire readily takes hold in chaff, fiber and hare's fur, but is quickly extinguished unless it attaches itself to some other substance which is capable of sustaining and feeding it, so the ardent physical passion that flares up between newlyweds should not be considered durable or well-established unless it is based on habit and achieves a state of vitality by clinging to wisdom.

5. Fishing with poison is a quick and easy way to catch fish, but it makes them inedible and worthless. Similarly, women who contrive to use love potions and magic spells on men and gain control of them through pleasure end up living with crazy, mindless fools. The men bewitched by Circe were of no use to her, nor did she have any need of them after they had been turned into pigs and asses; but she was very much in love with Odysseus, who possessed discretion and conducted himself prudently in her presence.

6. Women who would rather dominate foolish men than obey men of good sense are like people who prefer to guide the blind along the road instead of following those who can see and know where they are going.

9. Whenever the moon is at a distance from the sun she looks large and bright to us, but when she draws near to him she fades away and hides herself. Conversely, a virtuous wife should be most visible when she is with her husband, and ought to stay at home and hide herself when he is absent.

10. Herodotus was wrong in saying that when a woman takes off her chiton she also removes her modesty. It is just the opposite, for the virtuous woman puts on modesty in place of her chiton, and in their intercourse husband and wife find that the symbol of the greatest love is the greatest modesty.

11. When two voices sing in unison it is the bass which carries the melody. Similarly, in a virtuous household every activity is performed by husband and wife in agreement with each other, but it is nevertheless clear that it is the man who is in charge and has the power of decision.

12. The Sun once bested the North Wind. The wind blew violently and tried to rob a man of his cloak, but the man only pulled it closer and held it more tightly. But after the wind came the sun, and in its heat the man became warm, and then burning hot, so that he took off not only his cloak but his chiton as well. Most women act in a similar fashion. When their husbands try to take away their luxuries and extravagancies by force they become embroiled in endless fights and become angry; but if they are persuaded by reason they will merely put these things aside and become more even-tempered.

16. The legal wives of the Persian kings sit with them at dinner and eat with them. But when the kings want to have a good time and get drunk they dismiss their wives and call for the music-girls and concubines. They are right in doing this, in not living dissolutely with their wedded wives or allowing them to participate in their drunken frolic. Therefore, if in his private life a man who is intemperate and unrestrained when it comes to pleasure should commit a *faux pas* with a courtesan or servant-girl, his legal wife should not be irritated or upset. She should reason that it is out of respect for her that he shares his drunkenness, licentiousness and immodesty with another woman.

19. A wife should not make friends of her own, but ought to enjoy her husband's friends with him. The first and greatest friends are the gods. Therefore it is fitting for a wife to worship and know only the gods her husband worships and to exclude from her home all weird rituals and foreign superstitions. For no god is pleased by secret and stealthy rites performed by a woman.

20. Plato says that the happy and blessed state is the one in which the citizens most infrequently hear the words "mine" and "not mine." This is because the citizens strive to consider all things of real value as communal property. It is even more necessary that such words should be eliminated from the estate of marriage, with this exception: as the physicians tell us, blows on the left side of the body are felt on the right side; in the same way, it is a beautiful thing for a wife to be in sympathy with her husband, and he with her. Thus, just as intertwined ropes get strength from each other, so husband and wife, with each contributing the appropriate measure of goodwill, will preserve their fellowship by their joint action. Nature unites us through our bodies in order that, by taking and mixing a part of each person, she gives back an offspring which is common to both, so that neither can discern or distinguish his own part or that of the other. It is also quite appropriate for married couples to have such a partnership in property. They should pour everything they own into a common fund, mixing all of it together. Neither should consider one part as his own and the other as not his own, but each should think of all of it as his own and none of it as not his own. Just as we call a mixture "wine" even though the larger part of it is water, so the property and the house of a man are said to be his, even if the wife contributed the larger part.

24. Again, when a certain young man of the court [*i.e.*, of Philip of Macedon] married a beautiful woman about whom nasty rumors were heard, Olympias said: "That man has no sense; if he did he would not have married with his eyes." A marriage should not be made on the basis of what the eyes see or what the fingers feel, as is the case with some who calculate the size of a wife's dowry instead of determining what kind of companion she will be.

30. In Egypt there was an ancient custom that women should not have shoes, and this was so that they would stay at home all day. Most women, if you take away their shoes embroidered with gold, bracelets, anklets, purple clothing, and pearls, will stay at home.

31. Theano [*i.e.*, the wife of the philosopher Pythagoras] once exposed her arm as she was putting on her cloak. Somebody remarked: "What a lovely arm!" "But it's not for the public," she replied. It is not only the arm, but also the speech of a virtuous woman which ought to be "not for the public." The words which she speaks to outsiders should be modest and guarded, for they expose her. Her feelings, her character, and her disposition are all noticeable in her conversation.

A Misogynous Poet: Semonides of Amorgos, *Censure of Women*, 83–95.

Semonides of Amorgos, an iambic and elegiac poet of the seventh century B.C. whose work has survived in fragmentary form, has left us a poem in iambic verse which is probably the most misogynistic piece in all of ancient Greek literature. Drawing from the rich store of popular fables, Semonides compares different types of women to various animals in a degrading and insulting manner. Yet even this rabid misogynist concedes that the wife with the attributes of the bee is a great blessing in a man's life, as the excerpt given here shows. This poem was preserved in the *Anthology* of Stobaeus (73.61).

Another of a bee, and he who gets her is fortunate.
In her alone blame cannot be found;
because of her, life flourishes and increases.
Loving and beloved she grows old with her husband,
having borne fair and name-honored children.
Among all women she becomes the most splendid,
and is filled with a divine grace.
She does not enjoy sitting among women
while they discuss sexual stories.
These are the best and wisest wives
that Zeus, in his grace, grants to men.
All others, thanks to Zeus,
are and ever will be a sorrow to men!

The Beauty of Women:
Anacreonteia, no. 24.

This lyric poem, a hymn to the unconquerable beauty of women, belongs to the *Anacreonteia*, a collection of works inspired by Anacreon of Teos, the famous poet of the sixth century B.C. These poems often capture the witty and fanciful spirit of Anacreon. Although derivative rather than original in conception, they have influenced later English and European poets, especially the members of the *Pleiade* in France.

Nature has endowed bulls with horns,
horses with hoofs,
hares with swift feet,
lions with ravenous jaws,
fish with the ability to swim,
birds with flight,
man with wisdom.
But did she neglect woman?
No, nature gave her beauty,
a match for all the shields
and swords in the world.
Beauty, which is strong enough
to conquer steel and fire!

Women as Causes of War: Athenaeus, *Deipnosophists*, XIII, 560b–f.

This discussion of women as the causes of war is drawn from the *Deipnosophists* or *Sophists at Dinner*, a lengthy work written in the second century A.D. by the pedantic but erudite grammarian Athenaeus of Naucratis in Egypt. The "dinner" is a literary device which allows Athenaeus to bring together famous "diners," some of them actual historical figures, who represent such disciplines as philosophy, law, medicine and literature and express their views in a converstion which lasts several days. The *Deipnosophists*, which has survived in fifteen books, is a massive compilation of data on nearly every aspect of Greek life and society and is based on countless ancient authors. Thus, the following views on women and war reflect beliefs widely held in ancient Greece.

My friends, I don't think that any of you are unaware of the fact that even the greatest of wars have been fought for the sake of women. The Trojan War was fought for Helen, the war of pestilence for Chryseis, the wrath of Achilles was for the sake of Briseis, and the so-called Sacred War for another married woman, of Theban origin, named Theano. She had been abducted by a Phocian, as Duris says in the second book of his history. This war was also of ten years' duration, but came to an end in the tenth year when Philip formed an alliance with the Thebans. It was then that the Thebans occupied Phocis. Likewise, the war called Cirrhaean, as Callisthenes says in his work *On the Sacred War*, when the Cirrhaeans fought against the Phocians, also lasted ten years, the Cirrhaeans having abducted Megisto, the daughter of the Phocian Pelagon, along with the daughters of some Argives as they were returning home from the Pythian sanctuary at Delphi. In the tenth year of the war Cirrha was also overcome. Entire households have been turned upside down for the sake of women: the household of Philip, father of Alexander, by his marriage to Cleopatra; that of Hercules by his marriage to Iole, the daughter of Eurytus; of Theseus, for the sake of Phaedra, the daughter of Minos; of Athamas, by his marriage to Themisto, the daughter of Hypseus; of Jason, by his marriage to the daughter of Creon, Glauce; and of Agamemnon, for the sake of Cassandra. Even the Egyptian expedition of Cambyses was caused by a woman, as Ctesias says. Cambyses, having been informed that the women of Egypt differed from all others in sensuality, sent a message to Amasis, the king of the Egyptians, asking for one of his daughters in marriage. Amasis, however, suspecting that she would not enjoy the honor of a wife, but would be treated as a concubine, did not give him one of his own, but sent instead

Neitetis, the daughter of Aprias. Now, as a result of his defeat by the Cyrenaeans, Aprias had been deposed in Egypt and put to death by Amasis. But Cambyses, who had enjoyed Neitetis and had been greatly excited by her, learned everything from her, and when she begged him to avenge the murder of Aprias he was persuaded to fight the Egyptians. Dinon, however, in his *Persica*, and Lyceas of Naucratis, in the third book of his *Aegyptiaca*, say that Neitetis was sent by Amasis to Cyrus, who fathered Cambyses by her, and that it was to avenge his mother that he undertook his Egyptian expedition. Duris of Samos says that the first war to be fought between two women was that of Olympias and Eurydice, in which Olympias advanced like a Bacchant with tambourines while Eurydice armed herself in the Macedonian fashion, having been trained by Cynna the Illyrian.

Marriage and Politics—The Case of Philip II of Macedon: Athenaeus, *Deipnosophists*, XIII, 557b–e.

Marriage as a means of furthering political careers, of consolidating and extending power and of cementing relationships between states is nothing new in history. Philip II of Macedon, a ruthless, energetic and intensely ambitious master of the arts of diplomacy and war, often resorted to marriage in order to promote his ambitious schemes of hegemony in the Greek world. It was the misfortune of Philip, however, to have been married to a proud queen, Olympias, who would not tolerate his infidelities and multiple marriages. In the end, his use of women as political pawns proved to be his nemesis, as is shown by the excerpt from Athenaeus which is given below.

Philip of Macedon certainly did not bring women along with him in his wars, as did Darius, the king deposed by Alexander who, while fighting for his very survival, had with him three hundred and sixty concubines, as Dicaearchus relates in the third book of his *Life of Greece*. Philip, however, always married before fighting a new war. As Satyrus writes in his *Life* of Philip, in the twenty-two years of his reign he married Andata of Illyria and had by her a daughter, Cynna, and he also married Phila, the sister of Derdas and Machatas. Desiring to appropriate for himself the Thessalian nation, he had children by two women of Thessaly, one of whom was Nicesipolis of Pherae, who bore him Thettalonice, and the other Philinna of Larissa, by whom he fathered Arrhidaeus. Likewise, he came to possess the kingdom of the Molossians through his marriage to Olympias, by whom he fathered Alexander and Cleopatra. And again, when he conquered Thrace, the Thracian king Cothelas came to him bringing his daughter Meda and many presents. Philip married her, thus taking another wife besides Olympias. After this he married the sister of Hippostratus and niece of Attalus, Cleopatra, with whom he had fallen in love. But Philip threw his whole life into chaos by bringing her over to take the place of Olympias. For shortly thereafter, during the wedding celebration, Attalus remarked: "Now, indeed, real kings, not bastards, will be born." When Alexander heard this he threw the goblet that he held in his hand at Attalus, who responded by hurling his own cup at him. After this episode, Olympias fled to the land of the Molossians, while Alexander fled to Illyria.

Hipparchia of Maroneia—A Cynic Philosopher: Diogenes Laertius, *Lives of Eminent Philosophers*, 6.96–98.

A member of a distinguished family in the Thracian city of Maroneia, Hipparchia was converted to the Cynic sect by a disciple of Diogenes, the Theban philosopher Crates, who had given up a considerable fortune to follow the frugal life of a Cynic philosopher. Hipparchia, whose brother Metrocies was also a Cynic, married Crates and the couple lived the life of the poorest of beggars. Besides the few biographical data and anecdotes preserved in Diogenes Laertius, little is known of the life and philosophy of this remarkable woman.

She fell in love with the philosophy and the lifestyle of Crates and would not pay deference to any of her suitors, ignoring their wealth, their high birth, and their physical beauty. To her, Crates was everything. She even threatened her parents that she would kill herself if she were not given to him in marriage. They begged Crates to dissuade the girl, and he tried his best. But in the end, being unable to persuade her, he stood up, took off his clothes in front of her and said, "This is the bridegroom and these are his possessions. Consider them before you make your decision, for you will not become my companion if you do not accept my pursuits."

The girl made her choice and, adopting his form of dress, she followed her husband and lived with him openly, often going out to dinners with him. Once, when she came to a banquet offered by Lysimachus, she put Theodorus, called the atheist, in his place by proposing the following sophism: "Whatever Theodorus does which cannot be characterized as wrong cannot be called wrong if done by Hipparchia. Theodorus does no wrong when he strikes himself; therefore, neither is Hipparchia guilty of wrongdoing when she strikes Theodorus." He had nothing to offer in reply to this argument, but tried to pull up her cloak. Hipparchia was neither astounded nor perturbed, as is natural in a woman. And when he asked: "Is this really she who gave up the weaver's comb and loom?" she replied, "Yes, it is I, Theodorus. Do you think that I have been badly advised if, instead of wasting my time working at the loom,[3] I pursue an education?" These and countless other tales are told of the female philosopher.

---

3   Euripides, *Bacchae* 1236

A Hellenistic Queen—Cleopatra VII of Egypt: Plutarch, *Antony*, 27–28.

The last of the Ptolemaic monarchs of Egypt, Cleopatra VII is one of the most fascinating women of antiquity, although her true character and personality have been colored by Roman propaganda which described her as a serious obstacle to Rome's expansion into the Middle East and as the seductress of some of its best generals. A well-educated, competent ruler, she was also intensely ambitious and used her considerable charm and talents to gain and consolidate power. The legend of a scheming Cleopatra of irresistible physical beauty, however, is dispelled in the following account by Plutarch, who speaks of the true beauty of the Queen of the Nile in terms of a beguiling charm stemming from education and a brilliant mind.

The next day Antony invited her in turn to supper and made it a point of honor to surpass her in splendor and elegance; he found, however, that he had failed miserably in this, and was the first to mock the shabbiness and grossness of his preparations. But Cleopatra, seeing that Anthony's railleries savored more of the soldier and the commoner, accepted the situation without showing any sign of reluctance or reserve. They say that her actual beauty was by no means unparalleled or of the kind that struck those who saw her, but that her presence was irresistible to those who were familiar with her and that the attractiveness of her person, joined with her seductive conversation and the natural grace that attended all her words and actions, was magical. When she spoke it was a pleasure to hear the sound of her voice; her tongue was like an instrument of many strings with which she could effortlessly switch to whatever language she chose to speak, for there were very few barbarian nations with which she communicated through an interpreter. She personally responded to most of them, as, for example, the Ethiopians, Troglodytes, Hebrews, Arabians, Syrians, Medes, and Parthians. It is said that she also learned several other languages, whereas the Ptolemaic kings who preceded her had scarcely bothered to learn the Egyptian language, some of them even having lost the ability to speak Macedonian.

The Epitaph of Pantheia, Wife of a Physician: Kaibel, *Epigrammata Graeca*, 243b.

This interesting epitaph from Pergamum, which dates back to the second century A.D., is dedicated to Pantheia, a devoted mother, wife and household manager who is also lauded by her grateful physician husband for her knowledge of medicine, which was equal to his own.

Hail Pantheia, from your husband,
whose sorrow over your death is everlasting.
Hera, Mistress of Marriage,
never knew your equal in beauty and discretion.
You gave me children resembling me in every way;
you cared for me as well as them;
you took the helm of the household
and guided all its affairs,
enhancing even its reputation in medicine—
for though you were a woman
your healing skill was equal to mine.
And so your husband Glycon
has built for you this tomb
in which lies the body of the immortal Philadelphus,
and where I, too, will be buried
when I die.

Death in Childbirth—Socratea's Epitaph:
Inscriptiones Graecae, 12, 5, 310, 3–10.

This moving epitaph of the second century B.C. from the Aegean island of Paros records a common tragedy that plagued women in ancient times: death in childbirth.

My father was Nicandrus,
my country, Paros,
my name, Socratea.
When I died Parmenion, my husband,
placed me in the grave,
ensuring that future generations
would know of my honorable life.
The Erinyes of childbirth,
against whom no one is safe,
destroyed my delightful life
with a fatal hemorrhage.
All my labor could not bring the child forth;
he lies in my womb, among the dead.

The Lament of a Widowed Husband—
Nicon of Aptera: *Inscriptiones Creticae*,
II, iii, 44.

This third century A.D. epitaph from Aptera in Crete echoes the lament of a husband over the loss of his beloved wife, Sympherousa. The husband's epitaph follows his wife's.

I, Sympherousa, lie here,
thirty years old, a foreigner, Libyan by birth,
now dwelling with the gods because in all things
I conducted myself with virtue and gentility,
and because my ways pleased the noble city of Aptera,
which grieved for my sudden death
and sent me off to Hades in this tomb.
Hail to you who pass by, and to you people of Aptera,
who with solicitous care and honor
promptly placed my remains in a great urn.

It was Nicon, her husband, who wrote this;
but now I, too, am dead. I gave
my beautiful one to an envious Hades and,
as I've written, I've missed her much for her virtue.
But all in vain! I cry aloud, but she doesn't hear.
I love her still, and I always shall,
but to no avail.
Just like the wind, she simply vanished!

On the Death of a Young Woman:
Anthologia Palatina, VII. 167.

Here is a touching epigram which takes the form of an epitaph
for a young woman of eighteen who died in childbirth. It is sometimes
attributed to Dioscorides, an Alexandrian epigrammatist of the early
second century B.C., though without sufficient reason.

Call me Polyxena, wife of Archelaus,
daughter of Theodectes and unfortunate Demarete,
and a mother, too, at least as far as
the pain of childbirth.
But fate caught up with my baby before
his twentieth day,
and I myself died at eighteen,
having just become a mother
and so recently a bride—so utterly short was my life.

VI
The Greek Outlook: Drama and Poetry

The Gift of Fire: Aeschylus, *Prometheus Bound*, 1–262.

Aeschylus (525–455 B.C.) was the first great dramatist of Greece. He wrote about ninety plays, though only seven of these have been preserved. Among these is *Prometheus Bound*, the first play in a trilogy whose second and third parts have, except for a few fragments, been lost.

The *Prometheus* is based on a mythological tradition which describes the early history of the universe. Led by their king, Cronus, the Titans had long been its unchallenged rulers. But Cronus' children rebelled against their father and established the rule of the Olympians with Zeus as their king. Hesiod tells us that Prometheus, himself a Titan, had created man out of clay and taught him how to live in a civilized fashion. When Zeus decided to destroy the human race Prometheus came to the defense of humanity and finally gave fire to man by stealing it in the pith of a stem of fennel.

Prometheus' action, because it gave to human beings something which was the exclusive property of the gods, constituted a violation of the moral order of the universe which demanded punishment. Thus, the play begins with the chaining of Prometheus to a rock in the Caucasus by Hephaestus, the Olympian god of fire who had been led along with Prometheus to that remote place by Zeus's servants, Power and Force. Left alone, he laments his fate and recounts his sad story to the Chorus. He says, too, that he has knowledge of a secret (that if Zeus consummates his love for Thetis the Nereid their son will one day overthrow him) which he will not reveal until Zeus releases him. Though the ruler of Olympus threatens to send him down to Tartarus, Prometheus keeps the secret to himself. At the end of the play a bolt of lightning blasts his lonely rock and the Titan sinks into an abyss.

Fragments of the rest of the trilogy indicate that Prometheus was brought back to suffer greater tortures until the intervention of Hercules resulted in his release.

POWER

To the very end of the earth we've come,
to the narrow Scythian country, an untrodden wasteland.
And now you, Hephaestus, must attend to the commands
of the Father—to bind this villain here
to the towering, craggy rocks

258

in untiring bonds of adamantine chain.
For it was your flower—bright fire, which sustains every craft—
that he stole and gave to mortals. And now
he must pay to the gods the penalty for such a sin,
learn to accept the tyranny of
Zeus and be done with his love of humanity.

HEPHAESTUS

O Power and Force, the task enjoined on you by
Zeus is completed, and no obstacle remains.
But, as for me, I haven't the boldness to bind
by force a fellow god to this stormy mountain cleft.
And yet I must be bold,
for it is a grievous thing to ignore the Father's words.

(He speaks to Prometheus)

High-minded son of right-counseling Themis,
it is against my will as well as yours that I nail
you with unyielding brass to this lonely crag
where you will never hear another mortal voice or see a human form.
Scorched by the sun's bright flame, your fair
skin will shrivel, and you will be grateful when
the star-embroidered night hides the light of day
and, again, when the sun scatters the frost at dawn.
The burden of your present suffering will forever
wear you down, for he who would release you has not been born.
This is your reward for philanthropy.
A god yourself, you did not cower before the wrath of the gods,
but gave to men honors not rightly theirs.
And so you will stand watch on this unhappy rock,
standing upright, sleepless, knees unbending.
You will utter many cries and groans—all of them
useless. The heart of Zeus is unrelenting,
for all are harsh who are newly come to power.

POWER

To work! Why do you delay? Why this senseless pity?
Why do you not hate the god most hated by the gods,
the one who handed over to mortals a privilege that was yours?

HEPHAESTUS

The power of kinship, and time spent together.

POWER

I understand, but to disobey the words of the Father—
how can you do that? Isn't that more to be feared?

HEPHAESTUS

You are always ruthless, and devoid of compassion.

POWER

To lament him is no remedy for his fate. Don't
waste your efforts doing what will be of no use.

HEPHAESTUS

O my craft—how I hate you!

POWER

Why hate your craft? The plain truth is that
it is not the cause of your present troubles.

HEPHAESTUS

And yet I wish it had been given to another.

POWER

All things are oppressive except to rule over the gods.
Zeus alone is truly free.

HEPHAESTUS

I know. I can't deny it.

POWER

Quickly now. Throw the chains around him.
What if the Father sees you delaying?

HEPHAESTUS

Look, the chains are ready and close at hand.

POWER

Wrap them around his hands. Bind him fast
with strong hammer blows. Pin him to the rock.

HEPHAESTUS

I'm doing it, and quickly.

POWER

Strike hard. Bind him tightly. Leave no chain loose.
He has a talent for wriggling out of difficult situations.

HEPHAESTUS

There! This elbow is fastened so that it cannot be loosed.

POWER

Now buckle the other one securely, and let
him learn that his wisdom is foolishness to Zeus.

HEPHAESTUS

No one has just cause to criticize my work, except Prometheus here.

POWER

Now drive the unfeeling point of adamantine wedge
straight through his chest. Strike it hard!

HEPHAESTUS

Alas, Prometheus! I grieve for your sufferings.

POWER

You shrink from your task and grieve for the enemies
of Zeus? Take care, lest you grieve for yourself one day.

HEPHAESTUS

You see a sight hard to look upon.

POWER

I see someone who is getting his due. Now, throw the strap around
his ribs.

HEPHAESTUS

This is something I have to do. Don't urge me on too much.

POWER

But I *will* urge you, and exhort you too.
Now go lower; secure his legs with rings.

HEPHAESTUS

It is done, and without great effort.

POWER

Now, summon all your strength and pierce his feet with bolts.
It's a severe judge who appraises this work.

HEPHAESTUS

The words you utter are as ugly as you are.

POWER

You may be softhearted, but don't reproach me
for my stubborn temper and harshness.

HEPHAESTUS

Let us go. His limbs are bound.

POWER

(to Prometheus)

Let's see you commit your outrages now—now that you're chained
to the rock. Go ahead, cheat the gods out of their prerogatives and
give them to mortals.
What can mortals do to ease your suffering?
The gods name you falsely when they call you Prometheus
["foresight"], for foresight is something you will need more of if
you are to escape these bonds.

(Prometheus is now left alone on the rock)

PROMETHEUS

O divine aether and swift-winged winds!
O sources of rivers and immeasurable laughter of the
ocean's waves! O earth, mother of all, and
the all-seeing circle of the sun—I call on you.
Look at me! Look at what I, a god, suffer at the hands of gods.
Behold the tortures I will
endure as they break me down
through endless time.
This is the humiliating bondage which the
new lord of the gods has devised for me.
Alas! I groan for my present troubles and
for those to come, wondering if an end to
my suffering will ever be decreed.

But what am I saying? I know just what
the future holds; no sorrow can befall

me unforeseen. What fate has ordained I must bear
as lightly as I am able, knowing that the
strength of Necessity is unconquerable.
I cannot keep silent about my misfortune, but neither
can I speak of it. For I am he who gave
great prizes to mortals, and for that I am tied down in wretched
constraint.
I am he who sought out the source of fire, hidden
away in a reed stalk, and stole it, so that it became
the teacher of every art to men and their way to greatness.
This is the offense for which I must pay the price,
pinned down in chains beneath the open sky.

(The Chorus of the daughters of Oceanus enters)

Ah! What is that sound?
What sweet scent waits to me unseen?
Is it sent by gods, or mortals, or both?
Has someone come to this peak at the world's edge
to watch me suffer? What could he want?
Look at me, an unlucky god bound in chains,
the enemy of Zeus, hated by all the gods
who enter the court of Zeus
because my love for humanity was too great.
Ah! Again, what is that sound I hear nearby? The
rustling of birds? The air whispers
with the light beat of wings.
Everything that approaches me is a cause for fear.

CHORUS

Be not afraid. We are a band of friends
who come in hasty winged contention to your rocky peak.
With toil and trouble we persuaded the Father to let us
come, and were carried here by rushing winds.
Deep within our ocean cavern
came the echo of sounding steel,
banishing our solemn modesty.
Quickly, unsandaled, we came in this winged chariot.

PROMETHEUS

Alas!
Children of Tethys, the mother of many,
you daughters of Father Oceanus,
who encircles the whole earth
with his sleepless flood—
look! Look at the chains
with which I am fastened
to the rocky heights of this mountain crevice
to keep a watch that none would envy.

CHORUS

I see, Prometheus. Fear fills my
eyes with a mist of tears when I
see your body, wasting away on the rocks
in unyielding chains of shame.
New rulers hold sway on Olympus, and
Zeus, setting aside the old, rules with strange new laws.
The mighty Titans of old have been vanquished.

PROMETHEUS

If only I had been cast deep into the earth,
deeper even than Hades where the dead are received,
down into bottomless Tartarus,
savagely constrained in unbreakable bonds,
so no god or other being
might rejoice over my fate.
But now I am the wretched plaything of the winds,
and my enemies gloat over my suffering.

CHORUS

Who among the gods is so hard-hearted
that he takes pleasure in your pain?
Who does not share your indignation at
your torment—save only Zeus? For maliciously,
and with a will ever inflexible, he drives the
children of Heaven in yoked subjection,
and he will never cease until his heart is sated,
or another takes his rule—so hard to capture—
by trickery.

PROMETHEUS

And yet, though I am now cruelly tormented in
these fetters, the day will come when the lord of the Blessed
will have need of me to show him the
new plot whereby he will be
defrauded of his scepter and his honor.
But he will never win me over to
his side by enchanting me with honey-tongued
persuasion, nor will I ever be frightened
by his threats into revealing my secret
until he has loosed me from these brutal chains
and is willing to pay the price for
what he has done to me.

CHORUS

You are bold, and even in your
bitter misery you are unyielding
and too free with your speech.
A piercing fear troubles my heart,
and it is for your fortunes that I am afraid.
Where and when must it be that you will
find safe haven and see the end of trouble?
For the mind of the son of Cronus is hard to
move with prayer, and his heart is hard.

PROMETHEUS

I know that Zeus is harsh, and that justice is
his to define. But in time his
resolve will be softened—when he is broken.
His unmerciful anger will be calmed,
and he will come hurrying to me
desiring peace and friendship.

CHORUS

Reveal everything. Tell us your story.
For what reason did Zeus take you and
punish you so dishonorably and cruelly?
Tell us, if telling will bring you no harm.

PROMETHEUS

Even to speak of it causes me pain,
but silence, too, is painful.
There's misery everywhere.

Now, when the gods first became angry
with one another and factions arose among them—
some wanting to cast Cronus from his throne
so that Zeus might reign, and others urging the
opposite, that Zeus should never rule the gods—
I tried then with the best counsel
to sway the Titans, the children of Heaven and Earth;
but my efforts were in vain.
They scorned my wily schemes,
and in their arrogant pride they thought to
make themselves masters easily, by force.
But my mother, Themis—or Earth, for
though she is one her names are many—
had foretold more than once what was to be:
that the conquerors would come to power
not through force or strength, but by cunning.
Yet, when I told them this they thought my
words unworthy and averted their eyes from me.
The best course open to me then,
it seemed, was to take my mother
and willingly cast my lot with Zeus.
It is because of my counsel that
ancient Cronus and his allies are now hidden away,
engulfed by the blackness of Tartarus.
Having received this benefit from me,
the tyrant of the gods paid me back with evil.
Indeed, there is a sickness inherent in tyranny
which renders tyrants unable to trust their friends.
But you have asked why it is that he
tortures me, and this I will now explain.
As soon as Zeus sat upon his father's
throne he assigned to the various gods their
special prerogatives and apportioned power.
But for suffering mankind he had no
concern at all, since he planned to wipe out
the entire race and raise a new one in its place.
I alone stood against his designs.
I alone dared. I saved humanity from
destruction and from being cast down to Hades.
I am bent down by agonies painful
to endure and pitiful to look upon, for
I set pity for mortals above concern for myself,
never thinking this would be my fate. Pitilessly have I
been restrained, a sight which brings shame to Zeus.

CHORUS

Prometheus, he who does not share your indignation
at your adversities must be iron-hearted and
made of stone. I had no desire to see them,
and, now that I do, my heart is distressed.

PROMETHEUS

I am a wretched sight for friends to see.

CHORUS

Did you go beyond what you have already told us?

PROMETHEUS

Yes, I stopped mortals from foreseeing death.

CHORUS

What kind of remedy did you find for that disease?

PROMETHEUS

I made blind hopes to dwell in them.

CHORUS

A great benefit you gave to men.

PROMETHEUS

And I also gave them fire.

CHORUS

So mortals now have flaming fire?

PROMETHEUS

Yes, and they will learn many crafts from it.

CHORUS

And it is for these reasons that Zeus torments
you, and that there is no release from your pain?
Is there no end to the misery inflicted on you?

PROMETHEUS

None, save when it pleases him to end it.

CHORUS

But when will it please him? What hope is there? Don't
you see that you were wrong? It gives me no pleasure to
say that you erred, and for you to hear it is bitterness.
But let us speak no more of it. Try to find some
release from your ordeal.

Law and Conscience: Sophocles, *Antigone*, 635–943.

Sophocles (*ca.* 497–405 B.C.), the most prolific of the ancient Greek dramatists, wrote about 125 plays. Only seven are extant. In these he emphasized the heroic dignity of man—a dynamic and yet fragile quality won through suffering and lost through the imperfections of human character.

Sophocles' plays presuppose his audience's familiarity with the great stock of Greek mythological and legendary material. Thus, the individual who witnessed a presentation of the *Antigone* had most likely heard the story of Polynices, the son of the tragic Oedipus, who sought to remove his brother Eteocles from the throne of Thebes and take it for himself. He knew, too, that both brothers had died in a duel they fought over the city and that the new king, Creon, had given Eteocles a proper funeral but refused this necessary ceremony to Polynices, ordering that anyone who attempted to perform the rite should be put to death.

The play begins with Antigone's declaration of her intention to give her brother a ceremonial burial despite Creon's decree. Her sister Ismene tries to dissuade her, but Antigone is determined though she knows she is risking her life. She is arrested when a guard informs Creon that someone has defied his order by scattering dust on the corpse. Creon condemns her to death even though she is engaged to his son Haemon. In the excerpt which appears below Haemon tries unsuccessfully to reason with his father and Antigone is led away to die. But the tragedy does not end here, for it is Creon who ultimately suffers the worse fate.

Like other Greek tragedies, the *Antigone* deals with the sort of conflict which all men and women experience in life. In this case it is conflict between the laws of society and divine law. Both claim the loyalty of the individual but, for Sophocles, the latter must be seen as the higher authority.

HAEMON

Father, I'm your son. You, in your wisdom,
guide me with good counsel, and I obey you.
I'd never consider any marriage more important
than your good advice.

CREON

This, my son, is a thought you must keep in
your heart,
that all things should be subordinated to your father's will.
This is what men pray for, to have obedient sons
in their homes,
sons who punish the enemies of their father
and who honor his friend just as he does.
But he who sires worthless children,
what can be said of him except that he has
produced troubles for himself and much laughter for his enemies?
My son, never throw away your good sense for
the sake of taking pleasure in a woman, but know that
this is an embrace that grows cold—to share your
bed and home with an evil wife. For what ulcerous
wound is worse than a loved one who is wicked?
Spit her out as if she were your enemy,
and let her find a husband in Hades.
I caught her in the act—she was the only one
in the whole city—of open disobedience.
I'll not play the city false. No, I'll kill her.
So let her sing her dirge before Zeus, protector of kin.
Why, if I raised my own children to be ungovernable
I would have to expect the rest of the city to be full of malcontents.
For he who is good at managing his household
will show himself to be a just ruler of the city.
No one who transgresses and violates the laws
or presumes to give orders to those in power
will ever win praise from me.
Rather, he whom the city places in power must be obeyed
in things both small and great, just and unjust.
And I am certain that the man who is willing
to be ruled well would also be a good ruler,
and that in war's storm of spears he would stand
fast at his appointed post, a good and noble
comrade fighting by your side.
But there is no greater evil than anarchy.
It is anarchy that destroys cities, ruins homes,
and breaks the ranks of allies, throwing spearmen into
confused retreat. But of those who prosper,
most owe their security to obedience.
Thus, those who govern must be defended,
and they should in no way yield to a woman.

And, even if one must fall from power, it is better
to be ruined by a man and so escape the name
of one worsted by a woman.

CHORUS

To us, unless old age has robbed us of our sense,
it seems that you have spoken wisely.

HAEMON

Father, the gods endowed men with reason,
the noblest of all our possessions.
It's beyond my power, I don't know how,
to point to the error in what you've just said;
perhaps another might have something helpful to say.
You are my father, and so I watch to see
what men say and do, and what they complain
about—things which would displease you if you were to
hear them. The common people are afraid to meet
you face to face, but I have heard them
murmuring in the dark, lamenting this girl.
The whole city mutters that never was a woman
so unjustly condemned for so glorious a deed as hers.
She would not leave her fallen, butchered brother
unburied, carrion for wild dogs and birds.
Shouldn't she be honored with a prize of gold?
These are the dark words which are quietly spreading
throughout the city.
Father, there is nothing more important to me than
your good fortune. What greater glory is there for a
child than the prosperity and good name of his father,
or, for a father, that of his child?
Don't commit yourself just yet to the point of view
that you, and you alone, are right.
For he who thinks that he alone is wise,
that he is without equal in speech or mind,
is seen to be empty when the truth comes out.
It is no disgrace for a man, though he may be wise,
to continue learning, or to be flexible of mind.
Haven't you seen the trees on the banks of the swollen winter torrent,
how those that yield to the current's force keep every twig safe,
while those that resist are destroyed, roots and all?
It's the same with a sailor who keeps his sails trimmed too tightly;
if he doesn't slacken them the boat will capsize, and
his voyage will end with the deck down and the keel up.

Let go of your anger. Let yourself change!
I know that I'm just a young man, but let me say this:
it would be best if men were born with perfect wisdom
and understanding; but, since this is not usually the case,
it's good to learn from those who speak wisely.

CHORUS

Lord, you would do well to learn from him, provided
that what he says is relevant. And you, Haemon,
should do the same. Both of you are making sense.

CREON

Are men of my age to be taught how to think
by boys like him?

HAEMON

Yes, when justice is at stake. I'm young, but you
ought to judge me by what I have done, not by my age.

CREON

So, it's an achievement to revere the lawless?

HAEMON

I'd never encourage anyone to admire those who are evil.

CREON

But isn't that the disease with which *she* has been stricken?

HAEMON

There's no one in all of Thebes who thinks so.

CREON

Shall the city tell me how I should rule?

HAEMON

Don't you see that you are talking like a child?

CREON

For whom should I rule this city—for others, or myself?

HAEMON

One man doesn't make a city.

CREON

But isn't it generally held that the city belongs to
the one who holds power?

HAEMON

You'd make a good king of a desert—out there
by yourself, alone.

CREON

(to the Chorus)

It looks like the boy has sided with the woman.

HAEMON

You are right, if you are a woman. *You* are the one I
care for.

CREON

You're depraved, challenging your own father.

HAEMON

I see you sinning against justice.

CREON

Do I sin by respecting the prerogatives of my office?

HAEMON

But you don't respect them, not when you trample
on the honor of the gods.

CREON

Your mind is polluted. You're under the spell of a woman!

HAEMON

Perhaps, but at least I'll never submit to shame.

CREON

Everything you say is for her sake.

HAEMON

And your sake, and mine, and for the gods who dwell
below.

CREON

You'll never marry this girl, not while she's alive.

HAEMON

Then she must die, and her death will cause another.

CREON

Are you threatening me? How bold you've become!

HAEMON

Is it a threat to speak against your foolish opinions?

CREON

You'll suffer someday for teaching your empty wisdom.

HAEMON

If you weren't my father, I'd say you were
out of your mind.

CREON

You slave of a woman—don't push me!

HAEMON

So, you want to talk but refuse to listen?

CREON

Is that what you think? By Olympus, you'll not abuse
me with these taunts and get away with it!
Bring that despicable woman out here—she'll
die before her bridegroom's eyes, right beside him.

HAEMON

No, she will *not* die by my side. Don't even think it.
And you will never see me again. You'll have to do your
ranting and raving at friends who are willing to put
up with you.

(exit Haemon)

CHORUS

The man has gone, lord, hastened by anger.
A young mind like his can be dangerous when hurt.

CREON

Let him take—or plan—an action beyond human capabilities.
It won't matter. He'll never save those girls from their doom.

CHORUS

Do you intend to execute both of them?

CREON

Well-spoken; I'll not harm the one who wasn't involved.

CHORUS

What sort of death have you chosen for Antigone?

CREON

I'll take her to some remote place where no man has
ever set foot and hide her, still alive, in a rocky cave
with just enough food to keep the city untainted
by any stain of guilt for her death.
There she'll beg Hades, the only god she worships,
to spare her.
Or maybe then she'll finally realize that
to revere him is wasted effort.

(Creon goes into the palace)

CHORUS

Love, unconquered in battle;
Love, nothing is safe from your onslaughts;
Love, lying in wait behind a young girl's soft cheek,
roaming the seas, reaching even the far-off halls
of the wilderness.
No immortal finds refuge from you,
nor can any among ephemeral humankind escape.
Those whom you seize are driven to madness.
You warp the minds of the just to injustice,
leading them to destruction.
It was you who stirred up this quarrel between father
and son.
Love, you alone are victorious—
a warm longing, brilliant in the eyes of a happy bride,
a power enthroned alongside divine law.
Invincible Aphrodite, you toy with us for sport.

(Antigone appears, brought from the palace under guard)

Now, seeing this, even I feel myself moved to
defy the law.
No longer can I hold back the flood of tears,
watching Antigone arrive at the chamber
where all are laid to rest.

ANTIGONE

Look at me, people of my fatherland,
setting out on my last journey, seeing for the last
time the light of day, never again to behold the sun.
Hades who brings all to sleep leads me yet
alive down to Acheron's shore.
No wedding song was meant for me.
None will sing the bridal hymn.
Acheron will be my husband.

CHORUS

Glorious, then, and with praise,
you go down to the pit of the dead.
No wasting illness struck you down,
no blow of the sword your fate—
according to your own law, alone among mortals,
you will descend, alive, into Hades.

ANTIGONE

But I have heard of a more sorrowful death,
that of the Phrygian stranger Niobe, daughter of Tantalus,
on the Sipylian heights. There,
like tenacious shoots of ivy, stone overpowered her.
Men say that she wastes away,
the rains and snows never ceasing,
her stony neck moistened by the tears
streaming from beneath brows of solid rock.
My fate is to fall asleep much as she once did.

CHORUS

But she was a goddess, born of gods,
and we are mortals, born of mortals.
And yet it is a great thing to share the
fate of the godlike, now in life,
and later in death.

ANTIGONE

Oh, you laugh at me! Why, in the name
of our fathers' gods, do you abuse me while
I still live? Could you not wait until I am gone?
O my city, O you, her wealthy citizens,
O springs of Dirce, and sacred grove of Thebes
with chariots fair,
you, at least, will testify how with no friend weeping
and by what laws I go to my rock-enclosed tomb.
Unhappy, I am a stranger here and in the world below,
homeless among the living and the dead.

CHORUS

You took boldness to the very limit.
You assaulted the high seat of Justice my child,
and you fell.
Perhaps you pay the penalty for your father's ordeal.

ANTIGONE

You've touched the thought most painful to me,
turning over again and again in my mind my
grief for my father, for the evil which has
befallen our family—the brilliant house of Labdacus.
Alas, my mother's marriage-bed,
what horrors there as they slept—
mother and son embracing—
my father, my unlucky mother.
Such were the parents who gave me my wretched life.
And now I go, accursed and unwed, to be with them.
Oh my brother, unhappy in marriage,
your death has destroyed me.

CHORUS

Reverence deserves to be acknowledged,
but transgressions against authority are not forborne
by the man who holds power.
Your self-righteous anger has ruined you.

ANTIGONE

Unmourned, friendless, unmarried—I am led away,
a pitiful wretch, down the road prepared for me.
Miserable, the law says I should never again
behold the holy torch of the sun.
No tears are shed over my fate,
no friend laments me.

(Creon appears, coming from the palace)

CREON

Don't you realize that if one could postpone death
by singing his own dirges and laments, the chanting
would never end?
Now take her away—quickly! Wall her up in
the tomb as I told you, and leave her alone there
to decide for herself between death and a life entombed in stone.
We are innocent of this girl's fate.
She's to be deprived of her right to dwell here in the world above.

ANTIGONE

O tomb, my bridal chamber, my home—
deep-cut in stone, ever-vigilant.
I come to you, and to my family there,
most of them already numbered among
the dead embraced by Persephone.
I go down, the last and most unfortunate of them all,
before my appointed time has come.
I go, clinging fast to the hope
that my arrival will be welcome to my father,
and pleasing to you, my mother,
and you, brother [Eteocles].
When you died I washed and dressed each of you
with my own hands. I poured the libations upon your graves.
But now, Polynices, because I also prepared your
body for the grave, this is my prize.
And yet I honored you, and the wise would
say I was right in doing so.
Had I been the mother of children,
or if it had been my husband who lay dead and decaying,
I would never have taken up this labor against the state.
Do you ask what law I obeyed in all this?
A dead husband can be replaced,
and a child, too, if the first is lost;

but with both my mother and father hidden in the
shroud of Hades, no brother could ever
spring forth for me again.
In obedience to this law I honored you above all others,
but Creon thought this a sin, sweet brother,
and a terrible outrage. And now he takes me
in hand and leads me away.
Unwed, I never heard my bridal-song,
knew the blessing of marriage or nurtured a child.
But thus, bereft of friends, unlucky, I go
down alive to the hollowed caverns of the dead.
What divine law have I transgressed?
Why should I, miserable as I am, look to the gods?
Who is my ally? For it is my
piety that has condemned me for impiety!
All right then: if the gods deem this just,
then in my suffering I'll recognize my sin.
But if it is the others who sin
I would have them suffer no evil greater than
that which they impose upon me.

CHORUS

The girl is still subject to those same tempestuous
winds of the soul.

CREON

Yes, and for that reason her guards will have
occasion to rue their slowness.

ANTIGONE

Oh! That word brings death near!

CREON

I've no word of encouragement to cheer you. You are
condemned.

ANTIGONE

O land of Thebes, city of my fathers,
O gods of ancient birth,
they take me away, delaying no longer.
Behold me, lords of Thebes,
the last of your royal family,
and see what I suffer, and on whose order,
all because I respected what is right.

On Man: Sophocles, *Antigone*, 332–374.

This is one of the most famous passages from the plays of Sophocles. Sung by the chorus in his *Antigone*, it is a magnificent ode to the
genius and skill of humanity. But while Sophocles praises the human
potential for good, he is also aware that the misdirection of intelligence
can bring disaster.

Marvels abound everywhere,
but there is none more wondrous than man.
Man—who cuts his way across the hoary winter's sea,
driving his ships through surging tides,
who wears down even the most ancient of gods,
imperishable, untiring Earth,
scoring her year after year as horse
and plow go endlessly to and fro,
carving the furrows.

The lighthearted race of birds he snares,
and in the meshy folds of his nets
he takes wild beasts and creatures of the deep—
man, the cunning one!
With artful devices he subdues the wide-ranging
beasts of the hills. The shaggy-maned horse and
powerful mountain bull he brings under his power
with harness and yoke about their necks.

Language, wind-swift thought,
and a passion for the customs of civilization—
these he has taught himself, and how to
find shelter from the storm's fierce darts of
ice and rain.
He strides into the future, powerless against nothing.
From death alone he finds no escape, though he has
devised remedies for diseases once incurable.

Clever, ingenious man—
with skill beyond imagining he makes his way,
now to evil, now to good.
When he honors the laws, and his oaths, sworn
before the gods, to preserve justice, he stands highest
in the city. But that man is an outcast, and cityless, who
resolves to side with evil. May such a man never
share my hearth, nor even my thoughts.

On the Horror of War: Euripides, *The Trojan Women*, 620–781.

The Trojan Women takes as its subject the aftermath of the Trojan War, a struggle which, according to legend, began with the seduction of Helen, the beautiful Queen of Sparta, by Paris, one of the sons of King Priam of Troy. When they discovered that she had been carried off to Troy, the nobles of Greece sailed across the Aegean to lay siege to the city and, after ten years, finally broke through the Trojan defenses.

The play opens with a scene of utter destruction, an open area before the city which is littered with corpses and weapons. Hecuba, the widow of Priam, is there weeping, and as the play progresses she learns the full extent of the disaster. The captive women of Troy are to be divided among the Greeks. One of her daughters, Polyxena, has been murdered. Her grandson Astyanax, the child of Andromache and her son, the heroic Hector, is to be executed. The reconciliation of Menelaus and the hated Helen only increases her bitterness.

The Trojan Women is not the greatest of Greek tragedies, but it has real value as an example of Athenian social commentary. It was first performed in the spring of 415 B.C., when Athens was enjoying a brief peace after sixteen years of war with Sparta. By that time Euripides and many other Athenians had come to oppose the war, largely because of the outrages perpetrated by their city. Athens had already ruthlessly suppressed rebellions in Mytilene and Scione. Then, just a few months before the first performance of the play, Athens invited the tiny neutral city of Melos to become an ally. When the offer was rejected the Athenians destroyed the city, massacred all the men, and sold the women and children into slavery.

The similarity between the events at Melos and those at Troy could not have escaped the notice of Athenian audiences. It must have become evident to many that they could no longer claim moral superiority in their struggle with Sparta and that the suffering they had inflicted on innocent non-participants was hard to justify. It was Euripides' intention to bring all this home more forcefully by confronting his countrymen with a dramatic portrayal of the brutal consequences of war.

The following excerpt focuses on the misery of Andromache, who has been chosen from among the captive women by the son of Achilles. Her grief is made worse when Talthybius, the messenger of the Greeks, comes to her with more bad news. The chorus is composed of Trojan women.

ANDROMACHE

Your daughter Polyxena is dead. They cut her throat
above Achilles' grave and made her an offering to his corpse.

HECUBA

What suffering! Now I see what Talthybius meant
by those dark words. Yes, it's all very clear to me now.

ANDROMACHE

I saw her myself. I got down from this wagon
to cover her body with a cloak and sing the dirge.

HECUBA

Oh my child, what unholy butchery.
Alas, how cruelly you were slain!

ANDROMACHE

She died as she died, that's all. And she was
more fortunate in dying than I am in being left to live.

HECUBA

No, child—no life is like death;
death is empty, but in life there is hope.

ANDROMACHE

Mother, listen to me,
for my words will cheer you.
To die is the same as never to be born,
and death is better than a life of pain.
The dead feel no hurt and are insensitive to evil;
but the happy man, when his fortunes fail,
wanders in his soul back to the time of happiness.
For Polyxena it is as if she never saw the light;
dead, she has no knowledge of her misfortune.
As for me, I aimed at glory, and got it,
but I shot wide of happiness.

By hard work in the confines of Hector's house
I won that virtue which should be found in women.
Whether they deserve blame or not,
women who do not stay at home
are the subject of unkind speech,
and so I spurned my longing and remained inside.
I allowed no silly women's talk under my roof,
it being enough for me to be guided by the good
teachings of my own intellect.
In my husband's presence I kept a quiet tongue
and gentle eye.
I knew when to press my will,
and when to yield to him.
But word of me reached the Achaean camp,
and proved my ruin,
for Achilles' son, Neoptolemus, chose me from
among the other women, and took me as his own.
A slave I shall be, and in a house of murderers!
If I renounce the dear memory of Hector
and open my heart to this new husband
I will appear a traitor to the dead; and yet,
if I show Neoptolemus my loathing,
I will be hated by my master.
They say that one night together dispels
a woman's aversion to a man's bed,
but I spit on the woman who casts aside
the one she loved and gives herself to another
in a newer bed.
Even the young mare, when taken from her companion,
does not easily bear a new yoke; and yet
beasts are voiceless and without understanding,
inferior to us by nature.
Beloved Hector, in you I had a man,
and I was content with your intelligence and noble birth,
your wealth and your great courage.
Still pure when you took me from my father's house,
I gave you my virgin love in the marriage-bed.
Now you are dead, and I shall be taken across the sea to Greece,
a prisoner of war, to bear a slave's yoke.
Hecuba, are not my sufferings greater than
Polyxena's, whose death you now lament?
I have no hope, the one thing left
to mortals when all else is gone; nor do I
deceive myself, though it would be sweet to
think I might make life happy again.

CHORUS

You've come to ruin, and your laments remind
me of my own misfortune.

HECUBA

I've never been aboard a ship, though I've
learned of them through paintings and tales.
I know that while the storm winds are still moderate
the sailors are eager to save themselves by their own efforts,
one taking the helm, another the sails, and all
the rest pumping water from the hold.
But when the sea rises and pours in upon them
they abandon themselves to chance, consigning
their fate to the running waves.
And so it is with me, for I have suffered much;
beneath this overwhelming surge sent by the gods
I no longer have power even to speak.
Sweet child, think no more of Hector.
Your tears cannot save him now.
Honor your new master. Offer him your charms,
the bait which brings men to love.
You will gladden your friends if you do,
and if you raise this boy, my grandson,
to perform some great service for Troy.
Do this so that children yet unborn might one day
come to live again in Troy—so that the city might
live again.

But now my words must give way to another's.
Look, who is this who approaches in the service of
the Achaeans? Of what decision does he bring us news?

(Talthybius enters with an armed escort)

TALTHYBIUS

Wife of Hector, once the greatest of the Trojans,
do not hate me, for I come unwillingly to announce
the message of the Greeks and the brother kings of
the house of Pelops, Agamemnon and Menelaus.

ANDROMACHE

What is it? I sense the beginning of even greater evils.

284

TALTHYBIUS

It has been ordered that your son . . .
how can I say this?

ANDROMACHE

Is it that he and I will not have the same master?

TALTHYBIUS

No, no Greek will ever be his master.

ANDROMACHE

Will he be left behind here, a relic of ruined Troy?

TALTHYBIUS

I can think of no easy way to tell you this
terrible thing.

ANDROMACHE

I'm grateful for your kindness, if it is bad news
that you bring.

TALTHYBIUS

They're going to kill your son. It's a dreadful thing,
and now you've heard it.

ANDROMACHE

Oh god, now I hear a thing more evil than
these forced marriages!

TALTHYBIUS

It was Odysseus who proposed this to the council
of Greeks, and won their assent.

ANDROMACHE

Oh, this pain we suffer is beyond measure!

TALTHYBIUS

He said that the son of a Trojan hero should not
be allowed to grow to manhood.

ANDROMACHE

May such things befall his own sons.

*(The guards attempt to seize Astyanax, but Andromache
holds him close to her.)*

TALTHYBIUS

Your son must be thrown down from the wall of Troy.
Show your wisdom, and let it happen.
Do not resist what must be, but suffer these evils
as befits a woman of high rank.
Have no thought of force or strength, for there
is no help for you anywhere.
You must see things as they are:
Your city is destroyed.
Your husband is dead.
We have you in our power.
How can one woman hope to fight us?
Put aside your desire to fight,
and do nothing that will bring you shame
or call hatred down upon you.
I beg you to hurl no curses at the Greeks,
lest the soldiers be angered by your words
and leave your son unburied and without the funeral rites.
Keep quiet, accept misfortune gracefully;
perhaps then the child's body will not be left to rot,
and the Greeks will treat you kindly.

ANDROMACHE

My little darling one,
my child, how I love you!
But now you must die at the hands of our enemies,
leaving behind a mother miserable with grief.
The nobility of your father condemns you,
that same nobility which meant protection for others.
His valor works against you in this evil hour.
Unhappy the marriage bed, ill-fated the nuptial rites
which brought me into the house of Hector,
never thinking my son would be murdered by Greeks;
no, you were to be the master of fertile Asia.
Are you crying, my son?
Can it be that you sense your misfortune?
Why do you hold me, your tiny fingers clutching my cloak,
a little chick sheltering beneath my wings?
Illustrious Hector will not come from underground,
brandishing his spear, to carry you to safety,
nor any kinsman or Trojan friend.

Your ruin will be to plunge headlong from above,
and to lie unpitied as the spirit ebbs from
your broken body.
My child, how dear to your mother is this last embrace,
how sweet your body, your breath.
It was in vain that I wrapped you in swaddling clothes
and nursed you at my breast. For nothing I
suffered the pain of childbirth and watched over you,
torn and wasted, when you were sick.
Now, and never again, hug your mother
and give her a kiss.
Wrap your little arms around me and kiss me
for the last time.

(Andromache gives the child to the soldiers, and then speaks to them.)

Greeks! This is a barbaric plan you've devised.
Why kill this child? What has he done to you?
O Helen, daughter of Tyndareus, I say you are
not the child of Zeus, but were born of many fathers:
Vengeance was the first, then Hatred, Murder,
Death, and every wicked thing that thrives on earth.
No, I proclaim that Zeus could never father one such
as you, a plague to many, both Greeks and barbarians.
Damn you! Your beautiful eyes brought a
shameful destruction to the renowned plains of Troy.
Take him, then. Take him and hurl him down
from the wall, if that is what you want.
Eat his flesh!
The gods are destroying us; we cannot
save even a small child from death.

Cover up this wretched body of mine;
throw me into the ship.
I go to my wedding, having lost my child.

CHORUS

Unhappy Troy! Thousands are dead,
and all for the sake of one woman
and her hated bed.

Aristophanes Lampoons Socrates:
Clouds, 365–390.

Aristophanes, a genuine poet and the genius of Attic comedy, wrote his *Clouds* in 423 B.C. The play, in which he attacked not only the sophists but Socrates as well, was not entirely successful since the poet won only the third prize in the dramatic competition, while Cratinus won the first. Aristophanes unmercifully lampooned the great philosopher and the Socratic method in a crude and vulgar language which justifies the observation of a French scholar that, when compared to Aristophanes, even Rabelais appears to be almost decent. The portrait of Socrates in the play, however, bears a strong resemblance to the real Socrates, whose personality and mannerisms are presented with a disturbing accuracy. In the excerpt given below Socrates is conversing with Strepsiades, a conservative Athenian who clings to traditional religious beliefs.

STREPSIADES

But what about Zeus the Olympian, isn't he a god?

SOCRATES

What Zeus? Don't be silly; there is no Zeus!

STREPSIADES

What are you saying? Who makes the rain, then?

SOCRATES

The clouds, of course. And I can prove it to you. Have you ever seen rain without clouds? If it is Zeus who causes rain, then you would expect it on clear days as well, when there are no clouds!

STREPSIADES

By Apollo, you have spoken convincingly. I used to think that rain was caused by Zeus urinating through a sieve! But tell me, who causes thunder? That's what scares me.

SOCRATES

When the clouds roll around, that's thunder.

STREPSIADES

That's a daring idea, but how do you explain it?

SOCRATES

When they are saturated with water and forced together, the clouds hang down because of the weight of their moisture. Then, being so heavy, they bump into one another and burst with a frightful uproar!

STREPSIADES

But he that makes them bump, isn't he Zeus?

SOCRATES

Not at all. The Heavenly Vortex does it.

STREPSIADES

The Heavenly Vortex? That's a new one! So, Zeus does not exist, and the Heavenly Vortex now reigns instead. But you haven't told me yet about the roar of the thunder.

SOCRATES

Didn't you heard me say that when the clouds are full of moisture they bump against one another and burst with a terrible uproar because of their density?

STREPSIADES

But how can I believe that?

SOCRATES

Well, let me prove it by taking you as an example. When you have stuffed yourself with food at the Panathenaean festival, don't you get a bellyache and suddenly feel loud rumblings inside of you?

STREPSIADES

By Apollo, you are right, it upsets me right away. The food growls like thunder inside me and then bursts forth with a tremendous noise. At first, it goes gently "pappax, pappax" and then grows louder "papapappax," and when I relieve myself it thunders "papapappax," exactly like your clouds!

The Syracusan Women at the Festival of Adonis in Alexandria: Theocritus, *Idylls* 15.

Theocritus of Syracuse, born *ca.* 300 B.C., has been called the Hellenistic poet whose work is most relevant to our own world. He was a court poet who settled in Alexandria and even wrote an idyll in praise of his patron, King Ptolemy Philadelphus. In fact, Theocritus is considered to be the inventor of the idyll as a poetic form. One of his best works is the *Syracusan Women* which has been characterized as a masterpiece because of its vivacious character and lively realism. Many scholars, however, consider it to be a mime rather than an idyll and believe that Theocritus had been influenced by another Syracusan poet and writer of mimes, Sophron (*ca.* 470–400 B.C.). This view is supported by an ancient scholion which indicates that Theocritus had indeed adapted one of the mimes of Sophron. The following excerpt describes the visit of two young Syracusan women to the festival of Adonis in Alexandria, which was given by Queen Arsinoe, wife of Ptolemy II Philadelphus. As does the entire play, it reveals many important aspects of the social and religious life of the people of Hellenistic Alexandria and is especially valuable as a source for the social history of women in antiquity. The greater freedom enjoyed by women during the Hellenistic period is one of its most striking features.

GORGO

(to a slave who has opened the door)

Is Praxinoa home?

PRAXINOA

Dear Gorgo! It's about time! I'm here. The wonder is that you finally came. Eunoa, give the lady a chair and put a cushion on it.

GORGO

Oh no, that's all right.

PRAXINOA

Do sit down.

GORGO

My goodness! I've scarcely managed to get here alive Praxinoa, with those huge crowds, the many four-in-hands [*i.e.*, litters]. Big boots and men in uniform are everywhere. And the road is so long! You really do live far away.

PRAXINOA

That's my crazy man's fault. He went to the end of the earth to find a dwelling fit for animals, not for human habitation, so that you and I would not be neighbors. That's how he is, the jealous and spiteful wretch.

GORGO

My dear, don't say such things about your dear Dinon in the presence of your little boy. Look how he is staring at you! Don't worry, Zopyrion, sweet boy. She is not talking about your daddy.

PRAXINOA

By our Lady, the child understands.

GORGO

Nice daddy!

PRAXINOA

And this daddy of his, why, the other day I told him, "Daddy, go buy me some soap and rouge from the shop," and he came back with salt, that big oaf.

GORGO

My Diocleidas is the same way, a perfect spendthrift. Yesterday he paid seven drachmas apiece for dogskins, shreds of five old leather bags. They were trash, all of them in need of repair. But come, get your gown and cloak and let's go to the palace of mighty King Ptolemy to see the Adonis. I hear the Queen has arranged something splendid this year.

PRAXINOA

Among fine people everything is done finely!

GORGO

And think what tales you will be able to tell those who haven't seen it!

PRAXINOA

Idle people are always on holidays! Eunoa, you lazy creature, take up the spinning and place it in the middle of the room. Cats always like to sleep softly. Well, move! Bring water! Faster! I need water first and she brings soap! But give it to me anyway. Not that much, you wasteful thing. Pour the water! You wretch, why do you wet my dress? Stop it! Thank god, I've managed somehow to wash myself. The key to the big cupboard, where is it? Bring it here!

GORGO

Praxinoa, that dress with the ample folds suits you very well. Tell me, how much did the material cost?

PRAXINOA

Don't speak of it, Gorgo. It cost more than eight silver coins, and I put my soul into making it too!

GORGO

But you succeeded admirably, as you wished!

PRAXINOA

It's nice of you to say that. Bring me my cloak, Eunoa, and set my hat on my head properly! No, I will not take you with me, my child. Cry all you want, I will not have you lamed by the crowd! Let's get going. Phrygia, take the little one and amuse him, call the dog inside and lock the front door! O gods, what a crowd. How will we get through it? How long will it take us? They are like ants, impossible to measure or number! You have done many good deeds, Ptolemy, since your father joined the immortals. Nowadays no criminal sneaks up on the passer-by, in Egyptian fashion, to murder him in the streets. Oh, the awful games they used to play, the perfect rascals, all of them the same, all of them so strange! What shall we do, dearest Gorgo? The king's war horses! My good man, don't trample on me. The bay's rearing, look how fierce he is. Eunoa, you reckless girl, stay out of the way! He will kill the man that leads him. I am so glad I left my little child at home!

GORGO

Cheer up, Praxinoa. We are behind them already and they have entered their station.

PRAXINOA

And I am beginning to find myself again! Since I was a child horses and cold snakes have been the things I've feared most. But let's go on, there's a huge crowd behind us.

GORGO

Coming from the Court, mother?

OLD WOMAN

I am, my children.

GORGO

Is it possible to get in?

OLD WOMAN

The Achaeans took Troy by trying, pretty lady. Anything can be accomplished by trying!

GORGO

The old woman has given us quite an oracle, hasn't she?

PRAXINOA

Women know everything, even how Zeus married Hera.

GORGO

Praxinoa, look what a crowd has gathered at the doors!

PRAXINOA

Wonderful! Give me your hand, Gorgo; and you, Eunoa, take the hand of Eutychis; hold on to her, so that you won't be lost. Let's all enter together. Don't let go of me, Eunoa. Oh dear, Gorgo! My summer cloak is already torn in two! For heavens sake, sir, if you wish to be a happy man you'll be more careful with my cloak.

STRANGER

I'm sorry, I can't help it. But I'll try my best.

PRAXINOA

What a huge crowd. They push like a herd of pigs!

STRANGER

Courage lady, we are fine now!

PRAXINOA

Now and forever may you be happy, dear sir, for taking care of us. What an upright, considerate man! But Eunoa is getting squeezed! Push your way through, you cowardly girl. That's fine! All inside, as the bridegroom said when he shut himself in with his bride.

GORGO

Come here, Praxinoa. Look at the embroideries! How delicate and how graceful! You'd think they were garments of the gods.

PRAXINOA

Lady Athena! What weavers made the material, what painters designed that detailed work! How realistically they stand and move. They are living things, not woven patterns. It's amazing how clever people are! And the god him-self—how beautiful to see him as he lies on the silver couch with the first signs of manhood just appearing on his cheeks, the thrice-beloved Adonis, beloved even among the dead.

SECOND STRANGER

Do cease your endless cooing, ladies. These women will drive me crazy with their broadly pronounced vowels!

PRAXINOA

My god! Where did this fellow come from? Why should you care if we are cooing? If you want to order people about then go buy some slaves, but don't give orders to ladies from Syracuse. If you must know, however, we are of Corinthian descent, just like Bellerophon, and speak Peloponnesian. Dorians should be allowed to speak Doric, I suppose! Lady Persephone, may we never have more than one master! I will do as I please, sir, so don't waste your time with me!

GORGO

Quiet, Praxinoa. The daughter of the Argive woman, the same accomplished singer who performed last year, is about to begin the song of Adonis. I know she will give us something splendid. Look, she is beginning her performance!

THE DIRGE

Lover of Golgi and Idalium and Eryx's steep embrace, O Lady Aphrodite with the face of golden radiance, the soft-footed Hours even in the twelfth month have brought back to you Adonis from the eternal stream of Acheron. Slowest of the Immortals are the beloved Hours, but they bring gifts to all mortals, and so they are welcome. O Cypris, Dione's daughter, you have changed Queen Berenice from mortal to immortal by dropping softly on her breast the immortal stuff of ambrosia, as people say. And now, lady of many names and of many shrines, for your delight, Arsinoe, the daughter of Berenice, fair as Helen, tends to Adonis with all manner of beautiful things. Before him are placed all the fruits that trees bear and delicate gardens arranged in silver trays and Syrian incense in golden vessels. And every cake that women prepare on the kneading-board, blending blossoms with the white flower of wheat, everything made of sweet honey and cooked in liquid oil, every cake fashioned to resemble creatures that fly and creep—all lie before him. . . . You alone of all the demigods, dear Adonis, visit both this world and the stream of Acheron [in the land of the dead], as people say. For Agamemnon enjoyed no such privilege, nor mighty Aias, hero of the terrible wrath, nor Hector, the firstborn of the twenty sons of Hecuba, nor Patroclus who returned from Troy, nor even those heroes who came before them, the Lapiths and the sons of Deucalion, nor the sons of Pelops and the Pelasgian chiefs of Argos. Dear Adonis, be gracious for another year. Your coming has been dear to us now, and dear will be your next coming!

GORGO

Praxinoa, the woman is exceptionally gifted. She is fortunate in what she knows, and even more fortunate in singing so sweetly. But it's time to return home. Diocleidas hasn't had his dinner yet, and the man is full of vinegar; don't get near him when he is hungry! Farewell dear Adonis, and may you find us happy when you return!

Praise for a Wrestler: Pindar, *Nemean VI.*

Born near Thebes late in the sixth century B.C., the poet Pindar is famous for the odes he wrote in honor of the victors in the Olympian, Pythian, Isthmian and Nemean Games. Alcimidas, the young victor celebrated in the hymn below, belonged to the Aeginetan family of the Bassidai, whose members had won many crowns in wrestling and boxing. Curiously, their successes had been gained in alternate generations. Thus, Alcimidas' father Theon had not achieved personal distinction, but Theon's uncle, Praxidamas, had been a champion wrestler; Praxidamas' father, Socleidas, won no contests, but it appears that Hagesimachos performed some glorious deed a generation earlier. Pindar exploits this coincidence by suggesting that the key to the successes of the Bassidai is their similarity to the Earth; both must sometimes lie fallow in order to produce great harvests. The Aiakidai are another family of which Aegina was proud; the "double burden" which Pindar says he shoulders is most likely that of praising two great families. The Melesias mentioned at the end of the poem was an Athenian trainer whose name appears elsewhere in Pindar's works.

Of men and gods there is but a single race,
for both received the breath of life
from the same mother.
It is only a difference in power
that divides us,
for the one is nothing
while the other lives forever,
secure in the brazen heavens.
And yet we resemble the gods
in the greatness of our minds
and the strength of our bodies,
though we do not know the destiny
to which fate has decreed we must run
by day and by night.

To this Alcimidas is a witness, showing us
even now how his race is like the fruitful fields
that give abundant life to men
and then lie fallow to regain their strength.
He has returned from the well-loved Nemean Games,
a boy called to the struggle by Zeus,
a hunter who has had good fortune in the contest.

He follows in the footsteps of his grandfather,
Praxidamas; for he was an Olympian champion,
the first to bring home to the Aiakidai
the olive branches from Alpheus.
Five times he wore the victor's crown at the Isthmus,
thrice at Nemea, and he saved from oblivion
the memory of Socleidas, first of Hagesimachos' sons.

These three came home with the prizes of victory,
their glory won by toil;
by God's grace no house in all Hellas holds
more crowns.
I pray that my bold praise will hit its mark,
an arrow shot true.
Come, Muse, guide my verses straight and glorious
to this house. For men die,

but songs and tales bring back for them
the glory of their noble deeds.
In these are the Bassidai rich,
a clan of ancient fame who have brought through
their ship with a lading of praise that
could give the Muses many a hymn of their
splendid achievements.
Once Kallias, of the blood of this land,
his hands bound in the boxing-strap,
won a victory at sacred Pytho, delighting
the children of golden-haired Lato.
That evening by the waters of Kastalia
he grew radiant, bathed in the Graces' loud song.
The Isthmus across the untiring sea honored Kreontidas
in Poseidon's sacred precinct at the biennial games
that the neighboring peoples celebrate with
the slaughter of bulls,
and he was once crowned with the Lion's grass
when he was victorious in the deep shadows beneath
the ancient peaks of Phleious.

Wide ways on all sides are open
for tellers of tales to praise this island
clad in glory,
for the Aiakidai have given them proofs
of its surpassing excellence.
Their fame flies over the earth
and across the seas—as far as Ethiopia

it went suddenly when Memnon did not come home.
Heavy for them was the fight when Achilles
fell from his chariot

and struck down the son of the shining Dawn
with the edge of his angry sword.
All this is a way discovered by men of old,
but I follow it too, and carefully.
They say the wave that rolls against the ship's keel
is the one that shakes a man's spirit.
But I gladly shoulder a double burden
and come to tell the news of this twenty-fifth

victory in the games men call sacred.
Alcimidas, you have given this triumph
to your illustrious race.
Twice as a boy the Olympian garlands were
stolen from you and Polytimidas in
the precinct of Cronus by
an unlucky draw of the lot.
To a dolphin darting through the salty sea
would I liken swift Melesias,
charioteer of hands and strength.

A Pessimist's View of Life: Posidippus, *Anthologia Palatina*, IX. 359.

Little is known of Posidippus, the author of the cynical epigram given below. He probably belongs to the early Hellenistic period.

What path can one take in life?
In the marketplace are quarrels and bad deals;
at home, troubles;
in the fields, tasks aplenty;
at sea, terror.
Going abroad?
If nothing else, you'll be frightened.
Financial problems?
They're depressing.
Are you married?
You'll have your share of anguish.
Unmarried?
Your life will be lonely.
Children are troublesome,
but life without children is incomplete.
Youths are foolish,
but the elderly are feeble.
It all comes down to a choice of one of these two:
either never to be born, or,
as soon as you are,
to die.

An Optimist's View of Life: Metrodorus, *Anthologia Palatina*, IX. 360.

This epigram was written in reply to that of Posidippus. We know nothing about its author other than his name.

Take every path in life.
In the marketplace are honors and wise dealings;
at home, comfort;
in the fields, the beauty of nature;
at sea, profit.
Going abroad?
If nothing else, you'll find glory.
Financial problems?
No one but you knows you're poor.
Are you married?
Your household will be best.
Unmarried?
Life will be easier still.
Children are desirable,
but life without children is carefree.
Youths are strong of body,
but the elderly are revered.
It is not a choice, then, between these two:
either never to be born
or to die;
for all things in life are good.

The Limits of Life: Kaibel, *Epigrammata Graeca*, 1117a.

This cynical inscription is found on a herm now kept in a museum in Bologna.

I was not,
I was born,
I was,
I am not;
that's all there is.
If anyone says there is more
he is lying:
I will not be.

Epitaph of an Unhappy Man:
Anthologia Palatina, VII. 309.

At sixty I, Dionysius of Tarsus, lie here,
never having married.
Oh, how I wish that my father had not.

Mnesarchides' Character: Kaibel,
Epigrammata Graeca, 65.

The following Attic epigram of the Hellenistic period which bestows praise on Mnesarchides provides us with a good example of what the Greeks of that period considered to be the virtuous life.

If respect for the gods,
admiration of honest labor
and devotion to justice and friendship
constitute good human character,
excellence, and an unblemished life,
then, Mnesarchides, despite your modesty,
you have all these things.

The Death of a Son: Diotimus,
Anthologia Palatina, V. 261.

Tradition knows of several poets who bore the name Diotimus, but it is uncertain to which of these the following epigram should be assigned. It probably belongs to the Hellenistic period.

What's the use of enduring the agony
of childbirth?
Why give birth to children?
Let the woman who is fated to see the death
of her child not give birth at all.
For over young Bianor his mother heaped
this earthen grave,
though it should be the son who buries
his mother.

Death of a Virgin—Leonto of Larissa:
Inscriptiones Graecae, 9,2,649.

The tragic death of a young woman of fifteen is movingly recorded in this epitaph from Larissa in Thessaly.

I was still a virgin,
but I, Leonto, died—
a young flower blossoming
with its first petals.
I was only fifteen,
but just before my marriage
I came to lie among the dead,
resting in eternal sleep.

VII
Science

Greek and Chaldaean Scientific Education Compared: Diodorus, *Historical Library*, 2.29.4–30.2.

The Greeks admired the wisdom of the ancient Near East and Greek philosophers, scientists, and scholars often traveled there in search of knowledge, as tradition records. In fact, many of the most important scientific advances of the Greeks were accomplished in the East centuries earlier. We know, for instance, that the mathematicians of Babylon had discovered the Pythagorean theorem long before the Greeks. In Hellenistic times, when science made considerable progress, the Greeks came to know well the sages and scientists of the East, including the Chaldaean or Neo-Babylonian scholars who were renowned for their knowledge of mathematics and skill in astrology. This acquaintance of the Greeks with the great scientific traditions and practices of Mesopotamia naturally invited comparisons between Greek and Asian scientists; one such case, found in Diodorus, is given below. The Chaldaean scientists, priests and sages who were patronized by the state and felt secure in their hereditary positions are contrasted with the independent scientists of Greece, who were products of an educational system that is characterized by some as one of intellectual anarchy.

Chaldaean education in all of these subjects is not similar to the education of the Greeks who pursue such matters. For among the Chaldaeans scientific training is traditionally handed down in the family; the son receives it from his father and is freed from any further obligations to the state. Since they have as their teachers their own parents, Chaldaean pupils not only learn everything ungrudgingly but also devote themselves to their lessons with a greater faith in their instructors. Then, because they are brought up with these teachings from childhood, they acquire a great mastery of them since youngsters learn easily and devote a great amount of time to study. But among the Greeks the student who undertakes without preparation the study of many subjects comes into contact with scientific pursuits relatively late in his life and then, after devoting much effort to them for a certain period of time, is forced to give them up by the need to earn a living. Only a few really devote themselves to higher studies and pursue them as a profession; but these people are always attempting to offer new interpretations of the most important doctrines and do not follow the ways of their predecessors. Thus, the barbarians who always concentrate on the same subjects have sure knowledge of every detail of their specialty, while the Greeks, who hope to profit from their scientific expertise and who are always establishing new schools and quarreling with each other over the most important theorems and concepts, teach their pupils conflicting views and cause their minds to wander from one speculation to another; thus, their entire lives are spent in a state of intellectual confusion and they are unable to believe in anything at all with certainty. If a man were to investigate in earnest the most important schools of thought he would discover that they differ from one another considerably and that they hold opposing views regarding the most essential dogmas.

The Chaldaeans, on the other hand, say that the nature of the world is eternal and that the universe was neither created nor will it one day be destroyed. They also say that the order of things has come into being by an act of divine providence and that all things that transpire now in the heavens are the result not of chance or any spontaneous action but of some definite and firm judgment reached by the gods. And since they have made their observations of the stars over a long period of time and have known the movement and force of each of them more precisely than any other people, the Chaldaeans have the ability to reveal to humanity many of the things that will occur in the future.

Hippocrates on Epilepsy:
On the Sacred Disease.

Little is known of the life of Hippocrates of Cos, the founder of scientific medicine who lived in the fifth century B.C. (460–390). His works are lost, although a collection of ancient Greek medical texts bears his name. These texts were composed by various members of Hippocrates' medical school at Cos and are known as the Hippocratic Corpus. The excerpts given here are from a fifth century B.C. Hippocratic work entitled *On the Sacred Disease*, which is regarded as one of the earliest examples of rational medicine. The physician argues convincingly that the name given to epilepsy, the "sacred disease" should be discarded, for all diseases are "natural," *i.e.*, they have natural causes.

The following discussion concerns the disease called sacred. It seems to me that this malady is no more divine or sacred than others, since it has natural characteristics and a natural cause; people have considered it to be something divine because of their inexperience and wonderment at its unique character among diseases. . . . But if a disease is to be considered divine because it is wondrous then there would be not one but many sacred diseases, for I will show that several other diseases are no less wondrous and awe-in-spiring, and yet no one considers them to be sacred. Such are the *quotidian, tertian* and *quartant* types of fever which appear to me to be no less sacred and divinely caused than epilepsy, and yet no one believes that those who suffer from them have been touched by the gods. I also know of people who are mad and out of their minds for no apparent reason and who act in many importunate ways. I know many people who in their sleep groan and shout, some who choke, and others who get up and flee the house, being out of control until they wake up as healthy and sensible as before, although they are pale and weak. These things are not rare, but quite common. There are many and various other examples which I cannot discuss separately, however, since this would require a lot of time.

It appears to me that those who first attributed a sacred nature to this disease were similar to the characters we now call magicians, purifiers, charlatans and impostors—people who pretend to be extremely pious and to know something more than others. Such people, then, not knowing what to do and having nothing to offer for the benefit of the sick, hid behind superstition and characterized this disease as sacred so that their ignorance might not be revealed. With persuasive words they established a cure for the disease that protected them from blame, prescribing purification rites and incantations, forbidding patients from using the baths and from consuming many foods not suitable for sick people. . . .

They prescribed these cures because of the sacred character of the disease, pretending that they possessed some superior knowledge and using other excuses so that if the patient's health was restored their reputation for cleverness would be enhanced; if the patient died, however, they would have safe explanations to offer, for they could claim that they themselves were not at all responsible for the patient's death, but the gods! . . .

It seems to me that those who attempt to cure such diseases in this manner cannot really consider them to be either sacred or divine. For if they are cured by such purifications and therapeutic means, what prevents them from producing their attacks on men by other devices similar to them? In this case something human, not divine, is responsible for causing them. For he who by means of purifications and magic can remove such an affliction can also bring it on by similar devices and so, according to this argument, the claim of the divine origin of the disease is disproved. By these words and schemes then, they pretend to know more than others and fool people by offering them purifications and cleansings, and most of their talk reverts to divine and spiritual powers. In my own opinion their words reveal not piety, as they claim, but impiety, and imply that the gods do not exist; for what is pious and divine to them is in reality impious and unholy, as I shall prove. . . .

This malady which is called sacred is produced by the same causes which produce other diseases, by the things that enter and leave the body, such as cold, sun and the ever changing and never resting winds. These are divine things, so that there is no reason to classify this disease as unique and to consider it more divine than other diseases. Each of them has a nature and a power of its own and none is so invulnerable that it is beyond medical treatment. Most of them are cured by the very same things that caused them. A cure for one disease is food, for another disease it is something else, although now and then each of these cures may actually cause harm. The physician must know how, by discerning the appropriate time, to prescribe nourishment and growth for one thing and suppression and harm for another. For in the case of this disease and all others the physician must not increase the illness but fight it by prescribing what is most hostile to each, and not what is agreeable. For what is agreeable causes growth and increase, and what is hostile causes weakness and destruction. He who knows how to produce in people by regimen, moisture or dryness, heat or coolness, will be able to cure the sacred malady as well if he can determine the appropriate time for useful treatment and not resort to purifications and magic.

A Hippocratic Physician: Selected Excerpts.

This treatise from the Hippocratic Corpus was written at the end of the fifth century B.C. by a writer of some literary talent, a fact which has led scholars to believe that its author was not only a physician but a rhetorician or sophist as well. He ably defends the scientific brand of medicine practiced by the followers of the Hippocratic school and condemns philosophic or speculative medicine. His emphasis on proper nutrition as the essence of good health should be especially noted. The most impressive part of the treatise, however, is the advocacy of a scientific approach to medicine based on observation and research and the rejection of what the author calls *hypotheses* [prejudiced or irresponsible assumptions] in the art of healing.

1. All those who have undertaken to speak or write about medicine have set up for themselves various hypotheses—heat, cold, moisture, dryness or anything else they want—on which they base their discourses, thus reducing the causal principles of diseases and of death and attributing to all the same explanations, by postulating one or two things. These people are manifestly wrong in much of what they say, but they are especially deserving of blame because they are in error about an art which serves all people, an art which concerns matters of the greatest importance and whose craftsmen and practitioners are greatly honored by all. There are incompetent medical practitioners and there are others who are highly skilled, a distinction that wouldn't exist if medicine weren't an art at all and did not involve research and discovery, in which case all its practitioners would be equally inexperienced and inexpert and the treatment of the sick would be in all respects a matter of chance. But this is not the case in our time, for just as in all other arts the practitioners differ from one another considerably in skill and in knowledge, so it is also in medicine. For these reasons I do not think that medicine needs any such empty assumptions as do dark mysteries which, if one attempts to deal with them, require a hypothesis; for example, things in the sky or under the earth. If one were to know and discourse on the nature of these mysterious things it would not be clear either to the speaker himself or to his listeners whether his sayings were true or not, for there would be no way of testing his statements by comparing them with anything that is clearly known.

2. Medicine, however, has for a long time had all the means of dealing with these problems and has discovered both a principle and a method of procedure by which many excellent discoveries have been made over the years. What remains to be learned will be found if the investigator is competent, has mastered what has already been discovered, and proceeds

from this knowledge in conducting his research. Anyone who rejects and casts aside all these procedures, who seeks to make discoveries in any other way or by any other methods, and claims to have discovered something, is and has been fooled. To do so is not possible. I will try to show the reasons why it is impossible by explaining what the art of medicine really is. From this exposition it will become obvious that discoveries cannot be made in any other way. It is my opinion, however, that anyone who discusses the art of medicine must keep in mind especially what is familiar to the common people. For what he investigates and discusses is nothing more than the sufferings of these same people when they are sick and in pain. To them, because they are simple people, the understanding of their own sufferings, their causes and their cures, and the reasons they get worse or better, is not easy; but when this knowledge is gained and explained by another it is easy for them to understand it. For nothing else is required but for each person to refer to his memory when he listens to a description of his own experiences. If, however, one does not succeed in being understood by the common people and is unable to affect his listeners in this manner, he will fail. And for these reasons medicine does not need any assumptions.

15. But I wonder in what manner those who espouse the opposite practice, and depart from this procedure, basing their art on a hypothesis, treat people with their assumptions. For I think that they have not found an absolute hot or cold, dry or moist which is free from any other conditions. I do think, rather, that in their treatments they use the same foods and the same drinks that we all use, and that they attach to one thing the label of hot, to another of cold, to another of dry, to another of moist; for it would be impracticable to order the patient to take something hot, as he would promptly ask, "What kind of hot food?" So, they must be talking foolishly, or otherwise make use of some foods known to possess these qualities. If, however, one hot food happens to be astringent and another hot food is soothing and a third hot food causes belly rumblings—for there are many kinds of foods often possessing contrary powers—it would naturally make a difference whether one prescribes the hot astringent food or the hot soothing food or the food that is cold and astringent—for such a thing exists—or the cold and soothing food. For, as far as I know, each produces the opposite effect of that produced by the other, not merely in man but in leather and wood and in many other things which are less sensitive than man. For it is not heat that has the great power, but the astringency and the soothing quality and all the other characteristics that I have mentioned, inside and outside of the human body, when they are eaten or drunk and when they are applied externally as ointment or plaster.

Greek Medical Ethics—The Hippocratic Oath: *Corpus Medicorum Graecorum* I. 1. pp. 4–6.

The Hippocratic Oath constitutes the basic statement of Greek medical ethics and is one of the most influential of all the documents that have come down to us from the ancient world. Its ideals have inspired physicians of the Judaeo-Christian and Muslim traditions for centuries and are accepted by many medical practitioners today. The Oath, which was taken by ancient apprentices in the healing arts before they were admitted as members of the medical profession, has been attributed to Hippocrates, but its real author is unknown. It has been suggested that the spirit of the Oath is more Pythagorean than Hippocratic, since many of its essential elements, such as the prohibition of abortion and suicide, and the emphasis on brotherhood and silence, represent well-known Pythagorean beliefs and practices.

I swear by Apollo the Physician and by Asclepius and Hygeia and Panacea and by all the gods and goddesses, making them my witnesses, that I will keep this Oath and this Covenant to the best of my ability and judgement.

I will hold my teacher in the art of medicine equal to my own parents. I will share my life with him, giving him money when he needs it and considering his family as my own brothers, teaching them the art, if they desire to learn it, without fee or any other compensation.

I will impart the precepts and the oral and written instruction to my sons and to the sons of my teacher and to apprentices who have taken the physician's oath, but to no one else.

I will use my regimen for the benefit of the sick, to the best of my ability and judgement, and not for their injury or to wrong them.

I will not give a deadly drug to anyone if I am asked to do so, nor will I suggest such a thing. Similarly, I will not give to a woman a pessary to procure abortion; rather, I will keep my life and my art pure and holy.

I will not cut into my patients, not even if they suffer from stones, but will refer such cases to those who are experts in these things.

In whatever house I enter I will come for the benefit of the sick, abstaining from all voluntary wrongdoing and harm, especially from indulging in sexual intercourse with women or men, slave or free.

Whatever I see or hear concerning the lives of men during the practice of my profession, or even outside of it, I will not divulge, guarding these things as religious secrets.

If, then, I fulfill this oath and do not violate it, may I enjoy my life and my profession alike, praised by all men for all time to come; but if I transgress and violate my oath may the contrary befall me.

The Atomic Theory of Democritus:
Aristotle, *On Democritus*.

The philosopher and scientist Democritus of Abdera (*ca.* 460–*ca.* 370 B.C.) is usually credited for devising the atomic theory, although he inherited it from another atomist, Leucippus, who is considered to be the true founder of the doctrine. Democritus, however, systematized the theory of atoms and used this philosophic conception to formulate a new view of the world according to which nothing exists but atoms and empty space, all change being the result of the random movement of atoms. The views of Democritus, which have stimulated the thinking of people throughout the centuries, drew the attention and admiration of many ancient philosophers, including Aristotle who wrote a treatise *On Democritus*, now mostly lost; the brief account of his atomic doctrines given here is based on an extant fragment of this Aristotelian work.

Democritus holds the view that it is the nature of the eternal objects to be minuscule substances of infinite number. He also hypothesizes that they exist in a place of infinite magnitude which he calls by the names *void, nothing* and *infinite*; he variously designates each of the individual atoms as the *yes-thing*, the *dense* and the *being*. He considers these to be so tiny that they go unnoticed by our senses, and yet he conceives of them as possessing every possible form and shape, and as being of different sizes. It is through the combination of these atoms, which he treats as elements, that visible and perceptible objects (masses) are produced. As the atoms circulate in the void they are in conflict with one another because of their diversity and the other previously mentioned differences, so that in their movement, as they bump against one another or as they touch each other when they come together, they become intertwined and interlocked. Yet, this action never causes them to assume a single nature, since it is naive to suppose that two or more things could ever really become one. That these substances can remain joined over a period of time may be explained by the fact that they fit together easily and catch hold of each other; for some bodies are scalene, while others are hooked, concave or convex, and there are many other variations. Democritus thinks that they cleave to each other and remain together until they are shaken apart and dispersed by superior external forces.

The Migrations of Animals:
Aristotle, *Historia Animálium*, 596b, 20.

Aristotle's reputation as a zoologist and biologist is well established; in fact, it has been said that ancient zoology begins and ends with him. He studied the lives, breeding habits and structures of 540 different species of animals, and his scientific observations are often astonishing. He was, for example, the first to give an account of the unusual development of a species of dog-fish whose young are attached to their mother's womb by a navel cord and a placenta, a phenomenon rediscovered by scientists only a century ago. His discussion of the migration of animals, given here, shows that Aristotle had an understanding of the problems of biological geography and of the relationships between animals and their environment; in other words, he was acquainted with the basics of ecology.

All of the activities of animals relate either to breeding and the rearing of the young or to the acquisition of food and are adjusted so as to enable them to cope with cold and heat and the changing of the seasons. For all animals are instinctively sensitive to changes in temperature, and just as men resort to houses in winter, or those who control vast areas of land pass their summers in cool and their winters in warm regions, so it is also with all animals that can change their habitat. Some of them find in their ordinary haunts the means of protection against changes in temperature, while others migrate, leaving Pontus and the cold regions after the autumnal equinox in order to escape the coming winter and after the vernal equinox fleeing from warm to cold regions for fear of heat. Some migrate to nearby regions, others to the end of the world, as is the case, for instance, with cranes. These birds fly from the Scythian plains to the marshes of Upper Egypt where the Nile begins its flow. Here it is said that they fight with the Pygmies; this is not a fable, for there is truly a race of "little people," as they say, and of puny horses, and these people are *troglodytes* [*i.e.* underground cave dwellers].

Pelicans migrate from the Strymon to the Ister river, and it is there that they have their young. They travel in flocks, the first birds waiting for the last so that when they fly over a mountain range the birds in the rear of the flock will be able to see the birds in front.

In a similar manner fishes also change their habitat, some coming to and others leaving the region of Pontus. During the winter season they migrate from the deep waters of the sea towards coastal waters in search of heat, and in the summer they move from the coastal waters to the deep sea to avoid the heat. Also, weak birds descend to the plains for warmth in winter, while in the summer they fly up to the mountains to escape the heat. Weaker animals are the first to migrate in order to escape extremes of temperature; for instance, the mackerel precede the tunnies and quail precede cranes. The former migrate in the month of *Boedromion* [22 August–22 September] and the latter in the month of *Maimacterion* [22 October–22 November]. All animals are fatter when they migrate from cold regions than when they quit hot regions; thus, quail are fatter in the fall than in the spring. The migration from cold regions coincides with the end of the hot season. Animals also have more ardor for breeding in the spring when they migrate from hot to cold regions.

An Ancient Copernicus—Aristarchus of Samos: Archimedes, *Sandreckoner* (ed. Heiberg, II, 218.7–18).

Aristarchus of Samos (*ca.* 310–230 B.C.) was one of the most important mathematicians and astronomers of the Hellenistic Age. He is best known for his heliocentric hypothesis in astronomy; in other words, Aristarchus conceived what we now call the Copernician system by placing the sun, instead of the earth, in the center of the universe and by theorizing that the earth rotates around its own axis daily and around the sun yearly. This theory, advanced nearly two thousand years before Copernicus, has been preserved not in the few extant writings of Aristarchus, but in the work of his younger contemporary, Archimedes of Syracuse, who described it in his *Sandreckoner*, written before 216 B.C.

Aristarchus of Samos published certain writings consisting of some hypotheses, and in these writings it appears that he makes the assumption that the universe is many times larger than we now conceive it to be. He hypothesizes that the fixed stars and the sun remain unmoved, that the earth revolves around the sun in a circular path, the sun being situated in the middle of the orbit, and that the sphere of the fixed stars, located around the same center as the sun, is of such great size that the circle in which he hypothesizes the earth to revolve has such a proportion to the distance of the fixed stars as the center of the sphere has to its surface.

Eratosthenes Measures the Circumference of the Earth:
Cleomedes, *On the Circular Motion of the Heavenly Bodies*, I. 10.52.

Eratosthenes of Cyrene (*ca.* 275–194 B.C.), who served as head of the Library of Alexandria after Apollonius Rhodius, was one of the most versatile scholars of his time. His interests included philology, poetry, philosophy, mathematics, astronomy and geography. However, his fame rests chiefly on his geographical works; he is, in fact, considered to be the first systematic geographer. In his famous treatise *On the Measurement of the Earth*, Eratosthenes dealt with mathematical geography. The excerpt given here is preserved in Cleomedes, a second century A.D. astronomer, and describes Eratosthenes' method of measuring the circumference of the earth, which was astoundingly accurate. Other ancient scientists had also calculated the circumference of the earth—Aristotle's figure was 400,000 stadia and Archimedes' 300,000. Eratosthenes' estimate of 250,000 stadia— only 50 miles short of the correct figure of the polar diameter, and 77 miles less than the equatorial diameter, based on the equivalence of 9.45 Eratosthenian stadia to one mile. Amazingly, the error in Eratosthenes' method was not much more than one percent.

. . . Such, then, are the means which Posidonius first employed to measure the size of the earth, but the approach of Eratosthenes is based on a geometric method and appears to be somewhat more obscure. His sayings will become clear, however, with these presuppositions: first, let us assume here again that Syene and Alexandria are located under the same meridian circle; second, that the distance separating these two cities is 5,000 stades; third, that the rays emitted from different parts of the sun to different parts of the earth are parallel, for the geometers assume them to be so; fourth, let us suppose that, as the geometers have proven, straight lines falling on parallel lines create alternate angles that are equal; fifth, let us finally assume that the arcs subtended by equal angles are similar, which means that they have the same proportion and the same ratio to their appropriate circles, as has been proven by the geometers as well (for when arcs are subtended by equal angles, if one of them is, for example, a tenth of its appropriate circle, the rest of the arcs will be tenth parts of their appropriate circles).

He who understands these principles will not find it difficult to comprehend the investigative approach of Eratosthenes described below. He says that Syene and Alexandria are located under the same meridian. Since meridian circles are great circles in the universe, it follows that the circles of the earth that lie under them must also be great circles. Thus, whatever size he proves the circle on the earth that passes through Syene and Alexandria to be, that will also be the size of the great circle on the earth. He goes on to say, and rightly so, that Syene lies under the summer tropic circle. Thus, when the sun finds itself in the Cancer during the summer solstice and is exactly in midheaven, the indices of the sundials necessarily cast no shadows as the sun is located in an exact vertical line above them; and this is true, as it is said, over an area of 300 stades in diameter. At the very same point in time, however, the indices of the sundial in Alexandria cast shadows because this city is located rather to the north of Syene. Since these two cities lie under the same meridian great circle, if we trace an arc from the end of the shadow of the index to the base of the index of the sundial at Alexandria, this arc will become a part of a great circle in the bowl of the sundial, since this bowl lies under the great circle. So, if we imagine straight lines sent out from each of the indices through the earth they will all come together in the same place, *i.e.*, the center of the earth. But since the sundial at Syene lies vertically under the sun, if we imagine a straight line traced from the sun to the end of the index of the sundial, the line extending from the sun to the center of the earth will be one straight line. If we, then, imagine another straight line traced from the end of the shadow of the index of the sundial at Alexandria rising through the top of the index to the sun, this straight line and the straight line previously mentioned will be parallel, since they are straight lines extended between different parts of the sun to different parts of the earth. On these lines, then, which are parallel, falls the straight line which is traced from the center of the earth to the index of Alexandria, thus making the alternate angles equal. One of these occurs at the earth's center by the intersection of the straight lines which are traced from the sundials to the earth's center, the other at the point of intersection of the end of the index at Alexandria and the straight line which ascends from the end of its shadow to the sun through the point where it touches the index. But this angle subtends the arc which has been traced around from the end of the shadow of the index to its base, while the angle at the center of the earth subtends the arc which extends from Syene to Alexandria. However, the arcs are similar to each other as they are subtended by equal angles. Thus, whatever ratio exists between the arc in the bowl and its appropriate circle, the same ratio will occur in the case of the arc that extends from Syene to Alexandria. And the arc in the bowl of the sundial is calculated to be one-fiftieth of its appropriate circle. Thus, it must necessarily be that the distance between Syene and Alexandria is one-fiftieth of the great circle of the earth, and the distance between them is 5,000 stades. Therefore, the circumference of the earth measures 250,000 stades. This is the approach of Eratosthenes.

A Greek Geometer: Apollonius of Perga, *Conica* I, Preface (ed. Heiberg, I 2.20–4.28).

Apollonius of Perga in Pamphylia (*ca.* 262–190 B.C.) was one of the greatest of the ancient Greek geometers. His interest in geometry, however, was on forms rather than measurements. Although he was the author of many books, he is best known for his *Conica*, a work on conic sections. It is divided into eight books, of which the last is lost; of the remaining seven, four have come down to us in Greek and three in Arabic. The first three books of the *Conica* are dedicated to Eudemus of Pergamum, a mathematician and friend of the author. A summary of the contents of this great work is offered in the preface to Book I and is reproduced here. It reveals not only the general aims of Apollonius but also something of his modesty and lack of affectation.

Apollonius to Eudemus, greetings:

If you are physically healthy and all other things are as you wish them to be, everything is well. I, too, am relatively well. During the time I spent with you at Pergamum I became aware of how anxious you were to learn about my work in the field of conics. For this reason I've sent you the first book, which I have corrected, and will send you the remaining books when I am completely satisfied with them. I assume that you have not forgotten that I undertook the study of this subject at the urging of Naucrates the geometer when he visited Alexandria and spent some leisure time with me and that, upon the completion of my study in eight books, I delivered them to him in too great a hurry because he was about to sail from the city. I didn't have time to purge them of errors, but recorded those that came to my attention with the intention of correcting them later. These days, whenever I get the opportunity, I publish those parts of the work which have been revised. And, because it has happened that certain other persons who have been associated with me received the first and second books before they were corrected, do not be surprised if you run into them in a different form.

Of the eight books, the first four constitute a basic introduction. The first book contains the means of producing the three sections and the opposite branches [of the hyperbola] and their basic properties, these being worked out more completely and generally here than in writings previously published by others. The second book contains the properties of the diameters and the axes of the sections and the *asymptotes* and other matters which provide the general and necessary means of determining *diorismoi* [limits of possibility];

and from this book you will also learn my definitions of diameters and axes. The third book contains many and marvelous theorems which are useful for the syntheses of solid loci and for determining limits of possibility. Most of these theorems, and especially the best of them, are new; their discovery made me aware that Euclid had not really solved the problem of the synthesis of the locus with regard to three and four lines but had only chanced upon a part of it, and even that without much success since it was not possible to accomplish the above synthesis without a knowledge of the theorems that I've discovered. The fourth book deals with the problem of discovering how many times the sections of the cones can meet one another and the circumference of a circle, as well as other problems which have not been investigated in the works of those who wrote before me; I am speaking specifically of the problem of determining at how many points a section of a cone or a circumference of a circle can meet [the branches of hyperbolas opposite to them].

The other books are mostly supplementary material. One of them deals exhaustively with *minima* and *maxima*, another with equal and similar conic sections, another with theorems regarding the determination of limits, and another with determinate conic problems. Naturally, when all books are published it will be up to those who read them to evaluate them according to their own judgment.

Farewell!

Archimedes of Syracuse—Scientist and Engineer: Plutarch, *Marcellus*, 14–19.

The most brilliant scientist of the Hellenistic Age was Archimedes of Syracuse (287–212 B.C.), who has been called the greatest mathematician of antiquity and one of the greatest of all time. He was also a great physicist who discovered specific gravity and the principles of leverage. A gifted astronomer, Archimedes invented a planetarium which showed the movement of the stars and explained eclipses. He was also an inventor, engineer, and mechanic who constructed numerous machines for his own amusement, though he considered these only as gadgets or toys and refused to put them to any practical use. He is credited with the invention of compound pulleys, an endless and a hydraulic screw (the "Archimedean screw"), burning mirrors, and various weapons, both offensive and defensive. Archimedes also wrote several scientific treatises which are characteristically clear and illuminating. He died in 212 B.C. during the sack of Syracuse when Marcellus and his Roman force attacked his native city because it had sided with Carthage in the Second Punic War. The siege of Syracuse and the role of Archimedes in defending it with his war machines is well-known to readers of Plutarch. In his Life of *Marcellus*, the Greek biographer describes the patriotism of Archimedes, who applied his scientific expertise in the defense of freedom; but he also explains to us the scientist's real attitude toward science, for Archimedes generally adhered to the old Greek tradition of the classical age which ennobled pure science and viewed mechanics and all applied science as base, degrading and unworthy of a Greek.

. . . Then Marcellus left with his entire army and marched against Syracuse. He encamped near the city and sent ambassadors to explain to the Syracusans what had happened at Leontini. But this action did not bring any results; the Syracusans were not persuaded, since the partisans of Hippocrates were now in control of the affairs of the city. Then Marcellus attacked Syracuse by land and sea simultaneously with Appius in command of the land forces while he himself approached with sixty quinqueremes full of all kinds of arms and missiles. He constructed an engine on a great platform made of eight vessels chained together and advanced toward the rampart, counting on the great quantity and excellence of his preparations and on his own personal glory. But all this posed no threat to Archimedes and his machines. This great man did not view his inventions as serious work; most of them were for him nothing more than mere games of geometry. He had constructed them before the war in compliance with King Hiero's desire and appeal that he turn from the theoretical to the concrete and somehow mix his abstract knowledge with something tangible, thus rendering his theories, through practical applications, more comprehensible to the masses of the people.

The first pioneers of this highly-prized and renowned science of mechanics were Eudoxus and Archytas, who cleverly employed it to illustrate geometric principles and to solve by means of practical experiments and actual instruments problems which were not easily understood by logical and geometric demonstrations. Such was the problem, for example, of finding the two mean lines of proportion frequently required in constructing geometric figures. . . . Plato, however, was indignant at this practice and severely reproached them for corrupting and destroying the good of geometry by abandoning abstract and intellectual notions becoming involved with material bodies, which demand much degrading manual labor. So, its reputation fallen, mechanics became separated from geometry; and, scorned for a long time by philosophy, it became one of the military arts. However, Archimedes wrote to King Hiero, his friend and relative, that with a given force it is possible to move any given weight. And it is said that, relying on the strength of his demonstration, he even boasted that if he had another earth to stand upon he could move this one. Hiero, in amazement, begged him to put his theory into practice and to show him some great mass moved by a small force. Archimedes took a three-masted ship from the royal navy which had just been drawn out of the docks with great effort and the labor of many men and, placing in this vessel many passengers and the usual cargo, he sat some distance away and without any great effort, but by calmly pulling with his hand the end of the pulley, dragged the ship toward him smoothly and evenly, as if it were sailing in the sea. The king marveled at this demonstration and, having grasped the power of the art, convinced Archimedes to construct for him machines for all kinds of siege operations, offensive and defensive. The king never used these machines, however, since he spent most of his life in peaceful and literary pursuits; but now they were ready to be used by the Syracusans, their inventor himself being there along with them. As the Romans attacked the city on two sides at once, the Syracusans were at first struck with fear, thinking that they could not possibly resist such violence and force. But when Archimedes fired his engines he hurled on the land forces of the Romans all kinds of missiles and stones of huge size which landed with an unbelievable noise and violence that no man could withstand; for they crushed those upon whom they fell in heaps and threw their ranks into confusion. Some of the ships were suddenly seized by poles thrust from the walls and plunged to the bottom of the sea by the great weights which the Syracusans dropped on them from above; other ships they caught by iron hands or beaks resembling those of cranes and, lifting them up into the air by their bows, the Syracusans set them upright on their sterns and plunged them into the water; or, by using engines worked inside the city, they drew some ships out of the water, whirled them about, and dashed them against the cliffs and steep rocks found under the walls, inflicting heavy casualties on their crews. Frequently a ship would be lifted out of the sea into the air and—a horrible sight to behold as it swayed back and forth until the crew were thrown out or overcome with slingshots—it would crash, empty of men, into the walls, or would fall into the sea when the beaks were released.

The engine that Marcellus was bringing up on the platform, which was called a *sambuca* [harp] because it bore some resemblance to that musical instrument, was hit while still at some distance from the walls by a stone weighing ten talents [about 830 pounds], and then by a second and a third which fell with such great noise and force that the platform on which it stood was damaged, the result being that its fastenings loosened and it was completely dislodged from its base. Marcellus, not knowing what to do, promptly withdrew his fleet and ordered his land forces to retreat.

Then, in a war council, the Romans decided to assault the city walls again, this time by night, if possible; for the stretched cords which Archimedes used to fire his missiles, they thought, required long distances to be effective and would be entirely useless if fired at short range since the missiles would fly over the heads of the soldiers without causing them any harm. But Archimedes, in anticipation of just such an eventuality, had long before prepared engines effective at any distance, short or long, and shorter missiles; and from a series of small openings pierced through the wall, which were numerous and well-spaced, short-range engines invisible to the enemy and known as "scorpions" were waiting to be fired. As the Romans attacked, thinking that they would not be detected, they found themselves instantly exposed to a shower of darts and other missiles, and when stones fell upon them from above and they were shot with arrows from all parts of the wall they retreated. But then, as they were going away, missiles of a longer range were fired on them in their retreat, causing many casualties among the men and the collision of many ships; the Romans were unable to retaliate in any way against the enemy. Since most of the engines under the wall had been constructed by Archimedes, and since thousands of darts were falling on them from invisible hands, they thought they were fighting against the gods! Marcellus escaped the danger unscathed, however, and, deriding his own technicians and engineers, he asked them, "Are we to quit fighting this geometrical Briareus who, to our shame, is playing games with our ships, using them as goblets to draw water out of the sea, and who is surpassing the legendary one hundred-handed giants in hurling against us so many darts at once?" And, in fact, all the other Syracusans constituted the body of the organism created by Archimedes; he was the soul and mind that moved and directed everything. For all other arms were laid aside and the city used only his weapons for its defense and security. Finally, realizing that the Romans had become so afraid that if they merely saw a rope or a little beam over the wall they would turn and run away shouting that Archimedes was bringing some engine to fire at them, Marcellus abstained from all combat and assault operations, counting on a long siege to reduce the city. Archimedes possessed so elevated and profound a mind and had acquired such a wealth of scientific knowledge that although these inventions gave him a reputation of an intelligence not human, but divine, he did not want to leave behind him any writings on these matters. He considered mechanics and, in general, all the arts that touched on the needs of everyday life, as base and ignoble, and devoted his zeal only to those pure speculations whose beauty and excellence are not affected by material needs-speculations which cannot be compared to any others, and in which the proof rivals the subject, the one providing grandeur and beauty, the other accuracy and a supernatural power. For it is not possible to find in all of geometry more difficult and abstract propositions explained on simpler and clearer principles than in his work. Some attribute this to his natural genius, others to his excessive industry thanks to which each of his works seems to have been accomplished easily and without labor. For no one could discover through his own efforts the solutions to his problems, though as one studies them he is made to think that he himself would have found them, so smoothly and rapidly he leads one along the path of proof. Thus, one cannot doubt what has been said about Archimedes, that he was always bewitched by some familiar and domestic siren so that he would forget to eat his food and neglect the care of his person, that when forcibly dragged to be bathed and to have his body anointed and perfumed he would draw geometrical figures in the ashes of the fire, and that when his body was oiled he would trace diagrams on it with his finger, for he was prey to an extreme passion and was truly possessed by the Muses. He was the discoverer of many admirable things, and it is said that he had begged his friends and relatives to place on his tomb, after his death, a sphere enclosing a cylinder, and to indicate on it the proportion of the volumes of the containing solid to the contained.

On Genesis and Growth: Galen, *On Natural Faculties*, 2.3–4.

Galen of Pergamum (123–199 A.D.) was one of the most important Greek scientists and physicians of antiquity and exerted a great influence on later generations. He rose from humble beginnings to the enviable position of court physician at Rome and devoted all of his life to writing philosophical treatises and medical works. An admirer of Plato, Hippocrates and Aristotle, Galen excelled as a teacher and physician; he was also widely known as an anatomist and a physiologist who performed dissections and was able to show that both the arteries and the veins carry blood. His discussion of genesis and growth, given here, suggests the intellectual vigor and scientific sophistication of this remarkable physician of antiquity, whose reputation is comparable to that of the great Hippocrates.

That Nature which forms the parts and little by little adds to them is surely extended through all of them; for, in truth, she molds and sustains them and contributes to their growth, not only externally but throughout. For Praxiteles, Phidias and the other sculptors would embellish their material only on the outside where they could touch it, but left the inside undecorated, untouched and devoid of art and provision, since they were unable to penetrate and get into the midst of it, thus gaining access to all its parts. But Nature is not so, for every part of a bone constitutes bone, every part of flesh constitutes flesh, every part of fat constitutes fat, and the same applies to everything else, for there is no part left untouched, unworked or unembellished by her. But Phidias could not mold wax into gold or ivory, neither could he turn gold into wax, for each of these materials retains the character it had from the beginning and only by being dressed externally with an artificial form and shape becomes a perfect statue. Nature, however, does not retain the original qualities of any type of matter, for otherwise all parts of an animal would be blood, specifically the blood that flows from the pregnant female to the semen which, in the manner of wax, is one homogeneous substance submitted to the artist. For no part of the animal is created from this blood that is as red or moist as blood, since bone and cartilage and artery and vein and nerve and fat and gland and membrane and marrow are not blood, although they were created from blood. . . .

Suppose, for example, the heart to be initially so small that it does not differ in size from a small grain, or, if you prefer, a bean; and consider how it could become large in any way other than by extending outward in all directions and receiving nourishment throughout its entire body, as I demon-

326

strated shortly before in discussing the nourishment of semen. Even Erasistratus is unaware of this fact, the man who praises the artistry of Nature but who thinks that animals grow like some web, rope, sack or basket, each of which has entangled in its extremities other parts similar to those which constituted it from the beginning. This is not growth, but genesis, most wise sir! For a bag, sack, garment, house, ship and each of the other objects is still in the process of genesis when the proper form, for which it is created by the craftsman, is not yet completed. But then, when does it grow? When the basket, being already complete with a bottom and a mouth and a belly and the parts between them, becomes larger in all of these parts. And how is this possible, one may ask? How else than by the basket becoming all of a sudden an animal or a plant? For growth is characteristic only of living things. You may perhaps think that a house grows as it is being constructed and a basket as it is being weaved or a garment when it is being woven. But that is not the case. For growth is characteristic of those things whose forms have been completed, while the process of attaining the form of a thing which is still being created is called genesis, not growth. For that which *is* grows, and that which *is not* becomes.

A Greek Account of the Indian Caste System: Arrian, *Indica*, 11. 13.

Before the time of Alexander the Great the Greeks knew little about India and its inhabitants; in fact, they often confused it with Ethiopia and viewed these two lands as a single country. Alexander's invasion and conquest of the Punjab in northwest India, however, gave them the opportunity to observe closely this frontier region and its social structure. Later, the Hellenistic king Seleucus I may have reached as far as the river Jumma, but he was defeated by the Mauryan King Chandragupta and abandoned his Indian territories. Seleucus, however, sent an ambassador named Megasthenes to the court of Chandragupta *ca.* 305 B.C., and the latter wrote a book which is the main Greek source on India; fragments of it were preserved in Diodorus and Arrian. In spite of these extensive contacts, the fabulous subcontinent of India remained a land of mystery and fable to the Greeks and occupied a prominent place in their utopian literature. Even such enlightened Greek visitors as the admiral Nearchus, the ambassador Megasthenes and Onesicritus, the pilot of Alexander's fleet, idealized India in their writings, as the extensive fragments of their work clearly show.

The Indians are divided into seven castes. Among them are the so-called wise men, who are fewer in number than the other castes but most eminent in the honors and reverence they receive. These people are not required to perform manual labor and do not contribute part of their earnings to the public fund; neither is any other form of obligation imposed on these wise men except that of offering sacrifices to the gods on behalf of the entire Indian people. When a person performs a sacrifice in private the proceedings are supervised by one of these wise men, for without their supervision the sacrifice would not be acceptable to the gods. They alone among the Indians are also expert in foretelling the future, and no one else is given the right to prophesy. They reveal the future regarding the seasons of the year and prophesy any disasters that might befall the community; however, they do not reveal to individuals prophecies regarding their private affairs, perhaps for the reason that their prophetic power does not concern itself with insignificant matters or because they consider it unworthy of them to deal with these things. The man who errs three times in his prophecies is not reprimanded in any way except that he is required to abstain from foretelling the future for the rest of his life. And no one can compel a man on whom such a silence has been imposed ever to prophesy again. These wise men live their lives naked, spending their time in the sunshine out of doors during the winter, while in the summer, when the sun's heat prevails, they sit in the meadows and marshes under great trees whose shade Nearchus reckons to be five plethra all round, and which are capable of providing shade for ten thousand men each; that's how great these trees are! They subsist on seasonal fruits and the bark of trees, which is no less sweet and nutritious than the dates of the palm trees.

After the wise men comes the second caste, the farmers, who constitute the most numerous of all Indian castes. These people do not possess weapons of war, nor are they concerned with war, but cultivate the land; and they pay taxes to the kings or to those of the cities which happen to be autonomous. When war breaks out among the Indians the workers of the land cannot legally be touched; neither is it legal to destroy the land itself. Thus, while some Indians are fighting and killing one another indiscriminately, others nearby plough the fields quietly, or gather fruit, or shake the branches of trees or harvest.

The third caste of Indians is that of the herdsmen, shepherds of sheep and cowherds. These people reside neither in cities nor in the villages. They are nomads who spend their lives in the hills; they also pay taxes from their herds and hunt birds and wild beasts in the country.

The fourth Indian caste consists of craftsmen and shopkeepers. These, too, are workers who pay taxes from their earnings, except those among them who make weapons or war; these people receive payments from the community. To this caste belong also the shipwrights and the sailors who navigate the rivers.

The fifth of the Indian castes is that of the warriors, who are second only to the farmers in number. These people enjoy the greatest freedom and are the most spirited of the Indians. They are devoted exclusively to military pursuits. Other Indians make weapons for them and provide them with horses, and still others serve in their military camps, specifically those who care for their horses, maintain their weapons, lead the elephants and line up and drive the chariots. The warriors fight when it is necessary for them to make war but enjoy themselves in times of peace. The pay they receive from the community is so great that they can comfortably support with it other people besides themselves.

The sixth caste of Indians is that of the so-called overseers [episcopoi]. These people keep an eye on all that goes on in the countryside and the cities and make reports to the king in areas where kings reign, or to the proper authorities in autonomous regions. It is illegal to submit any false reports to these people, and no Indian has ever had a reason to lie to them.

A seventh caste is made up of those Indian people who deliberate with the king, or the magistrates in the case of autonomous cities, about public affairs. This caste is small, but in wisdom and justice its members are superior to all others. It is from this caste that the Indians select their chief magistrates and those who serve as provincial governors or lieutenant governors, treasurers, army officers and naval commanders, financial officials and supervisors of works relating to agriculture. It is illegal for people to marry outside of their own caste: for example, a farmer cannot marry an artisan. It is also unlawful for one person to be involved in two different occupations or to switch from one caste to another; for instance, it is not permitted to change from shepherd to farmer or from artisan to shepherd. Members of all castes, however, are permitted to join the wise men; for the responsibilities of these wise men are not easy, but the most demanding of all.

An Ancient Naval Explorer—Nearchus of Crete: Arrian, *Indica*, 20–21.2.

Nearchus of Crete was a friend, trusted associate and admiral of Alexander the Great. He shared the king's early exile and followed him in his Asian campaign, serving as an administrator and soldier. His most important mission, however, was to bring the fleet of Alexander from the Indus to the Tigris river by sailing along and exploring the coast of Asia from India to Mesopotamia. He left us an account of India which was used by Strabo and Arrian and a description of his sea voyage which has been preserved in Arrian's *Indica*. His honest and reliable discussion of his Indian and naval exploits is fascinating: he encountered the southwest monsoon near Karachi, observed pearl fisheries, a shoal of whales and other marvels. His work contributed considerably to a better understanding of a previously unknown part of the world.

Regarding these matters Nearchus writes as follows: It was the desire of Alexander to sail the ocean that extends from the land of the Indians to Persia, but he was hesitant to undertake this voyage because of its great length and the fear that he might encounter some desert region or some land without anchorages, or one that did not produce an adequate supply of the earth's goods, and might thus lose his entire fleet. This would put no small stain on his great achievements and might destroy all of his happiness. But his persistent desire to do something new and exciting finally prevailed. He was not clear, however, on the choice of the person who would be able to carry out this enterprise, for that man would also have to uplift the spirits of the men of the fleet, who were assigned on such a dangerous mission, so as to remove their feeling that they had been dispatched carelessly to obvious dangers. Nearchus, moreover, says that Alexander met with him and discussed the problem of selecting an admiral for the fleet. But as a number of persons came to mind, Alexander dismissed some as not committed enough to him to risk their lives for his sake, others as soft-hearted, and still others as obsessed with an all-consuming desire to return to their homes; and in each case he used one or another of these arguments. Then Nearchus spoke and said: "O King, I accept the command of your fleet, and may the gods help us to achieve our goals. I will lead your ships and crew safely to the land of Persia, if only this ocean is navigable and the venture is within the bounds of human possibility." Alexander responded that he did not want to expose one of his own friends to such great hardships and danger. Nearchus, however, did not give up his request, but persisted. Alexander was well-pleased with

331

Nearchus' zeal and placed him in command of the entire fleet. Then the soldiers who had been assigned to sail on this expedition and the crews of the ships felt relieved, for they realized that Alexander would not have exposed Nearchus to such a clearly dangerous mission unless they, too, were to be safe!

The impressive splendor of the preparations, the embellishment of the ships and the exceptional regard of the captains for the various services and the crews had encouraged even those who were previously dispirited to face with bravery and high hopes the entire enterprise. In addition, they contributed considerably to the cheerfulness of the army which Alexander had personally led down the Indus river and which had explored both of its mouths until it reached the ocean, where the king had offered sacrifices to Poseidon and all the other sea-gods and gave magnificent gifts to the sea. And with faith in Alexander's exceptional good fortune they were convinced that there was nothing in the world he would not dare and nothing that he would not accomplish. Then, as soon as the etesian winds [*i.e.*, monsoons] had calmed (those winds that blow from the sea to the land during the entire summer season), they embarked on their expedition. This occurred in the archonship of Cephisodorus at Athens, on the twentieth day of the month of *Boedromion*, according to the calendar of the Athenians; however, according to the reckoning of the Macedonians and Asians it was in [the name of the month is lost in the text], the eleventh year of the reign of Alexander [October of 326 B.C.].